ROUTLEDGE LI
SEMANTICS A

Volume 6

LEXICAL REPRESENTATIONS AND THE SEMANTICS OF COMPLEMENTATION

LEXICAL REPRESENTATIONS AND THE SEMANTICS OF COMPLEMENTATION

JEAN MARK GAWRON

Routledge
Taylor & Francis Group
LONDON AND NEW YORK

First published in 1988 by Garland Publishing, Inc.

This edition first published in 2017
by Routledge
2 Park Square, Milton Park, Abingdon, Oxon OX14 4RN

and by Routledge
711 Third Avenue, New York, NY 10017

Routledge is an imprint of the Taylor & Francis Group, an informa business

British Library Cataloguing in Publication Data
A catalogue record for this book is available from the British Library

ISBN: 978-1-138-69750-8 (Set)
ISBN: 978-1-315-52029-2 (Set) (ebk)
ISBN: 978-1-138-69451-4 (Volume 6) (hbk)
ISBN: 978-1-138-69474-3 (Volume 6) (pbk)
ISBN: 978-1-315-52733-8 (Volume 6) (ebk)

Lexical Representations and the Semantics of Complementation

Jean Mark Gawron

Garland Publishing, Inc. ▪ New York & London
1988

Library of Congress Cataloging-in-Publication Data

Gawron, Jean Mark.
Lexical representations and the semantics of complementation /
Jean Mark Gawron.
p. cm. — (Outstanding dissertations in linguistics)
Revision of the author's thesis
Bibliography: p.
ISBN 0-8240-5182-3
1. Semantics. 2. Grammar, Comparative and general — Complement.
3. Generative grammar. I. Title. II. Series.
P325.5.G45G39 1988
415 — dc19
88-23542

Printed on acid-free, 250-year-life paper
Manufactured in the United States of America

Preface

Since this dissertation was written in 1983, research in lexical semantics seems to have increased considerably within generative linguistics; thus, the pessimistic views advanced in Chapter One no longer seem completely justified. The reasons for this mini-boom are numerous. Partly the change can be traced to some success in dealing with areas of syntax lexical semantics seems to affect quite directly, areas such as auxiliary selection, impersonal passives, so-called "quirky" case marking, and resultatives, a host of phenomena which have, with varying success, all been treated under the banner of Unaccusativity. Partly it is due to an increased volume of literature on "thematic" roles; even where that literature has been sceptical, it has served to establish thematic roles as a genuine theoretical issue. Most directly, it is due to the acceptance of some sort of theory of role-assignment, however underspecified, within most of the currently dominant theories. The idea that the lexical semantics of a verb will have some decisive role to play in determining its syntactic nature has been around in some form or another at least since Fillmore 1968, possibly since Panini; it now seems firmly entrenched within the field of generative grammar.

How much does that affect the nature of what is said in Chapter One, and in succeeding chapters, and to what extent is what is said in this dissertation relevant to the new interest in lexical semantics?

Certainly there are issues discussed in this dissertation that are of more general interest than they were directly after its writing. That is often the way with such works; they go through periods of increased and diminished relevance to what is going on in their field, and their periods of greatest relevance do not always coincide with the filing date. The discussion in Chapter Three of the Saliency Hierarchy and its role in selecting grammatical functions is in direct dialogue with current linking theories; of particular interest is the fact that some of the Fillmorian semantic "primitives" appealed to there differ somewhat from those in most theories of thematic-roles. Also of interest is the attempt to apply that theory to the noun phrase, and particularly to an account of the Nominal Passive, or rather, to the lack of it.

Later work has shown me some shortcomings in the account of valence selection in Chapter Four, but in this preface, I will merely point out that chapter's chief virtue: the valence alternations discussed there seem to me to pose a central set of puzzles for any linking theory, particularly one making cross-linguistic claims, and indeed other researchers have found many of them central problems as well, both before and after this work.

However, there are some ways in which this work still falls out of the mainstream, at least in some of its points of departure. The view that the primary function of lexical semantics is to shed light on text understanding has certainly not been central to any of the work alluded to above; indeed, it is hard to imagine problems of text-understanding being a central concern of generative linguists unless generative linguistics changes its nature considerably. That view -- encapsulated in the slogan that words are just very short texts -- is what makes it plausible to view lexical semantics as a kind of micro-ethnography, and what motivates the choice of AI-style frames as the principle vehicle of representation. AI-style frames make good candidates because frames are a very general representational device, and because even the simple frame model used here has the crucial formal property: information about both relations and entities can be packaged up neatly and used in making larger packages.

This is not the place to linger on the shortcomings of this work that hindsight reveals. But one mea culpa does little harm. If I had to point out the central shortcoming of this dissertation, it is that it falls short of a genuine attempt to apply text coherence concepts to lexical semantics. The idea of figure and ground frames discussed in Chapter Two is perhaps the most "text-" oriented device, though borrowed from the perceptual domain, since a primary aspect of text-structure is the distinction between background and foreground. But the basic thesis of Chapter One, that complement selection involves direct inheritance, while in some way correct, seems only a first step, and one that might be motivated in various other ways. What the idea of words as texts suggests is that words and their complements might participate in more elaborate, more text-like relations, even within the bounds of a single clause. The obvious example that suggests itself is causality, a relation which supplies coherence links between sentences as well as between a verb and its complements.

Nevertheless, this dissertation does represent an effort to lay the groundwork for a general approach to lexical semantics that pays some heed to the needs of a theory of discourse interpretation, a theory of compositional semantics, and a theory of lexical rules. Within those bounds, it raises some interesting questions. Answers will have to await future work.

Acknowledgements

First thanks goes to my advisor, Charles J. Fillmore, who has seen this dissertation in a number of incarnations, and affected its final form at every level of the act of composition. The importance of his own work and ideas as a starting point for much of what follows will be obvious.

I also wish to thank Johanna Nichols for her role in my linguistic education and for her measured and thoughtful criticisms of this work. In particular, her views on grammar and meta-grammar have helped me understand what use a semantics of valence might be for a working grammarian.

I would also like to thank my colleagues at the Hewlett-Packard Computer Research Center. Working on the GPSG Natural Language Project for the last two years has transformed the way I view linguistic problems in general, and has inspired some very specific aspects of the analyses in this dissertation; it has also taught me a great deal about the values — and the dangers — of computational modeling. Among those on the project with whom I have had valuable discussions are Daniel Flickinger, Anne Paulson, Geoffrey K. Pullum, Thomas Wasow, and Ivan Sag, who has also served as a reader for this dissertation. I especially wish to thank Carl Pollard, for numerous revealing discussions about semantic issues both large and small.

There are a number of other people who have served as sources of ideas, data, or temperate criticism: Farrell Ackermann, Paula Chertok, Cathy O'Connor, Jane Simpson, Patrizia Violi, Jenny Walter, and Karl Zimmer. And a special thanks goes to Meg Withgott, who, as a reader of a late version of this dissertation, made a number of suggestions that improved it considerably.

CONTENTS

1. Prepositions and Verbs

1.1 Introduction: Methodological Preliminaries

For the last several years the trend in grammatical theory has been to grant an increasingly central role to the lexicon. Gone are the days when the lexicon served only as a repository for the arbitrary and intractable. In Lexical Functional Grammar (see Kaplan and Bresnan 1982) and a version of Montague Grammar espoused by David Dowty (Dowty 1978), the lexicon is the sole domain for relation-changing rules, the same "cyclic" rules that were once the central concern for transformational syntax. This increased awareness of lexical structure has not been limited to syntacticians. Over the last decade a large body of work in generative grammar has been focused on developing a theoretically interesting account of morphology, filling a gap that had opened between generative phonology and syntax, and yielding insights in both domains (see, for example, Aronoff 1976, Siegel 1978, and Selkirk 1982).

The lesson of this slow revolution seems to be the following: much of our knowledge of a grammar can be characterized as knowledge of lexical structures. The same formal mechanisms that piece words together out of morphemes can be understood as guiding central grammatical processes such as passivization. This style of thought has redrawn the boundary between syntax and morphology. It has even suggested principles of organization for the application of phonological rules, articulated by Paul Kiparsky in a theory he has called lexical phonology (Kiparsky 1982, 1983) The one domain in which the lexicon seems to have been slow in penetrating is semantics. Generative grammar still has no framework or vocabulary for addressing the issues of lexical semantics.

Why has this been the case? Why does the leading semantic tradition in American linguistics currently emanating from places like the University of Texas at Austin, UCLA, the University of Massachusetts at Amherst, and Stanford, still translate *believe* as *believe1'*?

It is certainly not the case that generative linguists have denied the existence of lexical semantic structure. The semantic theory laid out in Katz and Fodor 1963 was grounded in a set of lexical semantic representations on which projection rules operated to yield the semantics of meaningful constituents. In short order Katz and Postal 1964 proposed the celebrated Katz-Postal hypothesis, which held that syntactic transformations had no effect on semantic interpretation; taken together with the notion of Deep Structure outlined in Chomsky 1965, the hypothesis entailed that semantic interpretation could be performed at deep structure. Whatever the merits of that claim may or may not have been, the historical fact is that its greatest influence was on syntactic research. Little generative work was done to elaborate the original lexical representations in Katz and Fodor 1963; the current version of the theory descended from Chomsky 1965 is so different that it no longer even makes sense to speak of a semantic "component."

A somewhat different line of research is that pursued in Jackendoff 1972. Following a version of generative theory in which the Katz-Postal Hypothesis had been discarded, this work attempted to lay down an alternative framework for semantic interpretation where interpretation took into account both deep and surface structure facts. Again a system of lexical representation was proposed, different in a number of ways from that of Katz and Fodor — most notably in the adoption of a system of thematic roles; and again no significant body of research followed. It seemed that much of the business of generative grammar could be transacted without any reference to semantics — let alone lexical semantics.

Much will be said in the pages that follows about work following the line of Fillmore 1968. Two points need to be mentioned for historical purposes. First, that work, though it was concerned with lexical semantic issues, does not lay down a framework for lexical representations, nor is it intended to. It is addressed to one specific aspect of lexical semantics, the semantic relations holding between nominal arguments and their heads. Second, the influence of that work, while it has been considerable, has been more directly felt outside of generative circles.

The central hypothesis of generative semantics seems to have been that the same formal mechanisms that could be used to describe syntactic structure would extend into lexical structure. Whether correct or not, this hypothesis reflects an attitude that lexical structure is as interesting as syntactic structure. Unfortunately, and perhaps inevitably given the history of generative grammar, the core of the generative semantics position seems to be that lexical structure is interesting *because* it is like syntactic structure. When this theory-internal appeal was undermined, so was the interest in lexical structure. The upshot of the hoopla seems to have been: no, it isn't really like syntactic structure. So it isn't very interesting.

By the mid-seventies, once the influence of Richard Montague had begun to be felt in linguistic circles, it was no longer possible to say that generative grammar had no coherent approach to semantics. That framework is now fluorishing and its influence on the system of semantics developed here will be spelled out in detail below; yet despite the existence of an entire book with the word "lexical" in the title (Dowty 1982), it is safe to say that the Montague tradition has inspired no serious work in lexical semantics. Dowty's book is concerned largely with the issue of formulating lexical rules, and where he strays into purely lexical semantic issues (such as the formulation of the semantics of causation), he does so because a regular lexical alternation has forced him to. There is no effort to fit the various topics discussed here into a particular lexical system, and, indeed, there is no interest in any such enterprise.

It would indeed be easy for generativists to maintain that lexical semantics has already found its rightful place in current formal semantic frameworks, a place perfectly consonant with its contribution to the grammar. Montague grammarians have their meaning postulates to capture lexical entailments, and everyone has the distinction between equi and raising, which after all is a distinction involving the number of arguments (or theta-role assigned positions) that a particular predicate has. Beyond counting arguments, what else can a systematic semantic account tell you about lexical items? The fact is, there really isn't that much one can systematically say about word meanings; there is a certain amount of ground words have to cover. One way or another, words cover it.

But this characterization is a little too close to caricature. The question needs to be posed more seriously: why has the generative methodology led away from lexical semantics?

I think one reason is that the avowed purpose of generative grammatical theory is to explain the mystery of language acquisition, and there is no particular linguistic mystery about how children learn the meanings of words. Mystery there may be. But the mystery of learning the word *horse* can not be separated from the mystery of learning to recognize horses. Thus, in the sense that generative grammar has sought to focus on those areas of study which seal it off from the other human sciences, it has had nothing to say about word meanings. Nothing in the formal idealization called a Language Acquisition Device could possibly be devoted to recognizing horses. This is not something to argue with. It is true by definition.

I need to emphasize here that I am attempting a historical explanation, not a rigorous development of the arguments in Chomsky 1965. One can easily imagine purely formal, purely linguistic, restrictions on the semantic structure of a lexicon. But they would be exceedingly difficult to find and verify; and they do not, methodologically, make a very appealing starting point. One very obvious type of restriction, on what words can be about, does not offer much hope of interesting results ("No language has a single morpheme meaning undetached rabbit part.") It suffices to conjure up a culture not too far out of the human line of things in which the forbidden item has become important enough to merit a new coinage. More promising are constraints on how much can be packed into single predicates. In order not to fall back into the trap of the first attempt, such proposals tend to require a fair amount of theoretical baggage to fly. Take the claim: "No verb can have two actors." Why isn't the sentence "John exchanged presents with Mary," a counterexample, when every circumstantial test of verifying instances will give John and Mary equal status? Such a proposal makes more sense as a theoretical stipulation than as a genuine prediction. But this still leaves us waiting for the payoff. Finally, there is a much more difficult type of prediction, that could only be made with the foundation of a genuine typology of lexicons: lexicons with property x have property y. This has obvious appeal, but the current state of knowledge makes it difficult to formulate substantive calims about lexicons as a whole.

I will argue below that there are issues resolvable with an explicit lexical semantics which are of interest even to the most hardhearted generativist. That is, there are lexical semantic issues whose resolution has serious consequences for the organization of the grammar. I will certainly not be the first to so argue. But there are problems quite independent of grammar that motivate the study of lexical semantics; and I think a revealing approach to the subject requires a proper perspective on those problems. In a sense, lexical semantics must be independently motivated from outside grammar before it can make any claims on the grammar.

1.1.1 Motivations for Lexical Representations

In this section I want to address a question which will not be controversial for a number of readers: why should we have lexical representations? The issue arises because I will be making use of the formal apparatus and vocabularies of two different and sometimes opposed traditions: knowledge representation as it is commonly understood in Artificial Intelligence and model theoretic semantics as formulated most explicitly for natural language by Richard Montague. The most common methodological assumption for those working in model theoretic, or *denotational* semantics, is that semantic representations may be dispensed with entirely in favor of rules of interpretation in a model. Quite naturally, then, those working in this tradition have had little to say about the internal semantics of lexical items. I thus need to make a case that these two traditions can be blended in a coherent way.

I will begin by arguing for lexical representations on grounds which are far removed from the central concerns of this dissertation. The heart of the argument is that any theory of discourse understanding will need to be anchored in a fairly rich system of lexical representations. This is a somewhat peculiar place from which to launch the enterprise, because almost nothing I have to say in the rest of this dissertation will have any direct bearing on discourse understanding. The need for the appeal, I think, boils down to the matter of balancing profit versus effort.

Many of the following pages will be taken up with detailed discussions of matters relating to very small lexical families. Some of the statements made will apply only to one verb. Some will apply to three or four verbs and one preposition — one preposition in a special sense of that preposition. In Chapters 1 and 2, I will set up a broad framework for lexical descriptions, taking as my focus an account of the selection of prepositions by verbs. In chapters 3, 4, and 5 — which form the linguistic heart of the dissertation — I will discuss some of the grammatical payoffs of such representations. It should be conceded at the outset that much grammatical inquiry can proceed quite independently of lexical semantic questions. Those interested in pursuing the cross linguistic behaviors of long distance dependencies, bound anaphora, coreference, cliticization, and agreement will most likely find questions of which particular verb has been used peripheral to their concerns. I would even go so far as to venture that the grammatical payoffs alone are too small to justify the enormous research effort of constructing detailed lexical representations. The starting point of this dissertation is to *assume* on independent grounds that lexical representations are necessary. Once that is given, there are numerous questions of interest both to the grammarian and the artificial intelligence researcher. How do such lexical representations connect up with the grammar? How do they contribute to the semantics of sentences? What consequence does their existence have for the grammar as a whole? Can some things that used to be stated as "grammar" simply fall out of the lexical structure? Chapters 1 and 2 will deal with the first two questions, chapters 3,4, and 5 with the last two.

I wish to do two things in this section: first, present a plausibility argument for lexical representations independently of grammar, and second, argue that such representations can be coherently treated in a denotational (model theoretic) semantics.

In dealing with word meanings we are dealing with that part of language which is flush with the physics and the metaphysics of the world. If knowing the word *horse* means knowing horses, then the same can be said of *run* and running situations, and *in* and situations of containment. We seem to commit ourselves ourselves to a potentially endless enterprise. Clearly we need some formal definition of the object of description; and just as clearly that formal definition cannot come from within grammar. What we are interested in here is some approach to viewing the relationship of language with the world; presumably the domain of grammar is purely language internal relationships. We thus need to begin by defining some larger enterprise outside of grammar within which lexical description can proceed.

This larger enterprise is already a going concern, and it has been very clearly articulated by Charles Fillmore:[1]

> (1) I believe that the linguist, in his consideration of a number of issues in semantic theory, can profit from the exercise of examining these issues within a larger view of language production and language comprehension.... [T]he task I am taking on is that of locating a concern with meaning within a larger theory of language processing; the aspect that I will concentrate on here is text comprehension."

Suppose, then, that a theory of text comprehension were the goal. Surely such a theory would need to concern itself with extra-grammatical structures, with text conventions, story frames, character roles, models of reader and writer, with knowledge of the world and structured events in the world; but it will also need at some point to return to the chunks of text, to the language tokens and the language types they instantiate, and at some point it will need to have access to "meanings," and those meanings will finally bottom out at words. It will be crucial, in any theory of text understanding, to have some understanding of how words structure the world, and just what pieces of it they evoke. A theory of lexical semantics that has some promise of being of more interest than a dictionary is a theory that can contribute to an understanding of text comprehension. Indeed, the view of lexical meaning set forth in the article just cited, in which word meanings are represented with structured templates called scenes, is one that can be summarized: words are very short texts.

---

1. Fillmore 1977b, p. 77

It is a very short step to recast things in a totally language independent fashion. Suppose we call the object of study discourse understanding, using the term discourse to mean any interaction, however brief or extended, governed by social conventions. The best term for the sorts of social convention of interest is probably Saussure's term *sign*. A discourse in the broadest sense is an interaction involving those social conventions which have meaning. We see a man walk up to a door and take out a key. That we can in some sense be said to "understand" this event is shown by the fact that we have expectations about it. The same knowledge we use in understanding the event will play a role in our understanding of a text about it.

The question the linguist asks sometimes characterized: what do we know when we know a language? The somewhat different question of a student of discourse might be: what do we know when we understand the discourse of a culture? This second question has a way of sounding impossibly large, a domain of study from which it is impossible to exclude anything. At the very least it is clear that any representation of such knowledge will be far more complex than current representations of grammar.

The "knowledge" at issue here is sometimes referred to as the encyclopedia, sometimes, by linguists, as real world knowledge, usually to distinguish it from the linguist's business, which is linguistic knowledge. At this point I would like to introduce a term current in Artificial Intelligence circles, which will be in force for the remainder of this dissertation. The term is "knowledge representation;" knowledge representation in AI is a field quite separate from natural language processing (though of course often linked to it in actual systems); it is generally thought of as just one side of a coin whose other half is reasoning. The idea is that reasoning systems work better if they have a model of the world it is easy to reason with. In one guise this is just an extension of the idea that good programs need good data structures. In another it is the classic time/space trade-off. Clever knowledge representations can have a lot of "reasoning" built into them; but they tend to be more complicated. The point is that talk about discourse understanding often boils down to much the same thing, distinguishing what is known from what has to be figured out. The discourse theorist's encyclopedia is the AI researcher's knowledge representation.

The central proposal of this dissertation is that an illuminating lexical representation can be built by combining some ideas from the linguistic work of Charles Fillmore with a style of knowledge representation familiar to Artifical Intelligence Researchers, namely frame representations.

The particular work I refer to is FIllmore 1977b, already cited above, in which the problem of discourse understanding is investigated with the help of a concept of "scenes." To put it somewhat crudely, scenes are what texts evoke in us, and the problem of discourse understanding is the problem of how we use texts to build scenes.

Fillmore's work supplies us with an object of study, scenes and "conceptual schemata;" the knowledge representation tradition provides us with a suitable formalism, that of frames. I will defend the choice of frames as the right formalism later in the chapter (1.7). What is more important here is clarify the notions *scene* and *conceptual schemata*. I will present a definition which differs in some particulars from Fillmore's, but which I believe is in the same spirit.

Fillmore 1977b makes the following terminological proposal described in terms of an implicit cognizer: *scenes* are "real world experiences, actions,objects, perceptions, and personal memories of these." *Schemata* are the "categorization[s] of actions, institutions, and objects." In this work I will depart from this usage, and speak of *scenes* as the generic, categorizational objects, reserving the term *situation* for individual events and actions. Nor will I begin by assuming a cognizer. Instead I will merely speak of a system of categories recognized and institutionalized in some culture. I thus define an object of study which is not exclusively linguistic, but is still in a classical sense semiotic. We will speak of the lexical item *marriage* as linked with a MARRIAGE scene which is a cultural category in a system of categories that can only be defined by its position in that system. We may speak of it as a particular state involving two individuals linked to one another by a particular institution. But all the terms in that description, "state," "individual," and "institution," are themselves linked with categories of the same system. The notion *scene* is thus defined with the help of the Saussurean notion of a semiotic system. The point of avoiding the psychological interpetration is simply that it is difficult to use psychological terms — even highly abstract terms like competence and performance — without at the same time adopting a particular psychological theory. Methodologically, the choice of the Saussurean terms is an attempt to abstract away from psychological issues.

Rather paradoxically, I have chosen to call the network of scenes which describes an entire cultural system a knowledge representation. I think this is probably a bad term for the present purposes, but it seems to me inescapable for historical reasons. The structures which I will argue are appropriate for lexical representation are precisely those used by artificial intelligence researchers in the enterprise they call knowledge representation — in numerous applications, including vision, problem solving, text understanding, and, of course, lexical representation.

There are two dangers in choosing categories in a culture-based knowledge representation as the object of study. First, there is the ontological threat. In adopting the theoretical notion of a semiotic system, is one countenancing an ontology of Platonist objects? Does one necessarily commit oneself to the claim that the category of MARRIAGE is an actual object? It is not the place of a linguist to make final pronouncements in this domain, but I think that some recent semantic work by two philosophers offers a promising way of looking at this question. Barwise and Perry 1982 present a framework they call situation semantics and define the concept of categories within the general framework of a theory of information. The central idea is that organisms within the world are attuned to certain regularities in the flow of events around them, and all talk of categories may be reduced to talk about such regularities. When we speak of a semiotic system of a culture, then, we are moving one level of abstraction up, and speaking about the relationships between the regularities recognized by the particular group of organisms participating in the culture. Certain regularities, for example, are more finely grained than others; kissing is a kind of touching; a dog is a kind of mammal. A knowledge representation can be thought of as a set of statements about the relationships between these regularities.

The other danger is that in tying our study of lexical semantics to cultural semiotics, we can only do lexical semantics in a culture specific fashion.

This, I think, is not just a danger, but a fact. It is of course true that linguists are interested in uncovering universal facts about language; and nothing in principle should exclude us from making universal claims in the domain of lexical semantics. But to have culture specific categories does not preclude recourse to universal categories. The view adopted here is that it is not possible to describe the semantics of particular lexical items without making reference to culture specific categories. Yet, in Chapter 3 I will turn to the problem of a subject selection hierarchy that makes universal claims about the semantics of nuclear termhood. In doing so, I will necessarily make reference to particular components of lexical representations that are putatively universal. The strictly Saussurean view is that no category in one system can be translated meaningfully into any other. However, it seems to me a perfectly coherent modification of this strict view to abstract from within the larger system certain subsystems with an independent status of their own. Returning to the idiom of situation semantics: the same regularities may be recognized by organisms in different cultures. Or to put it in yet another idom: certain categories are simply human categories.

To sum up this discussion, the frames in a knowledge representation will represent the regularities among situations recognized and institutionalized in some cultural system. Among those regularities are some with the special status of being linked to lexical items. Knowledge representations will inevitably build in the biases of a particular cultural system. This, in a sense, is what they are for.

For the purposes of this dissertation, when we speak of an English frame representation, we will mean a formal construction which captures the appropriate meta-regularities for a rather idealized system called English culture.

In using the term knowledge representation I have made a commitment to describing a certain semiotic structure which I suppose to be important to discourse understanding; but it is worth pointing out here that the commitment is not so much to the idea of representation as it is to a set of crucial relations. One can distinguish between semantic theories that subscribe to some form of semantic representation, and semantic theories that are denotational; the latter formulate their semantics in terms of commitments to certain objects, objects which are in theory in the world (though in practice only in the model). The general argument in favor of the latter approach is that the task of semantics is to describe the relation between language and the world; any theory which outputs only semantic representations has only performed a translation into another, as yet uninterpreted, language. I think this is a valid criticism. But I think either kind of semantics can offer a useful basis for discourse understanding.

The crucial point is, again, the semantics of sentences. To be useful in explaining discourse, a theory of sentential semantics must output structures informative enough to enter into meaningful discourse relations. A theory that assigns the denotation "true" or "false" to a sentence obviously fails this test. I believe that a theory that assigns sets of possible worlds to a sentence also fails, but to argue this point here would take us too far afield. Yet even if both these claims were upheld, that would not rule out denotational semantics as a useful road to pursue in studying discourse semantics. In so far as I understand it, situation semantics is denotational; it makes an ontological commitment to certain objects called situations, and builds up its semantics in terms of situations and their parts. This seems a promising path towards a sentential semantics rich enough to support discourse.

I have nevertheless chosen in this dissertation to adopt a vocabulary which includes the word "representation." This choice is partly motivated by the same sorts of considerations that led me to reformulate Fillmore's definition of scene in non-psychological terms. It seems desireable to abstract away from terminology that makes commitments which are difficult to meet. The advantage of the denotational vocabulary is that it always keeps the ultimate goal — the semantic links between language and the world — in view. The disadvantage is that it necessarily embroils one in ontology, in talk about what there is in the world. The payoff in talking about representations is that any semantic representation necessarily underdetermines the ontology that goes with it. One can defer those questions and focus on the purely theoretical construct of semiotic relations. In the meantime, one is free to speak notionally of the MARRIAGE scene as capturing a certain set of regularities among situations in the world, without building an explicit model of what "capturing" means.

But what about the charge of circularity? Isn't semantic representation still just re-representation? And doesn't one just end up with another uninterpreted object language?

I think the danger of circularity is important to bear in mind, but I also think it is overemphasized. As is often the case in talk of semantics, a comparison with phonology is useful here. Phonologists make use of distinctive features in describing the regular sound processes of a linguistic system. These features are roughly explicable in terms of acoustic phenomena, but the actual reduction to a physical description is often quite difficult and controversial (take for example the feature "tense"). Perhaps in a properly articulated phonological theory the final reduction will be made, but for the moment it is only a distant theoretical ideal, and the idea of a "phonological representation" is an indispensable theoretical tool.

Of course the analogy I am trying to draw here is with semantics. It is an analogy that was noted by Hjelmslev 1961, when he revised the famous Saussurean relation between *signifiant* and *signifie*:

Form / Substance	Expression
Form / Substance	Content

The idea here is that the same relation can be thought of as holding on the level of Expression (roughly, how the sign is said) and the level of Content (roughly, what it means). Both levels involve some medium, some brute, formless *stuff*. Hjelmslev calls this stuff itself *purport*; *substance* is the structured stuff onto which some form has been imposed. The line drawn between Form and Substance, then, on both levels, expresses the mutual dependence of structure and structured. The *purport* on the level of Expression can be thought of simply as acoustic space; on the level of Content, as the unstructured stuff of the world (what John Perry has called, in lecture, the undifferentiated ontological kapoc). Both a semantics and a phonology thus impose form on their respective continua.

When we do semantics we are ultimately interested in the Form/Substance relation on the level of Content. The role of a semantic representation can now be stated a bit more clearly. One of the theoretical difficulties that the above diagram captures is that there is no general correlation between the form/substance relation on the level of Expression and the Form/Substance relation on the level of

Content. To put it crudely, the word *father* does not sound anything like the word *parent*, even though a father is one sort of parent. No representation can eliminate either of these two levels, but we might think of a a theoretically interesting semantic representation as an attempt to make the level of Expression transparent, to make both Form/Substance relations as alike as possible. Thus, the full semantic representation of *father* might look something like the full semantic representation of *parent*, where that likeness makes the semantic relation clear. An interesting semantic representation is iconic; it is a special kind of representation we can call modeling.

The same point can be made for phonological representations if we reinterpret the above diagram a bit. In that enterprise, we are interested in the "semantics" of the phonology/sound relation, so that becomes the "content" level of our phonological language. What we then do is design a system of expression that is as direct a map of that content as possible. Thus the expression of both the sounds "b" and "p" will include some inscriptions such as "+LABIAL, +STOP." The similarity of those two expressions models a similiarity in the form/substance relation on the level of "phonological content."

Let us return to the question we started with: how does the concept of scenes in knowledge representation help us build a model of discourse understanding?

The answer I give must necessarily be somewhat programmatic, because lexical semantics is only a small part of discourse understanding. The problem seems to best stated in terms of the ultimate goal. To understand a discourse means to assign some meaning to it, presumably by using, among other things, its parts; if the discourse is linguistic, it will have words among its parts. The simplest assumption is that discourse meanings and word meanings are the same kinds of objects. This is the view embodied in the slogan, "Words are very short texts." In terms of what we have thus far, this would mean that a discourse meaning was a scene.

What we would need, on this assumption, is some means of putting the scenes associated with words into text scenes. In this dissertation I have taken only a very small step in that direction; I sketch, along with the lexical semantics, a compositional semantics for sentences. If the program were being followed through with absolute faithfulness, a sentence would also be a short text, and its "denotation" would therefore be a scene. In fact, I have found the problem of having sentences denote (or "construct") scenes, when taken together with the problem of representing quantification and negation, quite difficult. What scene does "Every boy walked" denote, and how does it relate to the scene for "No boy walked?"

As a provisional stopgap, I have thus adopted a fairly conventional logical semantics in which sentences of English denote sets of sets (but sentences of logic still denote truth values). This means that there is an asymmetry between between the semantics of sentences and the semantics of lexical items. In effect, lexical items have representations, but sentences do not; the crucial chain to a discourse representation has been broken.

Althcugh this interim solution seems unsatisfactory, I have nevertheless included a compositional semantics tied in with syntactic phrase structure rules (following the GPSG framework) as a kind of plausibility demonstration. This compositional semantics terminates in what is, except for a few added ornaments, a fairly conventional model theoretic semantics. The moral is that there is nothing in the nature of the lexical representations adopted here that is incompatible with a rigorous, compositional semantics. The other point is that there is something very like a sentential representation available to us in the frame model, although it is not the "denotation" of the sentence. A sentence in the logic will be interpreted as asserting the existence of a certain kind of scene. Any scene matching that description will be a satisfying instance, and will, intuitively, be the kind of object that would be appropriate for a sentential representation.

This talk of model theory hard on the heels of all this talk of knowledge representation may seem a peculiar mixture of terminology and ultimately of theoretical metaphors. In particular it combines two theoretical traditions that have sometimes been at odds, which I have here been calling representational and denotational semantics. The fact is that the tradition of denotational semantics has been most explicit in proposing techniques for systematically composing big meanings out of little meanings, and this seems to a problem common to all semantic theories.

I have taken the simplest way of reconciling any possible conflicts between these positions, which is to weaken the denotational position. I will define a special kind of model called a frame model constrained to have a domain consisting only of frames. The price is that there will no longer be a trivial connection between truth in a model and truth in the world. The payoff is twofold; first, the domain will be just the sort of semiotic structure we have argued is necessary for an adequate semantics; second, we will have access to much of the formal semantic apparatus available in Montague Grammar (see Montague 1970).

To this end, I have taken some pains to show how ordinary predicates are interpreted in a frame representation; early on, in chapter one, I sketch a model theory which incorporates the lexical representations. I also assume the sort of phrase structure rules proposed in Gazdar 1981b and 1982, in developing a framework which has come to be known as Generalized Phrase Structure Grammar (GPSG). In that framework, each phrase structure rule has associated with it a translation rule specifying how the translations of the daughters are to be combined to yield the translations of the mother.

Schematically, the various components of the system are related as follows:

Sentence
|
Phrase Structure Rules <========== Lexicon
|
tree
|
Rules of Semantic Interpretation
|
(dispensable) Logical Representation
|
Model
(includes nondispenable
lexical representations)

The nonstandard move here is to make the knowledge representations part of the model. In fact, the model domain is the set of frames in some English (read "some particular culture which speaks English") frame representation; this will include generic frames (among which will be the lexical representations themselves), as well as individual frames, among which will be objects like GAWRON, CHAUCER, and particular situations of READING. Thus, objects in the model will also be objects in the lexicon.

To sum up. The road to a semantics of discourse must take us through some richly differentiated semantics of sentences, and that in turn must be founded on some rich lexical semantics. I have chosen as the conceptual unit on which to found the lexical semantics the Fillmorian notion of a scene, and located the enterprise of lexical semantics within the larger enterprise of cultural semiotics. The formal commitments are these: the semiotic system as a whole I take to be representable in what artificial intelligence researchers call a knowledge representation, using as a building block the notion of a frame, because it seems a flexible enough formal object to represent scenes. The charge of circularity sometimes leveled against representational semantics has been denied, because the representation's function as a model of linguistic content may still take us one step further than the language we started with. This leaves open the possibility that at some point the final denotational step may be taken, and all semantics may be dissolved into objects and processes in the world.

It is time to leave the larger issues behind now. In the next section, I will talk a bit more specifically about the particular linguistic issues at stake.

1.1.2 Lexical Semantics and the Grammar

I now want to discuss what the payoffs of an independently derived lexical semantics are for the working grammarian. To begin with, we will need a formulation of what kinds of facts lexical representations must account for. We have already placed a kind of upper bound on this formulation with the very broad requirement that lexical representations be informative enough to serve as a foundation for discourse understanding. What we need now is a more specific characterization that sets a lower bound. What, specifically, is the *least* that such representations can account for? Without much argument, I will propose four kinds of facts that must be deriveable from adequate lexical representations:

(1) Semantic compatibility. Lexical semantic representations should show which kinds of semantic objects combine with one another. Semantic selection is often appealed to; lexical representations must give sufficient information for such appeals to be plausible.

(2) Argument structure. Here I mean an illuminating account. Work done in formal semantics thus far tends to content itself with rough structural templates as its contribution to lexical semantics. That is, with statements of the form: object equi verbs take three arguments, object raising verbs take two arguments, the verb *give* takes 3 arguments; so does the verb *send*. Lexical semantic descriptions should show why verbs with similar semantics have similar argument structures. In other words, the grammatical properties that follow from argument structure ought to follow from a lexical semantic description.

(3) Entailments. This is a desideratum that is usually cited. If the information you need about entailments relating verbs like *like* and *please* isn't here, in the lexical semantic structure, then where can it be? One can adopt the position that lexical entailments are not part of the grammar nor the business of the grammarian, but I doubt if one can then continue to claim an interest in lexical semantics. The position adopted in this dissertation is that the semantic system of lexical representations is an integral part of a system of knowledge representations. But even someone who did not share this assumption, and maintained that the account of entailments was properly a part of the encyclopedia rather than the lexicon, would need to ground that account by defining some relation between lexical representations and the encyclopedia. The fact that *like* is an inverse of *please* is ultimately a fact about two verbs.

(4) Paradigm intuitions. By this I mean our lexical representations must show that certain lexical items live in a kind of referential dependence on each other, because they carve up complementary pieces of the same domain; a simple example is the directions of the compass, *north*, *south*, *east*, and *west*. Capturing such relationships might be viewed as a special case of capturing the "right entailments" (north implies not east, south, or west), but this is unsatisfactory on two counts; first, semantic paradigms yields a special class of entailments which deserve some special status; *divorce* and *alimony* will be tangled up in some lexical entailments, but they are not part of the same paradigm; second, not all paradigm intuitions can be stated easily in terms of logical consequence; for example, one can be both a president and a vice-president, yet the words clearly enter into one or more paradigms together.

Some additional comments are in order. First, the notion of semantic compatibility is meant as something more general thar selectional restrictions as they are usually understood. The seler restrictions of Fodor and Katz 1963 combinations of predi referential arguments (verbs or adjectives with noun frightens sincerity" is semantically deviant because frightened, and emotions like sincerity are not animate. Selectional restrictions, then, are about the referential range of a head's arguments: what kinds of things can be frightened?

The term semantic compatibility will cover such cases, but they are not the sort I am chiefly interested in. Consider a sentence like:

(1) * Thirty seconds had elapsed with the clock.

Here, my concern is the suitability of the preposition for the verb. (1) appears to be unacceptable under any interpretation of *with*, but consider particularly the *instrumental* use common with action verbs. It appears that *instrumental with* is never appropriate with *elapse*, a fact which, if anything, is a semantic fact. But this time the semantic fact has to do with the combination of a preposition and a verb rather than a verb and an argument. Generally verbs and prepositions are not viewed as referential categories, though in the semantics I will propose, both prepositions and verbs will be associated with particular situation-types, provided for as objects in the frame representation. Under this treatment, the formal mechanisms for handling verb/preposition compatibility can be the same as the mechanisms for handling selectional restrictions. To the charge that I have neglected important differences between these kinds of semantic anomalies, I must plead guilty, though the guilt is not of the indelible sort. The fact that the theory recognizes one very broad class of semantic anomalies does not preclude any finer distinctions being articulated within that class. I will not, however, be concerned with such distinctions in this dissertation.

The first two chapters of this dissertation are devoted to developing a theory of compatibility for prepositions and syntactic heads of all categories (though the focus will be verbs). The aim will be to devise lexical descriptions which semantically characterize for a given head a set of possible valences.

Finally, there is the question: what does this all do for the grammar? In this dissertation, I will argue that explicit lexical representations give us a useful vocabulary in which to talk about some problems which have been addressed before using the various names thematic roles, semantic roles, deep case roles, and participant roles. In particular, in chapter three I will state some semantic generalizations about the realizations of nuclear terms (subjects and direct objects). Some of these generalizations have been noted often in the literature. They are easily formulated in the current framework, and stated within an integrated system of lexical representations, they become testable.

In chapter 4, I turn to the general question of valence alternations and semantically governed lexical rules. Given a prior semantic account of possible valences, and an account of the semantics of nuclear terms, it becomes possible to ask whether such lexical rules are ever needed. For example, I propose an account of Dative Movement on which the different valences are simply options left open by the rules for realizing direct objects; in general, verbs falling into that semantic class have an option to choose either valence, both, or neither. It becomes possible to formulate questions about the boundaries of grammar and lexical semantics in a fairly precise way.

1.2 Terminological preliminaries

Let us follow the convention adopted in X-bar theory (Chomsky 1970, (Jackendoff 1977) and refer to Adjectives, Nouns, Prepositions and Verbs as the major lexical categories. Besides defining lexical syntactic classes, the X-bar notion of major category also defines a set of phrasal categories which are spoken of as *projections* of the lexical categories. For example, besides nouns we have phrasal projections of nouns, which are constituents having a noun as their syntactic head. The notion head is a theoretical primitive; the only intuitive concept I know of to explain it is the notion of modifier or dependent; the non-heads of a constituent modify or are dependent on the head. A *maximal* projection of some head H is a constituent with H as its head which cannot be a subconstituent of any constituent which also has H as its head (this definition probably needs some revision because of coordinated categories, but it will do for our purposes here). The maximal projection of a noun is usually called a noun phrase. The maximal projection of a verb is sometimes taken to be a verb phrase and sometimes a sentence; in what follows it will be convenient to adopt the latter terminology.

My definition of complement will be English specific because it will be based on constituent structure. Ultimately when we enter into matters of semantics, talk of constituent structure will be dispensable; but for the moment the syntax offers a convenient entry point. By the complement of a lexical head in English I mean those constituents that meet three conditions:

(1) They are maximal projections following H.

(2) They are contained within the maximal projection of H.

(3) No other maximal projection contained by H contains them.

For the case of verbs, this definition excludes subjects and includes direct objects, indirect objects, adverbs, and all adjective-, verb- and prepositional- phrases in the same clause (but not embedded in some other maximal projection). Sometimes it will be necessary to talk about relationship of the internal structure of a complement to the head it is a complement of. In these cases the term head will be ambiguous because complements have their own heads. The terms *governing head* and *complement head* will supply the necessary distinction. When we view a prepositional phrase as the complement of a verb, the verb is the governing head and the preposition is the complement head. The term governing head covers only lexical categories, since only lexical heads can have complements (by the above definition). No matter how high up in the tree an adverbial complement is placed, its governing head will be a verb.

This dissertation will begin its search for adequate lexical representations by examining preposition distributions. The question at hand is how to represent preposition meanings in some way that reflects regularities in their distribution. I will proceed from the syntax down, considering the problem of subcategorization first, and argue that semantic regularities in subcategorization ought to be captured with a set of lexical redundancy rules, which can refer to lexical representations. I will then move to the treatment of prepositions in our compositional semantics, and from there to their representations in the lexical semantics.

One of the preliminary problems to address in the treatment of prepositions is this: what are the differences between subcategorized-for PP's and adjuncts? Where in the grammar should these differences, if any, be described?

I assume, following X-bar theory, and ultimately Chomsky 1965, that subcategorized-for complements are sisters to their governing head. I also assume that all complements that are sister to the head are subcategorized-for. The rule schema for subcategorization can thus be written as:

<X1 -> X C1 C2....>

X1 stands for any phrasal category with one "bar." There is an important convention of X-bar theory which I will not be enforcing here. In Jackendoff 1977, the convention for every phrase structure rule is that the mother has a bar level one higher than than the daughter that is the head. This means any X1 contain a lexical category (since bar-level 0 means "lexical"). I will allow rules expanding X1's with X1's as their heads, for example:

<V1 -> V1 P2>

This means a V-bar expands as a V-bar plus a prepositional phrase (P2 is the maximal projection of a P). Although I relax this restriction on phrase-structure rules, I will maintain the constraint that subcategorized-for constituents must be sisters to their governing head. Thus, any P2 introduced by the above rule is not subcategorized-for. Like Jackendoff 1977, we will have a structural distinction between subcategorized-for complements and non-subcategorized-for complements.

We now have a structural definition for a subclass of complements we call subcategorized-for. Let us refer to all other complements as adjuncts.[1]

We turn now to syntactic evidence for a distinction between subcategorized-for complements and adjuncts. First, there are facts involving word order:

(2a) John decided on the boat. (ambiguous)
(2b) On the boat John decided. (not ambiguous)

(3a) John tired of his pet duck in London.
(3b) ?John tired in London of his pet duck.

---

1. In chapter 3 we will discuss a third kind of complement, the predicative P2, but for the purposes of this preliminary discussion we can ignore that subtlety.

(4a) John rented the car on Tuesday in London.
(4b) John rented the car in London on Tuesday (with his American Express card).

There are of course various ways of making these facts fall out; the facts in (2) might be captured by first generating adjuncts freely both sentence initially and in post-V1 position. If, as we have already assumed subcategorized-for complements are generated only as sister to the verb, then the lack of ambiguity in (b) will follow. (3) also follows from the generating subcategorized-for complements only as sisters to S, because then the must always appear lower in the tree than adjuncts. (3) follows from generating adjuncts either recursively or iteratively, so that they occur in any order and any number (the rule we gave above, introducing a P2 as both a daughter to and a sister to a V1, would qualify) Restricting our attention to prepositional-phrase complements, all three facts would follow from something like the following set of rules, where only the first introduced subcategorized-for PP's.

<1: V1 => V P2>
<2: V1 => V1 P2>
<3: V2=> P2 V2>

Here V2 is equivalent to S, which is being treated as the maximal projection of a verb.

Although there are problematic cases with some of the generalizations cited above, on the whole they seem the most reliable of a number of syntactic claims made on behalf of subcategorization.

Other, more controversial facts have been claimed to follow from the structural status of subcategorization:

(5) *John kept his car in the garage, while Louise did so in the carport.

(6) John made his fortune in Turkey, while Louise did so in China.

(7) ?Who did John sell a book about to Mary?

(8) Who did John sell a book about on Tuesday?

Lakoff and Ross 1967 and Kuno 1974 make use of the difference in tree topologies between subcategorized-for constituents and adjuncts to explain the pairs of contrasts in (4). Yet the judgements here are far from certain and problematic cases are easy to find. For our purposes here it will be sufficient to concede that some syntactic contrast is desirable, without deciding exactly how much mileage can be gotten out of it.

Given this uncertainty about just what syntactic facts subcategorization is supposed to predict, it is natural that we will sometimes have trouble knowing just when to call a particular constituent subcategorized-for.

One minimal assumption seems implicit in most treatments of subcategorization: if a head only occurs with a particular kind of complement, then that complement is subcategorized-for. This assumption certainly does not follow from the structural place assigned subcategorized-for complements, but it does follow from the place of subcategorization in syntactic theory (a place which seems to have descended from the treatment in Chomsky 1965). Subcategorization is supposed to exhaust the things that a particular lexical head can constrain about its syntactic environment. If a certain kind of syntactic constituent must always follow a particular verb (but not all verbs), that constitutes a syntactic requirement idiosyncratic to that verb, a requirement that must be included among the verb's subcategorization specifications.

From the fact that subcategorization must include all syntactic requirements peculiar to a head, we can conclude that something must be said about any obligatory complement. But nothing has yet been said about how much. Is it enough merely to say that a complement must be there, to subcategorize for an X2? Or must the major category be specified? Or must more be specified?

In this dissertation I will chiefly be concerned with the subcategorization of prepositional phrases, and the assumption I will make is that a verb's syntactic subcategorization specifies a particular preposition. This stipulates a good deal more than the strict subcategorization information of Chapter 2 of Chomsky 1965, which gave only major category, but has as its precedent the treatment in Gazdar 1982, where subcategorization by rule number in effect determined particular prepositions.

In the next sections, it will be argued that this much stipulation is unavoidable. Given such stipulation, subcategorization facts will in general be redundant with, but not predictable from, lexical semantic facts. I will reserve until chapter 3 an explicit discussion of how such redundancies can be stated. Prior that we need an understanding of the semantic relation of a governing head to a preposition, and that will lead in short order to semantic representations for both.

1.3 Prepositions

The reader may wonder why a dissertation putatively devoted to lexical matters has devoted so much space to setting up syntactic terminology and examining a syntactic distinction. One reason is that I believe that the syntactic distinction reflects a lexical semantic fact; by the end of this chapter we will have a specific proposal for how the lexical representation of a head determines what that may subcategorize for. In doing so, we will have set up a lexical semantic analogue to the distinction between subcategorized-for complements and adjuncts. In this section I want to explore the semantic nature of that distinction. In particular I want to argue against one view of it, that subcategorization is *all* syntax, and that there is no corresponding semantic relation except the trivial one of argumenthood. This is in contrast to adjuncts, whose distribution is governed (by default) by semantics. In what follows I argue that semantic selection must enter into the choice of subcategorized-for complements as well; thus, semantic selection can not be a semantic criterion for distinguishing subcategorized-for complements from adjuncts.

Consider the English verb *long* in a typically acquisitive occurrence:

(9) Beatrice longed for a Buick.

Now the prepositional phrase here is obligatory and the verb must therefore subcategorize for it. For the discussion that follows, we will need a straw man who says the following: subcategorization is entirely a syntactic dependency. Since the relation is entirely syntactic, the preposition as such has no meaning. All the meaning is in the verb, and we can simply assign the prepositional phrase the meaning of the noun-phrase inside it.

It is fairly easy to see the problem with our straw man's position. To ignore the preposition entirely misses some fairly obvious regularities in the distribution of the preposition *for*. So we have, alongside (9):

(10) Batman wished for more time with Robin.
hoped
prayed
applied
tried
yearned
opted

All of these for-taking verbs could quite naturally be called verbs of longing; it is not necessary to argue that all of them subcategorize *for*, only that *long* does. Then if the meaning of *for* is ignored entirely in representing the semantics of sentences *long*, a fact of semantic "selection" will be ignored as well. *for* has a meaning that makes it compatible with verbs of longing. In honor of the first case grammarian let us call that meaning *karman*, Panini's name for the karaka that meant "desired object." Note that heads of categories other than verb will be compatible with the same semantic object:

(11) Batman was eager for more time with Robin
anxious

(12) Batman's desire for more time with Robin
need

What kind of statement captures the relevant generalization? Before answering this question, we need to confront a basic distributional problem for anyone's analysis of these facts. To put it in terms of our chief example: being a verb of longing is neither a necessary nor a sufficient condition for subcategorizing for the preposition *for*.

(13) John aspired towards a deeper understanding of metaphysics.

(14) Marybeth wants some tunafish.

(15) The fat man headed for the beach.

(16) Being a verb of longing is neither a necessary nor a sufficient condition for subcategorizing for the preposition *for*.

Let's tackle necessity first. If we are to extract usable generalizations about the classes of verbs *for* occurs with, we need to think of *for* as having more than one meaning. This is not really a problem, but a complication. If some linguists have found massive polysemy hard to take, no lexicographer has ever dreamed of doing without it. The troublesome preposition *for* will have at least the meanings listed below:

(1) *karman*
Beatrice longed for a Buick.

(2) *displacement, substition*
I substituted salt for the white pepper.
I mistook Abbott for Costello.

(3) *exchange*
I traded my bazooka for a bicycle.
I did my homework for a dollar.

(4) *benefactive*
I made a sweater for Mary.

(5) *condition*
I tested him for rabies.

(6) *goal,target*
He left for Rome.
She sailed for Byzantium.

This is not intended as a definitive list, but it gives a little of the flavor of the relevant data. *for* may be a particularly bad case, but few, if any, prepositions will live up to the ideal of "one form, one function."

But the other half of our problem is more serious than polysemy. Verbs that fit comfortably into the semantic class we have defined, do not subcategorize for *for*. This means that our apparent regularity is not so regular. At the very least it competes with other regularities; so besides the verbs of longings with their *for*"s, we have *hanker after*, *seek after*, *lust after*, and *thirst after*. The problem is this: the occurrence of *for* with *long* is clearly something more then an accident, and less than a rule.

The semantics of particular prepositions constrains but does not determine their subcategorization possibilities; if semantics alone will not account for the particulars of PP subcategorization, then syntactic stipulation is required. This leaves us in a bind. If we stipulate that *long* subcategorizes for *for*, we have lost a semantic generalization. If we leave the subcategorization to semantic selection, we will incorrectly predict the same subcategorizations for *long* and *hanker*.

This sort of recalcitrance is a familiar pattern in encounters with the lexicon; there are basically two sorts of mechanisms available for dealing with it:

(1) The exception feature: this toggle switch has a long and checkered history in every level of linguistic description except possibly pragmatics, where it would be hard to notice. The strategy here would be to mark verbs like *aspire*, *want* and *hanker* [-FOR]. How they get the subcategorizations they DO get would be a matter for the rest of the grammar to decide; if some rule governed, say, the transitivity of *want*, it would get its [__NP] for free(while the other verbs of longing might have to be marked [- __NP] if they also fell in that rules domain); if not the feature [__NP] could only be stamped on *want* at some cost in the evaluation of the entire grammar.

(2) The morphological redundancy rule. I have in mind the sort of redundancy rules proposed for the full-entry lexicon of Jackendoff 1975. The idea there is that the lexicon is written out longhand in advance, as if no fact related to any other, but generalizations are recovered in the application of the evaluation measure to the grammar. One of Jackendoff's examples is the English "causative" rule relating, for example, the transitive and intransitive forms of verbs like *open*. Both forms are entered in the lexicon, but there is a morphological redundancy rule telling us that when we have an intransitive verb, there is no extra cost for having a transitive form pronounced identically with appropriately modified semantics. Thus accidental gaps cost nothing, but patterns that are not fully productive can still be

appealed as rendering the grammar more "learnable."
Both these devices are extremely powerful, but obviously, something of this flavor is in order if our lexicon is not to over- or under-generalize in the domain of preposition selection.

Presentation of an actual formal mechanism to handle this problem will be deferred to chapter 3, when we have a general theory of the semantics of valence, but some foreshadowing can be indulged in here. Briefly, the valence of a lexical item will be partially determined by its lexical representation. Any subcategorization features that satisfy certain semantic requirements will be "generated" freely on a lexical entry. In the case of preposition selection, the semantic requirement will be that the preposition have a semantics capable of selecting a "participant" from among the head's participants. The procedure will not be completely deterministic because at times more than one preposition will be capable of marking some participant. This is presumably the case for the *karman* meanings of *for* and *after*. In such cases, any arbitrary choice is allowed by the generation procedure. Crucially, *some* choice is always made, and particular heads *do* have particular subcategorizations. Thus, the grammar as a whole will mark "John longed after Mary" as ungrammatical, because *long* subcategorizes only for *for*, even though no principle says it must be so.

This sort of mechanism is more in the spirit of lexical redundancy rules than exception features, because the subcategorization procedure amounts to a characterization of a possible subcategorization, just as the causative rule was a characterization of a certain class of possible lexical items. Note that the exception feature approach may embroil us in some unnecessary feature traffic. Consider:

(17) John desired a tootsie roll.

(18) John's desire for a tootsie roll.

(19) John's aspirations *for fulfillment
towards fulfillment

Now the generalizations in question are semantic, and it would be desirable for the preposition selection of a noun like "desire" to follow in some way from the fact that it is a predicate of longing. But under the exception-feature account, the only way that can happen is if the nominalization rule removes the exception feature [-FOR] from the verb, and this seems an unpleasant complication, involving either special lexical stipulations in the rule or special rule stipulations on the lexical item. Nor do we want to say that nominalization ALWAYS strips off exception features, because of facts like those in (19).

What the case of the verbs of longing has shown is this: particular meanings of particular subcategorized-for prepositions are compatible with a certain semantic class of heads; they occur with them, to borrow a phrase from another context, "with overwhelmingly greater than chance frequency."

1.4 The Problem for Logical Form: a first solution

The existence of semantic regularities in the distribution of prepositions is no surprise to anyone. In fact just about every generative syntactic theory accounts for the distribution of some prepositions with some kind of semantic selection. But explicit appeal to semantic selection is usually made only in the case of adjuncts. That is, since the selection of subcategorized-for PP's is handled by syntactic stipulation, only adjuncts REQUIRE a semantic appeal. My point here is that semantic selection also plays a role for subcategorized-for PP's. Parsimony suggests that we account for both kinds of selection with the same mechanism; the most natural such account, it seems to me, would be to give both kinds of PP the same kinds of semantics. This in turn poses a challenge to theories that make a type theoretic distinction between adjunct PP's and subcategorized-for PP's; a popular recourse for theories making this distinction is to give subcategorized-for PP's the same type as NP's. This is the treatment counseled in Gazdar 1981b and Sag and Klein 1982 for example.

Note that the penetrations of meanings like *karman* into the domain of subcategorization does not constitute a refutation of all analyses that gives subcategorized-for PP's NP-type meanings. All we have shown is that one should not throw away the meaning of the preposition. For those who still wish to treat subcategorized-for PP's as having NP-type denotations, there remains the possibility that a lexical rule operates to combine the meanings of heads and prepositions, at the same time marking the heads syntactically. In this way, the relevant verbs of longing could fit a common rule description before being marked [FOR], or some such, and the prepositional phrases could still be given NP meanings in the logic. The prepositions could, as it were, be incorporated presyntactically. But this path would at least take some motivating before it could be called a happy one.

There are various unintuitive aspects to such an analysis. For example, in the case of a verb like *give*, which subcategorizes for an obligatory *to*-phrase the form *give* itself would have be treated as something like a bound stem, since the verb would never occur without having first undergone an "incorporation" rule with *to*.

But past experience with the technical ingenuity of linguists suggests we should never dismiss an idea simply because of a few technical hitches. The strongest argument against the incorporation approach is to present a clean alternative to the treatment of PP's as bare arguments. The general problem of preposition meanings is knowing what to do with them.

For the moment let us think of a verb like *want* as a predicate with arguments. Let us begin by considering only semantic representations that use function-argument application. If a preposition like *for* is to enter meaningfully into the relation of the verb with its arguments, it must either mediate that predication, or modify it. That is, our choices seem to boil down to:

(a) (V P N2)
(b) (V (P N2))

Here, N2 stands for N-double-bar, the maximal projection of N, usually called a Noun Phrase. The particular N2 at issue in the above predication structures is the object of the preposition. Naturally choice (b) will be favored in an approach that prefers a transparent relation between its predicate argument structure and its syntactic constituent structure. But even, for such a theory, say Generalized Phrase Structure Grammar (hereafter GPSG, see Gazdar 1981b), the rules of semantic semantic combination can be kept simple, at the expense of more complicated lexical semantics. So we might mimic the choice (b) with the following toy lexicon and syntax.

```
<for :P: (LAMBDA NP (LAMBDA V ((V FOR) NP)))>
<wish : V : WISH>
<P1 => P N2: (P N2)>
<P2 => P1: P1>
<V1 => V P2: (P2 V)>
```

The format of the rules here is taken from Gazdar 1981b, with the material before the colon intended as a syntactic statement, and the material after as a semantic statement. In GPSG, every phrase structure rule must be accompanied by translation rule expressing how the translations of the daughters are to be combined to yield the translations of the mother. In the example rules given, the actual lexical predicate argument structure is concealed in the entry for *for* and is that of choice (b). If we insist on heads as functors, in our syntactic rules, we need only complicate the translation of *wish* to be (LAMBDA PP (PP WISH)). A decade of lambda conversion has taught us that the notions of function and argument are fixed only when there is some independent theory of the denotations of the objects being combined.

The moral to be drawn from lambda shuffling is one about the underdetermination of our logical representations. We need whatever help we can get when confronting the wealth of choices they offer. Thus, a theory that constrains the logical type of non-lexical syntactic categories, like that of Klein and Sag 1982, is welcome because it immediately rules out choice (b) above, which forces P2 to assume a disallowed type.[1] The specific choices of that theory, however, are problematic for me, because the type it DOES choose for P2's is that of N2. And the assumption I have made is that prepositions contribute to meaning.

I would like to investigate an alternative kind of constraint on our choices: suppose instead of constraining nonlexical syntactic

1. The idea of constraining syntactic categories was not first suggested in Klein and Sag 1982. It is fully explicit in Montague 1970, though his notion of a syntactic category was somewhat different than the one linguists are used to.

categories we tried to work things bottom up. Acquisitionally speaking, lexical items are where semantics starts, so there is some potential payoff in stipulating that their logical forms, at least, be simple (as we shall see later in the chapter, the conceptual structures behind those logical forms can still be arbitrarily complex). I have in mind letting prepositions be of type <e, <e,t>> and giving them semantics that uses conjunction and variable binding instead of function-argument application. I also have in mind a system of logical representations in which situations are entities, and sentences denote sets of properties of those entities. The payoffs in making situations entities will be threefold: (1) we will find it easy to make S's and NP's the same semantic types; (2) our logical representations will largely be simple first order logic; (3) both verbs and prepositions will be representable as first order predicates.

I will present the proposal top down, beginning with the semantics for an entire sentence. Here is the proposed semantics for our star sentence:

```
(EXISTS* SIGMA (EXISTS X (AND (LONGING SIGMA BEATRICE)
                              (FOR SIGMA X)
                              (BUICK X))))
```

Here *sigma* is a situation, a situation of longing; (Exists* sigma wff) should be thought of as

```
(lambda P (Exists sigma (and wff (P sigma))))
```

This allows the translation of a sentence in the logic to have type <<e,t>,t>. One advantage of this treatment is intuitive. The denotation of a sentence is the set of sets containing situations that match the situation the sentence describes. This is a little more intuitively satisfying than having a truth value as a denotation, though it still falls short of anchoring us in a particular situation. The chief technical advantage of this treatment is that it lets us handle embedded sentences just as we handle ordinary NP-arguments, because sentences are now the same type as NP's.

If we ignore the jacked-up type of the above logical expression, then we can interpret it as saying that there is a longing situation involving Beatrice, and the relation FOR holds between that situation and some Buick. Ontological liberties aside, the chief oddity of this representation is that the Buick is not an argument of the predicate LONGING, despite the fact that we have agreed that the for-phrase is subcategorized for. What I propose is that the actual arguments in logical representations be limited to just those participants realized by the grammatical roles subject and object (this will be revised in Chapter 5), and that all prepositional phrase complements be represented alike. Let us adopt the conventional assumption assumption that temporal modifiers are adjuncts. Then, if Beatrice's longing is to restricted to a particular Tuesday, I propose the logical representation be:

(EXISTS* SIGMA (EXISTS X (AND (LONGING SIGMA BEATRICE)

(FOR SIGMA X)
(BUICK X)
(ON SIGMA TUESDAY))))

Two points need to be made about the treatment of the adjuncts here. First, note that using the situations as entities evades a difficulty encountered in some treatments of adjuncts. Since we can represent recursive modifiers as "inserted" conjunctions we avoid having to posit operators that increase the valence of predicates; we avoid having to turn the "long for" relation into the "long for...on" relation. Because of this, facts about the commutativity of adjuncts fall out from the commutativity of logical "and". Thus "longing for a Buick on Tuesday in Rome" is logically the same as "longing for a Buick in Rome on Tuesday." On an account that resorts to valence increasing operations, some special stipulation needs to be made to capture these facts. I am indebted to Carl Pollard for pointing this out to me.

Second, note that there is no distinction here between the representation of the for-phrase and the temporal adjunct. Obviously there is something missing here about the semantics of longing; what I propose to do is make up for this lack in the conceptual structures that the lexicon accesses for both the meanings of *for* and the meanings of *long*. The strategy is to make the logical representations and the rules of combination simpler; what results is a logical representation with no difference between subcategorized-for complements and adjuncts. As we shall see that distinction can be made at the level of lexical representation.

On anybody's account there is a great deal of conceptual work that needs to be done to ascribe to adjuncts the correct *role* in the situations they are associated with. My point is that whatever mechanisms will do that work can do it for ALL the participants. I have stopped short of doing it for subjects and objects as well (as case grammarians of another age would) simply because there are no morphological markers for semantic roles in those cases.

It remains to exhibit the lexical entries and rules that could output the above representations. I will limit myself to just the V1, V2 (= S), P1, and P2 rules, and the entries for the verb and the preposition:[1]

---

1. The notation in these rules is a departure from a convention introduced by Montague whereby:

(i) (lambda x (lambda y [love (x) (y)])) (j) (m)

is equivalent to

(ii) love (j) (m)

which is in turn equivalent to:

(iii) (love m j)

I will write (i):

((lambda x (lambda y (love x y))) j m)

There will be no "relational-notation" convention.

```
<long: V: longing>
<for: P: for>
<V1 => V P2: (lambda sigma
               (lambda y (and (V y sigma)
                              (P2 sigma))))>
<V1 => V1 P2: (lambda sigma
                (lambda y (and (V1 y sigma)
                               (P2 sigma))))>
<V2 => N2 V1: (exists* sigma (N2 (lambda z (V1 sigma z))))>
<P2 => P1: P1>
<P1 => P N2: (lambda sigma (N2 (lambda z (P sigma z))))>
```

The conjunctive form of the semantics of these rules is not unique; call that form "(lambda x (and (P x) (Q x)))" property conjunction. property conjunction is a general compositional strategy resorted to with modifiers of property-denoting constituents, modifiers such as relative clauses and some adjectives. The proposal here thus seems to me compatible in spirit with the approach in Klein and Sag 1982, where the rule-to-rule hypothesis is abandoned and general type-driven semantic principles compose the translations that accompany phrase structure rules.

I assume that verbs and prepositions are associated with true first-order predicates, and not with higher-type predicates capable of taking NP denotations as arguments. This is why the NP's in the rules above are not arguments, but are quanitified-in.

Note that the V2 (= S) rule thus gives the subject scope over the verb phrase, just as the treatment in Montague 1970 does. One of the motivations for that decision is facts about scope of conjunction:

(20) A fish or a unicorn walks and talks.

The only available reading for this sentence is one on which the *or* has scope over the *and*. That is, the sentence asserts that either it is the case that a fish walks and talks or it is the case that a unicorn walks and talks. With conjunction scope reversed, the reading is wrong: the sentence would assert that A fish or a unicorn walks and a fish or a unicorn talks.

Although giving the subject scope over the VP gets the conjunction facts right, it does not get the facts about intensionality right — if one has a scopal treatment of intensionality:

(21) A unicorn appears to be approaching.

If subjects always have wide scope over VP's, this sentence should only have a *de re* reading, given a scopal treatment. Alas, the facts are otherwise, and so it would appear that any treatment giving subjects wide scope over VP's is doomed. My semantics above is one such semantics.

In fact, I think the truth is that one or both of the above scopal treatments must be wrong, either a scopal analyis of intensionality, or a scopal analysis of conjunction. The crucial examples are those like the following:

(22) A fish or a unicorn appeared to be approaching.

My claim is that the above example has a *de dicto* reading on which the *or* outscopes *appear*, that is, a *de dicto* reading that can be paraphrased: a fish appeared to be approaching or a unicorn appeared to be approaching. Rooth and Partee 1982 call such readings wide-scope *or* readings, and propose a treatment involving type-ambiguity; although I know of no technical objections to such a treatment, type ambiguity is undesirable on independent grounds, and any alternative account of intensionality that could avoid it would be preferable.

I confess that I have no such alternative account to offer. I present these facts here because they undermine a standard argument against a semantic treatment that gives subjects scope over VP's. Indeed, if one assumes that a scopal analysis of conjunction is correct, they provide a challenge to any scopal treatment of intensionality.

In the next section we will move away from logical issues to examine several other examples cut from much the same cloth as the examples of the verbs of *longing*. We will have two goals:

(1) To show that the phenomenon of systematic semantic compatibility is pervasive among all prepositions, whether subcategorized-for or adjuncts.

(2) To ask what the distributional facts about prepositions tell us about both the semantics of governing heads and prepositions. In 1.8 we will turn to the question of lexical representations that can capture these distributional facts.

1.5 Some more preposition meanings

In this section I want to look ahead to the business of constructing lexical representations and introduce some terminology which was breifly discussed in the introduction. Two terms which will prove quite useful even at this early stage are *scene* and *participant*. As stated in the introduction, we will assume that our lexical representations are statements of culturally salient categories, where these can in turn be thought of as culturally salient types of situations. These situation-types we will call *scenes*. The entities that can regularly be individuated in instances of a scene, and spoken of as playing roles in that scene, we will call participants.

In the last section I argued that prepositions have meanings that are systematically related to their distribution, even in contexts where they must be subategorized-for. In this section I want to continue to make that case, and to ask what the consequences of that claim are. The most significant consequence I believe, is that we shall want lexical representations rich enough to enable us to read off the semantic compatibility of a preposition with a head. However, let's defer tackling the lexical representations to get a bit clearer on just what facts we are trying to account for.

I want to leave the domain of verbs of *longing* now to consider a more celebrated example. This is the verb *decide*.

(23) John decided on the boat.

Chomsky 1965 cites this as a clear example of a verb subcategorizing for a preposition, and argues for a distinction from adjuncts on the syntactic grounds we mentioned before. Specifically, this kind of *on* phrase doesn't prepose, and it doesn't alternate position with adjuncts. Although we don't have the ironclad guarantee of obligatoriness in this case, let us assume for now that the PP here is in fact subcategorized-for, purely on syntactic grounds. The question is: how semantically "unpredictable" is this use of *on*?

First compare (24) and (25):

(24) John counted on Jim's coming

(25) John bet on the Yankees

None of examples (23)-(25) exhibits *on* in what one might call its prototypical locative sense, yet one might plausibly argue that a single peripheral meaning was exhibited in all three sentences, a meaning roughly paraphrasable as "impending object or event." Evidence that there is a single fact about *on* linking all three of these examples is a corresponding use of *against*:

(26) John decided against the boat

(27) John counted against Jim's coming

(28) John bet against the Yankees.

If one were to ask the average native speaker what the opposite of *on* was, the answer would probably be *off*; for *for*, the answer would be *against*. I would like to suggest that there is another antonymic axis, less central for both prepositions, linking *on* with *against*. That one word should have more than one antonym is, of course, a common lexical occurence. A typical example is *short*, with polar opposite *long* in one sense, and *tall* in another.

Note, however, that although we can claim the uses of *on* and *against* are not semantically unique in these cases, we can hardly claim that they were entirely predictable, as some near synonyms show:

(29) *He put money against the Yankees.

(30) *He relied against Mary's coming

(31) He opted for the boat.

Note also that *opt* might have been included among our verbs of longing in the last section. The *karman* meaning of *for* and the meaning of *on* discussed here are not very different, if any systematic difference can be drawn between them at all; in the last section we saw that *after* competed with *for* for some of the same verbs; here we see *for*, in its *karman* meaning competing with *on*. This kind of indeterminacy in the selection of prepositions by heads seems to be fairly common, and a fairly natural consequence of the underspecified meanings of prepositions. It is the chief source of helplessness a foreigner feels before the awesome complexities of the English preposition. It is not my aim to belittle those complexities. I emphasize again that my aim is not to predict the distribution of prepositions, but to characterize what constraints there are on that distribution, and to learn what I can about how to adequately represent prepositions (and their governing heads) from those constraints.

A natural approach to this enterprise is to look at semantically delimited class of verbs, and see what prepositions turn up often.

Recall that the "natural" antonym of *for* was *against*, thus suggesting there is another natural paradigm linking these two prepositions. It's not hard to come up with verbs that take both: *argue, come out, battle, speak out, struggle, fight, campaign*. Call these verbs *campaign* verbs. In this class I mean to include all the verbs involving situations of conflict; thus, *speak out* qualifies because it is a special lexicalized kind of speaking which implies an audience that is being challenged. Of course, the more general verb *speak* also takes *against* in what we would clearly like to call the same meaning, but let's put that point aside for a bit. Call the meaning of *for* associated with them *favored-cause*, and the meaning of *against* *contended-force*. If we need an example of one of these meanings occuring with a syntactically obligatory prepositional phrase, we have one in the verb *pit*. *Pit* also differs from the other verbs mentioned in that it takes *against*, but not *for*.

There seem to be a number of heads like *pit* in that they only allow *against*:

(32) We must always guard against complacency.

(33) There is no defense against good intentions.

(34) The Hungarians revolted against the Austrians.

(35) We shall always have the forces of fate to contend against.

However there seem to be no examples of *heads of campaigning* that take the *favored-cause* meaning of *for* but not the *contended-force* meaning of *against*. There is a rather straightforward account of this, given that we have limited ourselves for the moment to situations of implicit conflict: situations of strife naturally involve protagonists and contended-forces, but favored-causes are quite dispensable. At the moment, without any tools for representing situations, we have no very good way of talking about this; but we can try the following tentative and entirely descriptive conclusion: all *heads of campaigning*, with one qualification reserved for the next paragraph, are semantically compatible with the *contended-force* meaning of *against*; a subset is compatible with the *favored-object* meaning of *for*. One way of talking about this is to say all *heads of campaigning* have lexical scenes including a *contended-force* participant. The *contended-force* meaning of *for* is appropriate to mark that participant. Some *heads of campaigning* have, besides, a *favored-object* participant, for which *for* in one meaning is appropriate. We will develop this style of talk further in the next section.

Still another set of verbs, those we might call true verbs of clashing, take the preposition *over* , using it to pick out yet another of the participants in a typical conflict scene, a participant we might call the *bone-of-contention*. This class will include *fight, battle, argue,* and *debate*. We might at first be tempted to say that the verbs of clashing make up a subset of the verbs of campaigning. Note, however, that the verb I chose to name the class does not allow *against*.

(36) * We clashed against Bill.

In fact there seem to be a number of verbs, all of which could be notionally classed as verbs of *campaigning,* that do not take *against*. These include *quarrel, quibble,* and *haggle*. What they have in common is that they are obligatorily symmetric; that is while they conceptually allow a *contended-force,* to be grammatically realized that argument must either occur in the same Noun-phrase as the protagonist, as in "Bill and I quarreled, or after the preposition *with,* as in "I quarreled with Bill." This too could be called a semantic fact about the verbs in question, though it is a fact not so much about the sort of situations they describe, as about their argument structure. More importantly, though, is that the fact that a verb is symmetric and a verb of *conflict* does not preclude its taking *against*. So we have *argue,* taking both *with* and *against*, but apparently in slightly different functions:

(37) I argued with Mary.

(38) ?I argued with Mary's proposal.

(39) I argued against Mary.

(40) I argued against Mary's proposal.

The crucial fact is that *argue* does not entail an obligatorily symmetric situation; for many speakers, *with* chooses the symmetric situations; *against* does not. For those speakers (38) sounds peculiar. Some speakers accept (38), but everyone seems to agree that there is a difference between (37) and (39), in that in (37), Mary must be an active participant, but in (39), she must be a topic: "The panel narrowed down the list of candidates to Boswell, Bogdan, and Mary; I argued against Mary." Thus *argue* is not obligatorily symmetric, like *quarrel, quibble,* and *haggle.* and the contrast between these verbs and *argue* may still be made on semantic grounds.

To summarize: there is a class of non-symmetric verbs we can call the verbs of *campaigning,* including an obligatory participant called a *contended-force,* which can always be marked with *against*. Call the scene with which these verbs may be associated CAMPAIGNING. There is another semantically related class of verbs which are symmetric, and make reference to the CAMPAIGNING scene in their semantic composition. Something about their lexical semantic structure guarantees that they are no longer compatible with *against*; and the fact that are symmetric guarantees they are compatible with*with*. Note that this approach, though I have been quite vague in characterizing it, makes one important claim. It claims that symmetric verbs are semantically more complicated than other semantically close, but non-symmetric verbs. We will not return to symmetric verbs until Chapter 4, when a treatment compatible with these brief remarks is proposed. The only significant point to note here is that one kind of semantic relatedness which will need to be expressed in our lexical representations is that of shared components. The verbs of *campaigning* and the symmetric verbs of *campaigning* share some semantic component even though they are not compatible with exactly the same prepositions. We might speak of this component as the CAMPAIGNING scene.

In this section we have looked fairly closely at two examples of semantically related groups of verbs taking the same preposition. A few minutes leafing through works like Householder 1964 and 1965 is probably a more convincing demonstration than this sort of piecemeal approach. These works are both painstaking compendia of verb classes, where the classes are defined entirely distributionally. It becomes clear after only a brief inspection that there are numerous semantic generalizations to be drawn among verbs that appear on the same page. Consider the following list from Householder 1965, p. 27: *forbid, inhibit, dissuade, stop, hinder, prevent, keep, restrain.* All of these verbs appear in the frame Noun-Phrase + Verb-Phrase + *from* +

Verb-Phrase-ing (example: Bill stopped Harry from smoking). The semantic relatedness is obvious; my conclusion here is that something about the representations of these verbs and the relevant meaning of *from* must predict this distribution. Another example, p. 65: *goad, inveigle, intimidate, maneuver, manipulate,pressure, provoke, scare, shame, wheedle.* All these verbs occur in the frame Noun-Phrase + Verb-Phrase + *into* + Verb-Phrase-ing: (example: Bill goaded Harry into striking back).

I think paradigms like this are the rule rather than the exception, and that there are very few semantically unmotivated occurences of prepositions.[1] This view appears to be incompatible with a treatment like that adopted in GPSG, where PP's have NP-type meanings — unless that account can be supplemented with some mechanism for allowing prepositions to contribute to the semantics. On the other hand, the version of LFG adopted in Simpson 1983 takes a very different tack: there subcategorized-for prepositions are assigned a single grammatical function OBLIQUE, reserved for "semantically complex arguments, where a semantically complex argument is "a

---

1. One kind of exception it would be reasonable to make: some prepositions might have a purely grammatical function; this seems a plausible line to take with the *of* we often find in nominalizations, or the passive *by* with verbs (though in chapter 3 I will suggest that *by* with nouns is distinct).

predicate which in turn takes arguments."[1] An account of this form though it might differ in detail is in the same semantic spirit. A question arises though over the issue of subcategorization. The only proposal I know of in LFG is to subcategorize heads by the grammatical functions of their complements. But if OBLIQUE is the only function for subcategorized-for complements, then that leaves the choice of particular prepositions to semantic selection; what we have argued in this section is that semantic selection can narrow down the choice of prepositions to a few, but that it can not always determine the "correct" one (cf. *long* vs. *hanker*).

1.5.1 Individuating Preposition Meanings

The direction we have taken leads to a partitioning of verbs into semantic classes according to the prepositions they select. Throughout this dissertation I will be using such semantic verb classes to help construct lexical representations for verbs.

However, there is a serious problem involved in this classificatory enterprise that I have not yet addressed; this is the individuation of the preposition meanings. We are dealing with generalizations here that sometimes involve very small classes of verbs. The *impending-object* use of *on* we first saw with *decide* could be argued to cover perhaps

---

1. p. 50.

seven verbs *bet, wager, decide, count, rely, plan, and depend.* But only five of these also allow *against*. Should there be two preposition meanings here, or one? More generally, how do we halt the atomization of preposition meanings that results from resorting to finer and finer verb classes? At its most absurd extreme, pursuing this course would yield a different preposition meaning for every verb that subcategorized for na preposition, which would put us right back on an even footing with a theory that selects all its prepositions by arbitrary syntactic marking. On the other hand, the opposite extreme is the one-form/one-function view, which leaves us with lexical characterizations so intolerably vague that they can be of no use either in prediction or interpretation. Even among the few examples I've discussed, some problematic cases can be adduced. What allows me to distinguish between the *karman* meaning of *for* discussed in 1.5, and meaning in 1.6 called *favored-cause* (which occurred with some verbs of *campaigning*). There are three points to make here:

(1) If there is a theoretically interesting way to decide when one preposition meaning ends and another begins, it cannot possibly be made on a case-for-case basis. The decision needs to be made on the basis of the lexical system, in light of an overall understanding of how the forms associated with some semantic domain carve it up, where they overlap, where they diverge, how they can co-occur.

(2) There may simply BE no theoretically interesting way to rule out all the possibilities. But this is equivalent to saying that the question of how many meanings a preposition has just may not be that important. The only theoretically significant point we need to make here is that neither extreme will work. Preposition selection is not arbitrary syntax, and preposition

forms do not determine single meanings.

(3) It will not do to characterize preposition meanings purely in terms of the classes of heads they occur with; this is not just because of the risk of circularity; it is because they exhibit those meanings in other places.

Points (2) and (3) need some clarification.

The claim in (2) is that the question of how many meanings some form A has is not intrinsically very interesting. This, however, does not entirely close the matter. It is interesting if all the meanings that belong to one form cluster closely together. This is what answers the question of whether it is arbitrary accident that A's various uses have all accrued to one form, or an example of linguistic systematicity. To put it somewhat differently, counting meanings is not a very good evaluation measure unless there is a general metric for measuring meaning distances available.

It should be fairly clear that what is in store for if we continue pursueing this line is lots of preposition meanings. The verb classes we have talked about are small; the English prepositions are relatively few; therefore each one will have to shoulder a number of semantic loads. I do not count this a great drawback, however, because I leave open the question of how to relate those meanings. The preposition *for* has arisen in two different ways so far, once in paradigmatic opposition to *against*, once in the meaning I have called *karman*. I have no doubt that these meanings are in some way related; on the other hand it would be no great surprise to me to find them carried by different forms in some other language, if they were entifiable units of meaning at all. In Chapter 2, once we have presented a modest framework for lexical representation, we will look at three clearly different meaning representations for *for* and see that although different, they share some structure. This, however, is not sufficient motivation for abstracting that structure out and calling it *the* single meaning of *for*. In the first place, there will be no single piece of structure shared by all the *for's*. Rather the relations will be of the family resemblance type; *karman* may share some structure with *favored-object for*, which may share some completely disjoint structure with the next meaning. In the second place, even if such an abstraction were possible, the meaning chosen would be so vague that it would predict the compatibility of *for* with far too many heads. There is a dependency between the decision to worry about semantic compatibility and the move towards polysemy.

Turning now to to point (3) above, the claim that preposition meanings cannot be characterized exclusively in terms of the heads they occur with. This is crucial because it shows that not only does an account that discards preposition meanings lose generalizations about the classes of heads particular prepositions occur with; it loses any unifying account of the preposition itself, because prepositions can occur as predicators on their own, without any lexical head available. So, alongside the occurence of the *favored-cause* meaning of *for* with verbs of campaigning, we also have:

(41) I'm for capital punishment.

They also occur in predicative position, a phenomenon we will be examining in detail in Chapter 5, but which has been recognized in a number of different syntactic analyses:

(42) He set it behind him.

(43) He set it in front of him.

(44) He set it under him.

(45) He set it over him.

The crucial point here is that a number of different prepositions can occur in the same syntactic slot.[1] What the verb seems to select semantically is a certain kind of predication, here locational, and all the prepositions with appropriate locative meanings will do. Here is an example involving one of the preposition meanings we have considered:

(46) He set her against him

This is our *contended-force* use of *against*. (45) arguably involves a different verb *set* from that in (46), yet it still appears to allow a number of different prepositions in the same grammatical "slot:"

---

1. Also of note here is that all the examples given, a coferential reading is possible between the subject *he* and the object *him*. This poses problems for a clause-bounded account of reflexivization which a predicative analysis can resolve (see Chapter 5).

(47) He set her at her task

(48) He set her to her task

(49) He set her on the right track.

This suggests a predicative construction. Note also that there is nothing in the semantics of *set* which suggests a situation involving conflict. That semantic component only appears when *against* appears.

A third sort of case is that of a preposition occuring with some head to narrow its unmodified meaning. This was the sort of example we passed up before with *speak*:

(47) She spoke against him

(48) He used her own words against her

(49) He ran against the Danes at Millrose.

(50) She voted against the bottle tax.

Obviously, *speaking, using, running,* and *voting* describe situations which may be unspecified for any *contended-force*; yet using them with the preposition *against* introduces an antagonist. There are two lines one might take with examples like these; and the plausibility of either depends, I think, on the particular verb; first one might say that it is the collocation of Verb + Against that introduces the meaning of conflict, that is, essentially, that there is a lexical entry for that verb which is marked for syntactic coocurence with *against*, which has a different meaning from the unmodified head. This is the road that must be taken if the of the verb-preposition collocation is a bit more than the sum of its parts, that is, if the new meaning is too specific. Then the right treatment for *run against* may simply be to enter a composite verb in the lexicon, since that verb-preposition pair so strongly suggests a race that it might just as well be viewed as a lexicalization of a racing situation.

The other kind of account is more appealing for the cases like *use* and *speak*. This is to say simply that among speaking situations there are those involving conflict and those not, and that the use of *against* narrows it down to the former. This more or less compositional *semantic narrowing* seems to be the strongest sort of argument for the meaningfulness of prepositions, and one of the clearer litmuses for just what those meanings are.

The central problem of this dissertation, then, can be posed independently of the question of subcategorized-for prepositional-phrases versus adjuncts: prepositions have meanings, just as other heads do; those meanings determine their distributions in all their syntactic roles. The interesting problems begin once this rather simple point is granted. What sorts of lexical representations would we need to read off the basic "predictable" facts of semantic compatibility? Once we have such representations, we will see that they will be useful in making other kinds of syntactic predictions.

In the next section I will briefly present the conceptual

framework in which the lexical representation of this dissertation is set. Following that we will move to the frame representations themselves.

1.6 A proposal concerning English Prepositions

Let us return to the notions introduced at the beginning of the last section, scenes and participants: Fillmore's canonical example of a scene is the commercial event. He says:[1]

> The elements in a prototype commercial event scene are the buyer, the seller, the money that changes hands, and the goods that change hands.

Fillmore's suggestion is that the information about what scene a verb is associated with is part of its lexical entry. The lexical entries for verbs like *buy, sell, spend, cost, purchase, pay,* and *price* will all make reference to the commercial event scene. Presumably so will the entry for nouns like *cost, price, sale, purchase, goods, buy, buyer,* and *seller,*, and adjectives like *expensive* and *cheap*.

Fillmore's advice to the lexicographer, then, is that she take on some work not very different from that of a good ethnographer. A culturally significant type of situation is isolated and its central features are described. Lexical items encode particular perspectives taken on this material. The notion of such a "perspective" will not be incorporated into our lexical representations until Chapter 2. Until then, we will simply relate verbs directly to scenes. As noted in the introduction, the chief motivation for the notion scene is that it offers a

---

1. Fillmore 1977b, p.103

lexical foundation for a theory of discourse understanding.

I now lay down some necessary background assumptions for the pages ahead.

First, the whole point of exploring lexical semantics is to illuminate lexical relations. Thus, we must be able to talk about the relation of one scene to another. As a simple first step in that direction, I propose that there be a hierarchy of scenes. A scene like the commercial event scene will lay towards the more specific end of the hierarchy of scenes. It will not be primitive because a verb like *trade* ought to share some elements of the commercial events scene and not share others. I think a useful way of talking about this is to say that *trade* involves another kind of scene that is more general than the Commercial Events scene. Call it an Exchange scene. And the Commercial-Event scene is a kind of Exchange scene.

Within the Commerical-Event scene we will make statements about the relationship of certain participants to one another, of buyer to seller, and buyer to money. At the more general end of the hierarchy of scenes, we will want to make statements about more general participant relations as well, and the kind of participant relations we talk about in very general scenes will be very like those called case roles or thematic roles. But there will be no particular limit on the number of levels in the hierarchy, and there will be scenes which are less general than "case role" scenes, and still more general than the Commercial-Event. For example, there are semantic generalizations to be made about the use of prepositions like *from* and *to*, that cannot be stated in terms of a Commercial Events scene.

It will be convenient to be spared the burden of deciding which scenes are primitive. We will not begin with any basic inventory of scenes out of which all others must be constructed, but will make them up as needed. Even in Chapter 3 when we turn our attention to "case role" scenes, our only concern will be to capture certain obvious generalizations about the semantics of nuclear terms. The case role scenes will of course be very general and will be components in a number of other scenes, but there will be no claim that every verb must include in its make-up a case role scene. Although there will be a single root scene called THING, of which every scene is a generalization, this is only a formal convenience; being a kind of THING just means being a scene, and does not embody a semantic claim.

Prepositions will have scenes as verbs do, but with two differences; first, prepositions tend to suffer from polysemy, and become associated with a multitude of scenes; second, prepositions tend to have vaguer scenes that specify things like motion through some kind of space, or conflict. In certain simple cases, verb scenes will simply be more populated and more fully specified version of some preposition scenes.

With all this apparatus in place, the next section will finally present some first attempts at lexical representations.

1.7 Lexical representations

The real question for any theory of the facts two sections back has not really been addressed yet. What we are talking about is lexical meanings, more than that, relatedness of meaning, not only within semantic verb classes, but also between verbs and prepositions. The goal is to design lexical semantic representations that will make these relations manifest.

There are a number of formalisms that could encode the right kind of information. The one I have chosen is appealing because it is open-ended and capable of representing information of arbitrary complexity. It is also appealing because Fillmore's work on scenes suggests that we can represent their structure chiefly in terms of the relationships of the participants in them. This, of course, is a view of things inherited from Case Grammar, but it differs crucially from that framework in that participants of scenes are much more specific than classical case roles; in a sense, *all* of a verb's meaning is decomposed into participant relations. Frames offer a very natural way of representing the resulting structure.

The idea of frames as a representational tool is usually credited to Minsky 1975, although the necessary concepts seem to have been around in AI work for some time before that (see Winograd 1975 for an excellent discussion of the relevant historical background). It is hard to do better than Winograd's explanation[1] of the basic idea:

> (1) A frame is a structure which represents knowledge about a very limited domain. A frame produces a description of the object or action in question, starting with an invariant structure common to all cases in its domain... A critical point is that the frame, as the unit of represented knowledge, is quite large. Rather than being on the order of a single property or relation attributed to an object, it is on the order of a description of the object with additional information indicating relations with other frames.

The frames we will be concerned with will mostly be frames defining scenes, the invariant structure that objects (situations) of a certain type must show. The "cases" in such a frame's domain will be individual situations instantiating the scene. The "invariant structure" will largely be participant structure.

The syntax of my lexical representations will be modeled on FRL (for Frame Representation Language), which is a knowledge representation system developed by Goldstein and Roberts (Goldstein and Roberts 1977, 1979). The system as developed has a good deal more machinery than is needed for the discussion here; so I will make do with a very curtailed version that employs two of the principal ideas of FRL. The first is a particular data structure for all frames, both generic and individual, and the second is the idea of inheritance.

The computer language that most AI work is done in is called

---

1. p. 152

LISP. In LISP terms, an FRL frame is a property list of the following form:

```
(frame
(slot1 (value1))
(slot2 (value2))

(slotn (valuen)))
```

The slots may be thought of as attributes of the frame, and the values as their values. What I shall be doing is identifying the frame with a particular situation type, and the slots with its participants.

The idea of inheritance is what will make things run. In FRL there is no structural distinction between generic objects and individuals. Information about people in general can be encoded in frame called PERSON (which can have various slots with or without accompanying values), and information about GAWRON in another frame very much like it. The relation between these two frames is encoded in a special slot called AKO (mnemonic for "a kind of"). So we might have

```
(PERSON
 (AKO (THING))
 (NAME (FNAME :FRAME))
 (ADDRESS)
 (PERSONAL_HISTORY))

(GAWRON
 (AKO (PERSON))
 (NAME)
 (ADDRESS (SUNSET_BLVD))
 (PERSONAL_HISTORY (BIRTH
                    GRADE-SCHOOL
                    HIGH-SCHOOL
                    COLLEGE
                    GRAD-SCHOOL)))
```

Here PERSON is AKO THING, which is the root frame; everything is ultimately AKO THING. Gawron is AKO PERSON. In virtue of that he inherits all the slots of a person. Slots may have procedures attached to them instead of values. Those procedures may be used to calculate the value for that slot when none is stipulated; so GAWRON inherits the procedure for calculating names (which I have not bothered to copy over) in addition to the NAME slot, and that procedure tells us that the name of a person is the same as the name of the frame. In this way various kinds of default information about people can be encoded in the generic PERSON frame and passed to the non-generic children. This includes AKO information. Thus, in virtue of being AKO PERSON Gawron is also AKO THING. We call GAWRON an individual frame, and PERSON a generic frame.

We are now ready for the skeleton of our first scene, the scene of LONGING, which will have two participants:

```
(LONGING
 (AKO (THING))
 (KARMAN)
 (LONGER ))
```

I have called this scene the LONGING scene because we have been speaking generically of the class of verbs that take *for* in its *karman* meaning as the verbs of longing. It was necessary to choose some name for this abstract scene, but in doing so I do not wish to distinguish the verb *long* in any way from the other verbs of longing. I might just as well have called this scene BEATRICE, except that the name would be less mnemonic. I mean for the structure of this scene to be shared by all of them. We can guarantee this by associating with each of the verbs of longing its own generic frame, into which will be encoded the specific information that distinguishes their meanings, and making each of those scenes AKO LONGING. This means they will each inherit the two slots KARMAN and LONGER.

Now for some terminology. The term *scenes* will be used for generic objects like the one represented by the LONGING frame, the term situation for the entities that instantiate those scenes, that is, particular situations of longing. More conventional individuals like Gawron, that table, this book, or that chair will be called *individuals*. The cover term for generic objects, whether their instantiations are situations or individuals, will be *sort*. Thus, PERSON and LONGING are both sorts.

The term *sort* will also be used of one-place predicates in the logic. In general, for every frame FRAME, there will be a one-place predicate FRAME'. We will talk a bit more explicitly about the connection between the logic and the frame representations in the next section.

The term role will be used to distinguish those slots that carry actual grammatically realized material from those like AKO which simply carry structural information. Later when our lexical representations grow more elaborate we may have a number of slots all with the same filler. The term participant will be used to designate the single filler of all those related roles. To put it differently, the term role will always correspond to one and only one slot in a frame; the term participant may correspond to a number of slots.

There will be an important distinction between actual lexical scenes and the more general structure of scenes erected above them, which will capture the relations between lexical scenes. The LONGING scene is an abstract scene which captures a shared semantic component among a group of verbs. There will also be a WISHING scene, a HOPING scene, a WANTING scene, a LONGING-L (L for "lexical"), and so on, all of them AKO the LONGING scene, all of them distinct in some way that captures the individual lexical differences among the verbs.

The question of distinctness is an important one for any theory of lexical semantics. Consider some candidate representations for HOPING and WANTING:

```
(HOPING
 (AKO (LONGING))
 (KARMAN)
 (LONGER))

(WANTING
 (AKO (LONGING))
 (KARMAN)
 (LONGER))
```

As I have written them, the only thing that distinguishes these frames is their names. Clearly, marking the distinction in this way does not constitute much of a semantic analysis; the only analysis consists in positing a similarity of structure inherited from the LONGING frame. I would like to view the differences between these two frames as being encoded in procedures that relate the two participants, which are not spelled out in the schematic representations given above; these procedures should be thought of as attached to one or both of the frame's slots. In what follows, I will have occasion to present a number of such "procedural attachments" to slots in a frame, but no frame in this dissertation will ever be complete — complete in the sense that it semantically distinguishes a lexical item from all other lexical items in English. Representations that detailed will have to await a complete specification of the procedural language of frames; it seems likely that in many cases the procedures will serve a function quite similar to that of distinguishers in Fodor and Katz 1963; that is, there will be "procedures" that occur in only a single lexical item. The procedures we will attend to in this dissertation will be those relevant to a semantic theory of complementation.

We have made a proposal concerning a rather sketchy semantic representation for a small class of verbs. But this still leaves open the problem that has dominated this chapter, the meaning of prepositions, in particular the preposition *for* in the special sense we have been concerned with. If we follow the proposal outlined in the last section, then prepositions will have scenes too, though these will be more general structures than the lexical scenes of verbs. As the lexical scene for the preposition *for* in its meaning of *karman*, I propose that we use the LONGING frame itself. Thus, *for* in this meaning can be thought of as a two place relation between a *longer* and a *karman*. It is simply a more general version of the lexical scenes with which it is semantically compatible.

But this leaves us with one last problem. The predicate *for* in the logic was a relation between an individual and a situation, not a vanilla flavored relation between individuals. It appears that something peculiar will have to be said about the mapping from the preposition frame LONGING to the preposition predicate FOR. But the peculiarity here is only apparent. Scenes in general will have an arbitrarily large number of slots, inherited from all of the frames up the sort hierarchy. Only certain specially selected slots will be encoded into the logical predicates that represent lexical items; for the time being, let us say that predicates will always have one argument position reserved for the scene itself. Thus, in the logical representation for "Beatrice longed for a Buick," we made LONGING a three-place relation holding between a situation and two individuals, and we made FOR a two-place relation holding between a situation and an individual. In both cases, the situation took the first argument position, and in both cases that argument position corresponds to the entire frame we are accessing in the frame representation. Call that argument position the "frame" position. Then, to complete the mapping from representations to logical predicates, the remaining argument positions must be determined by grammatical fiat. The following conventions will do as a first pass:

(1) intransitive verbs: these always translate into two-place relations between a situation and a participant. Thus *run* is a two place relation between a running situation and a runner. (RUN SIGMA JOHN) is true just in case SIGMA is a situation which is AKO RUNNING whose *runner* is JOHN. *runner*, of course, may be one of several slots in the RUNNING scene. Which slot in a scene corresponds to subject will be specified for each verb. (The exact mechanics of this specification will be given in the next section).

(2) transitive verbs: these are always three place relations between a situation and two participants, one the subject, one the object. Again, the slots corresponding to subject and object will be specified.

(3) prepositions: these are always two place relations between a situation and an individual; that individual is always grammatically realized as the object of the preposition. Again, specification will be required to determine which slots in the preposition's lexical scene correspond to which argument positions in the two-place relation.

This is a sketch of a procedure for mapping from scenes into logical predicates; one of the unsatisfying aspects is the stipulation involved in the mapping from particular slots to particular grammatical roles. To avoid this stipulation, the procedure would have to be able to look at the participants in a scene and determine from its structure which of those participants would make the best subject, the best direct object, or the best object of a preposition. There are numerous suggestions as to the semantics of the first two cases in the literature of case grammar. The third, I believe, is just a simpler example of the same thing. Thus, we have all heard statements like "Agents tend to be subjects." It would be quite useful, then, to have something like a Fillmorian subject hierarchy to mediate the mapping from scenes to predicates, with the added proviso that this hierarchy should help determine the "grammatical functions" for preposition meanings as well as verb meanings (and presumably for the other major categories as well).

However, I want to defer discussion of such a hierarchy till chapter 3, when our representational apparatus has become more sophisticated. The point to make here is simply this: the representations I'm proposing are explicit about the structures of the situations associated with lexical items. A question then arises about the mapping from situational structures to the logical predicates. If there is nothing interesting to say about this mapping, then it is arbitrary and must be stipulated and we are no worse off than with a theory that has nothing to say about such matters. In other words, the appeal to something like a subject selection hierarchy is dispensable. The claim it makes is that there IS something interesting to say about this mapping.

To strike up the chorus, here once again, is the logical form of our star sentence.

```
(EXISTS* SIGMA (EXISTS X (AND (LONGING SIGMA BEATRICE)
                              (FOR SIGMA X)
                              (BUICK X))))
```

What this means is that there is a situation which is an instance of both the scene associated with the verb *long* and the scene associated with the preposition *for*. This is consistent with our frame representations of the verb scene and the preposition scene, since the verb scene is AKO the preposition scene. It will be a stipulation about the predicate LONGING that its second argument maps onto the *longer* slot, and about the preposition *for* that its second argument maps onto the *karman* slot. Thus there is a single LONGING whose *karman* is a Buick and whose *longer* is Beatrice.

The above logical expression denotes a set of properties, the set of all properties true of a LONGING situation with Beatrice as *longer* and a Buick as *karman*. An example of a such a LONGING situation is:

(LONGING-1

```
(AKO (LONGING))
(LONGER (BEATRICE))
(KARMAN (BUICK-1)))
```

1.8 The logic of frames

In this question we will address the question of how we get from the logical representation (or directly from an English sentence, if the logic is dispensed with), to particular situations in the frame representation.

We have implicitly begun the task of associating particular lexical items with particular frames. Suppose that lexical items can be broken up into two classes. First, there will be those whose denotation is a logical constant (for convenience, call these closed class items, although they will not include everything generally thought of as closed class). This class will include items like *and*, *or* and *every*. Second, there will be those whose denotation must be "associated with" (in a way outlined below) a "lexical frame". For convenience, call this class of items the "open class" (though it will include prepositions, which are not generally thought of as open class). Then, if our enterprise is finite there is some correct set of lexical frames for the open class items of English.

In the introduction, we used the term English frame representation. The goal stated there was that the English frame representation be a single system capturing all the formal relations of the culturally salient categories. The implicit assumption was that an English frame representation must include all the open class lexical frames (the closed class items will be dealt with shortly). We will keep that assumption here, but we will give this master frame representation a special name. The unique frame representation that contains the entire English cultural system (including the open class lexical frames) will be called the *core English frame representation*.

Frames, however, can do more for us than represent word meanings and cultural categories. They can also represent states of the world. We can have a LONGING frame defining a structure for all LONGINGS, as well as a LONGING-37 frame, involving BEATRICE and BUICK-1. To represent a particular state of the world as viewed through "English" culture we will need a frame representation with both "core" frames and individual frames. There are an infinite number of frame representations describing different particular states of the world, containing the core frames of English, and consistent with them. We will call this infinite set of frame representations the set of English frame representations. In order to be a well-defined English frame representation, a frame representation must include a particular set of formal objects, namely the core frames of English, and it must be consistent with them (we will expand on the relevant notion of consistency below).

Talk of a system of representations that says everything systematic about a culture may sound ambitious, but in practice it is no more ambitious than the business of lexical representation is in the first place. At any given time we will only be concerned with a very small number of frames, and in this dissertation, those frames will always either be lexical, or they will components used in building lexical frames. In practice, then, we will have little truck with ethnographers. Why then embed the lexical representations in a general semiotic representation? The answer, ultimately, is theoretical parsimony. The full theory of discourse will clearly need something like a full blown semiotic account; it will need to know the meaning of a STOP sign, which is not deduceable from the meaning of *stop* (after you stop, you are allowed, under special conditions, to go again). The claim made by folding the lexicon into this general semiotic representation is that there is no separate level of lexical categorization. This means the two kinds of categorization should "feed" one another. Lexical categories should be used in building purely cultural categories, and vice versa. Clearly, the word *marriage* in all its meanings is founded on the existence of a certain social institution. Just as clearly, STOP signs, even those in airports with diagrams and no words, make reference to the same semantic notion as the word *stop*. I am not making any claims about epistemological priority. In fact, in locating both kinds of category at the same level, I am claiming that neither linguistic, nor non-linguistic categories, are specially distinguished.

I propose the formal connection of the frame representation to the grammar be the following: we replace the notion of truth in a model under an interpretation with truth in a frame model. Along with a number of those who work in the framework proposed by Montague, I regard the logical representations we have exhibited as merely a convenience and ultimately dispensable. However, the frame models, like models, are not dispensable.

How happy people will be with such a proposal will depend on two factors, first, how easy it is to define truth in a frame model; second, on whether there is some extra work that frame representations can do that classical models can't do, or at least, can't do without considerable augmentation. This second point was argued for in the introduction. If frame representations can also be linked to our truth conditions for English, this is a bonus.

We first need to say what language we are building models for. The rules we presented before for building the semantics of syntactic constituents were set in the framework of Gazdar 1982, although many of the semantic particulars differed. Gazdar 1982 uses the IL (of Montague 1970) as his logical language, maintaining, as Montague himself did, that the logical language was dispensable. We will make the same claim, and use the logical language merely as a convenience; because of its simple syntax, truth conditions are easy to formulate. However, we will not use IL, but rather IL without intensions (call it LL, for Logical Language) and without higher-order non-logical constants; LL will thus include first-order quantifiers, lambda, all the variable types countenanced by type-theory without intensions, and equality. We will have to beg some very difficult questions having to do with the success of intensional logic in handling problems of intensionality. I have no clear proposal for how the sort of frame representation proposed here can substitute for intensional logic in this domain, but I think that the initial success of situation semantics with intentional attitudes provides at least a plausibility argument for the possibility of an extensional account (see Barwise and Perry 1981).

The definition of truth in a frame model is actually quite simple, because for all but atomic formulae it will be the same as the definition for truth in a model. To establish this will require a bit of background.

Let us associate with frame representations models we can call frame models. A frame model will have the usual structure <*A*, *In*> where *A* is a set of objects and *In* an interpretation, but with several added restrictions. First *A* is contrained to be the set of frames and slots in some frame representation. Next, *In* is an interpretation function with two unusual features:

(1) First, the way *In* interprets predicate constants will be a bit unconventional. More on this below.

(2) Second, *In* must be told that words have particular meanings. It must be prevented from mapping the predicate associated with *dog* onto the frame intended for *cat*. To this end, *In* will be defined by the English lexicon. In the lexicon, each open class lexical entry will be associated

> with a denotation in a frame representation for English. That denotation will consist only of elements taken from the core frames of English. Since closed class lexical items will be logical constants, *In* will be entirely determined by the lexicon. In fact, there is only one *In* for English, although there are many different frame models, since there are many different *A*. The key to this result is that all lexical denotations must be built up from among the core frames, which by definition must be included in every English frame model.

To summarize the oddities of frame models, first, where the ordinary formal definition of a model is quite indifferent as to what objects are chosen for the domain, I insist it be a particular kind of formal object, either a frame or a slot, moreover, one that is well-defined in some English frame representation; next, I require *In* to be the same particular function for all English frame representations, a function whose range can only include objects in the core English frame representation.[1]

As far as ontology goes, let us assume that a frame model has all the

---

1. Two caveats are in order here. First, nothing we have said provides for the predicate constants in LL. So the verb *want* must, besides its frame theoretic denotation be provided with an LL predicate WANT, with the same denotation. Since the form of this predicate is immaterial, we will assume the form of the English word itself is used. Thus, the symbols for the constant predicates of LL will be a subset of the symbols for words of English. (We will still make a typographical distinction and type predicates in capital letters). Second, proper names might seem to offer an obstacle to a single Interpretation function for all English frame models, at least if we consider proper names part of English. Again I will appeal to the work of situation semantics (Barwise and Perry 1982); there proper names are treated in way parallel to properties; they must be relativized to particular resource situations. This is to account for the somewhat obvious fact that there is more than one person named John.

usual objects required for the interpretation of IL, minus intensions and possible worlds. Thus, there will be functions from entities to truth values, functions from functions from entities to truth values to truth values, and so on. In essence, all our frame representation adds to a basic model theory is internal structure for the objects; it enforces a particular definition of what a well defined object is. We might thus interpret it as simply defining a theory, a class of models under interpretation, which is to say, not in any formal sense an augmentation of model theory. The choice made in the current formulation reflects a view that such constraints on the structure of objects do not belong as axioms in some logical piece of syntax, but in the internals of the model itself. The fact that all dogs are mammals is not represented as a fact about two English words, but about the cultural categories those words are associated with. To rephrase it in the language of Barwise and Perry, it is fact about two separate uniformities among situations, where one one is finer-grained than the other.

Let us now turn to the general treatment of predicates: For our purposes, we will only need one-, two-, and three-place first-order predicate constants; The interpretation function *In* will map one-place predicates onto members of *A* and the others onto ordered tuples of A, (not subsets or sets of ordered tuples of *A*). Calling the denotation set of one-place predicates D/P1, two place predicates D/P2, and so on, we have:

D/P1 ε A
D/P2 ε A *X* A
D/P3 ε A *X* A *X* A

Here "A *X* A" means the Cartesian product of the set A with itself, or the set of ordered pairs consisting of members of A; "A *X* A *X* A" is then the set of ordered-triples. (For typographical purposes, I have used the set of ordered-pairs consisting of members of *A* here in place of the equivalent notion of the set of functions from A onto A. The latter fits a bit more neatly into the type theory, It will be convenient nevertheless to think of something whose denotation is in A *X* A as of type <e,e>.)

The logical syntax of LL will be the usual one; predicates of n arguments form a sentence when followed by n terms; quantifiers will bind variables and prefix sentences. Lambda's with a variable can prefix any meaningful expression. The standard logical connectives among sentences will be allowed. [1]

The interpretation rules of LL will, with one set of exceptions, be the same as the interpretation rules for that subset of IL that is LL.

---

1. Another modification in the syntax of LL is also required, to be perfectly proper here. In Montague's IL, expressions of the form (A B) where both A and B denote things of type *e* (*e* for entity) are simply not well-formed. However, we have defined a class of predicates of type *e*, *<e,e>*, and *<e,<e,e>>*. We not only need the syntax to allow expressions consisting of such predicates and their arguments to be written; we must also define the type of the resulting expression, which in this case is *t* (for truth-value, the type of all sentences in the logic).

The exception is the interpretation of atomic predicates. Let us begin with the simplest case and work our way up. For any expression E in the logic, (*In* E) is its denotation in the frame model. We will retain the standard assumption that the interpretation of a sentence of logic is a truth value. Then, for a one place predicate P and and a term (name or variable) T.

(I (P T)) = True iff (I T) is AKO (I P).
(I (P T)) = False otherwise

This is a replacement for the standard first-order interpretation which assigns to a predicate P a set and to a term T an individual:

(I (P T)) = True iff (I T) ε (I P).
(I (P T)) = False otherwise

In the model theoretic definition ε in the metalanguage denotes set membership. I have replaced this set theoretic metalanguage with frame theoretic metalanguage. AKO denotes AKOness in the frame representation. If one asks how do we know whether one thing is AKO another, the response is, the same way we know about set membership in a model, by inspection of the relevant structures. There is nothing in principle more problematic about AKOness than set membership; *as used in the above truth definition*, both are formal relations on formal objects. Truth in a model is truth in a certain kind of formal object; truth in a frame model is truth in a slightly different kind of formal object, for which we have a slightly unconventional descriptive language. Note that resorting to AKOness instead of set membership denies me direct access to the language of set theory only in interpreting atomic formulae. I can still refer to sets of frames, and sets of sets of frames; by writing expressions with lambda abstractions; so the set of objects that is AKO P is "(LAMBDA X (P X))", because lambda abstraction will have its usual interpretation.

By now it should be fairly clear how *In* can be the same function for all frame models of English. The lexical entry for *cat* will be associated with a particular lexical frame CAT, part of the English core and thus common to all English frame representations. *In* is thus constrained by the English lexicon to map *cat* onto CAT.

The case of two- and three- place predicates is slightly more complicated. The denotation of a two place predicate is a pair each of whose members is in A, such that the first member is a frame and the second is a slot. For R a two-place predicate, let (*In'* R) denote the first member of this pair and (*In''* R) denote the second member. Then if T1 and T2 are terms:

(*In* (R T1 T2)) is defined iff (*In* T1) is AKO (*In'* R);

and, if defined,

(*In* (R T1 T2)) = 1 iff
(get (*In* T1) (*In''* R)) = (*In* T2)

(*In* (R T1 T2)) = 0 otherwise.

Here "get" is a function of two arguments, which for a given frame and slot returns the value of that slot. The intuitive content of this definition will be clearer with an example:

(KARMAN LONGING-37 Buick-1)

Suppose the denotation of KARMAN is <LONGING, KARMAN>. Then this atomic formula will be defined just in case LONGING-37 is AKO LONGING, and, if defined, it will be true just in case Buick-1 is the value of the *karman* slot in LONGING-37.

The definition for three-place predicates is quite parallel:

(*In* (R T1 T2 T3)) is defined iff (*In* T1) is AKO (*In'* R);

and, if defined,

(*In* (R T1 T2 T3)) = 1 iff
(get (*In* T1) (*In''* R)) = (*In* T2) and
(get (*In* T1) (*In'''* R)) = (*In* T3)

(*In* (R T1 T2)) = 0 otherwise.

Putting an undefined value into the definitions gives us, in effect, a three-valued logic; we will adopt the interpretation that says, for any operator, if one of its arguments is undefined, the value of the operator is undefined. For example, (*In* (AND True UNDEFINED)) = undefined. For quantifiers, the value of a quantified expression is undefined if its matrix is undefined for all variable assignments. That is, (*In* (EXISTS X PHI)) is undefined if PHI is undefined for all assignments of the variable X.

Besides being three-valued the logic is, intuitively, sorted, since undefined values can be returned for certain arguments of the right type (type-theoretically). Thus the definition above, together with the above denotatation for KARMAN, will assign UNDEFINED as the denotation of "(KARMAN WALKING-12 BUICK-1)" if (*In* WALKING-12) is not AKO LONGING. This is a way of importing the notion of semantic compatibility into the logic. The intuitive motivation for this is that it seems to undermine the notion of a truth definition for a language to assign truth values to semantically incoherent strings, that is, to strings which do not belong in the language in the first place. This point will be elaborated at the end of this chapter, when we have revised our mapping from frames to predicates a bit.

A final point about the logic. We have granted that it offers no obvious way to handle the problem of intensionality, but that admission needs to be qualified a bit. Note that *some* of the work left to intensions in a Montagovian system is carried off merely by the nature of the ontology here. In a first order reduction of the Montague semantics, the interpretation of a common noun *dog* would simply be the set of dogs. This is somewhat inadequate as a characterization of *meaning*, because each time a dog is born or dies, the meaning of the word changes. Adding a level of intensionality resolves this simple intuitive problem. The interpretation of *dog* is associated with a function from possible worlds to sets.[1] What the interpretation of *dog*

---

1. We are simplifying certain non-relevant details of the actual semantics Montague gives in Montague 1970.

gives you, then, is a specification, for each possible world, of a set. The interpretation doesn't change from one possible world (or moment) to another. Note that in this system, no such layer of intensionality is necessary to capture the intuition relating interpretation to meaning. The interpretation of *dog* is the frame DOG, which is the same frame for all English frame representations, irrespective of what set of objects is actually AKO DOG.

Lest it be thought that such intuitive considerations do little actual semantic work, we can illustrate the need for intensionality in common noun denotations with adjectives. Suppose that the meaning of an adjective like *competent* were a function from common noun denotations to common noun denotations. That is, the expression *competent programmar* denotes the same kind of object as *programmer*. If common nouns denoted merely sets, that object would be a set. Consider a world in which the set of programmers is coextensive with the set of linguists. Given our treatment of *competent*, in such a world, one would be a competent programmer if and only if one was a competent linguist. Given that each noun denoted the same thing, *competent* would have the same set as its argument, and being a function, would have to give the same set as its output. But one can easily imagine a a world where programmers and linguists were coextensive, but competent programmers and competent linguists were not. Montague resolves this problem by having adjectives like *competent* be functions from the intensions of sets to sets. Thus *competent* takes the intension of *programmer* as its argument, and this is quite a different thing from the intension of *linguist*.

Again, in the semantics offered here, the basic ontology solves this problem without any layer of intensions. The denotation of *linguist* will be the LINGUIST frame. The denotation of *programmer* will be the PROGRAMMER frame. These are two different objects, so that there is no reason that an adjective that combines with them, *however* it combines with them, should ever output the same denotations. The semantics of the words has been made independent of extensions to begin with, and there is no reason to introduce a level of intensionality to create that independence.

The kind of intensionality for which there is no obvious treatment in this framework is the most celebrated and troublesome kind, non-specific intensionality:

(51) John seeks a unicorn

Nothing we have said gets around the fact that *seek*, unlike most verbs, is just not a relation among individuals. Montague offers what seems to be a fairly workable scopal treatment using possible worlds and jacked-up denotations. I noted several sections back a challenge to any such scopal treatment involving the scope of conjunctions. Another problem, noted in Bennett 1974, is the need for stipulating the following entailment on Montague's treatment:

(52) John seeks a white unicorn

(53) John seeks a unicorn.

Pollard (in preparation) suggests that this entailment can be captured with a general constraint that all natural language verbs are upward monotonic on all argument positions. That is, if a predication holds of some property set, then it holds of any property set bigger than that property set. This very general axiom gets the above entailment. However, it seems to me too general if applied to *seek*, since it also predicts an entailment between the following two sentences:

(54) John seeks a unicorn.

(55) John seeks a unicorn or a fish.

All in all, I think there are enough residual problems with Montague's treatment, so that it does not, in itself, offer any strong motivation for intensional logic.

There are two fairly serious charges that can be made against the hybrid enterprise just sketched, one from each flank. The first is that it undermines the notion of semantic interpretation that makes models useful to model theorists. A model is a well-defined formal object which has an intuitively satisfying connection with important notions like soundness and consistency. Because models are interpreted in terms of set theory, and because we understand set theory, we can say of logical theories that they are consistent if they have a model. The same can not be said of a frame representation, because surely we can construct a "contradictory" one. Then, although the frame model we place on top of it will be set theoretically sound, the interpretation we give to the objects will be nonsense.

This brings us back to the notion of a "consistent" frame model. What does it mean for an entire frame model to be consistent with the core frames? Indeed, what does it mean for the core representation to be internally consistent (the two questions probably have the same answer)? The only real answer to this question is a complete formalization of what it means to be a frame representation, a formalization which would rule out "inconsistent" representations as non representations (just as "models" which require an object to be both in and not in the same set are not models). A complete formalization of that sort would take us too far afield here, but we can concede it as a desideratum without abandoning the whole enterprise.

The kind of situation such a formal definition would rule out is the following:

```
(FOO
 (SLOT1 (= SLOT 2))
 (SLOT2))

(FOO-1
 (AKO (FOO))
 (SLOT1 (BAR))
 (SLOT2 (BAZ)))
```

Here, the annotation on SLOT1 should be interpreted as stating that the value of SLOT1 must equal SLOT2. FOO-1 is a "frame" which is AKO FOO frames but does not meet a basic condition on FOO frames. The value of SLOT1 does not equal SLOT2. Our formal definition of frame must not countenance FOO-1 as a well-defined object.[1]

The second kind of criticism might come from those who are used to working in frame representations and ask, what do you need models for? The answer is simple: the framework of model theoretic semantics offers the best analytical apparatus for doing compositional semantics, for building the semantics of large expressions out of the semantics of small expressions. For example, the logical treatment of quantifiers and variables seems to me the best thing going in that line; I know of no current frame-based system that has as general a treatment for quantification as that in Barwise and Cooper 1981, and that treatment is stated in an extension of Montague's framework. Similarly, model theoretic work in plurals and tense seems like the most promising,and any transplantation into a new framework will very likely carry over the

---

1. As a matter of fact, current implementations of FRL do not implement any such requirement. In fact the ability of frame representations to supply "default" values for a slot which can be overruled by individuals is often cited as a basic difference between such representations and their "equivalent" formulations in logic. The important point here is that we need some way of formalizing absolute restrictions imposed in a generic frame. The fact that we may then need some notational means of distinguishing default from absolute properties does not alter this need.

same principles. The proposal here is simply an attempt to perserve the advantages of that approach, while incorporating the very different descriptive power of a representational system. The payoff will be two-fold. When we write the specifications for a particular frame representation, we will have a state description which induces a model. And the model will be accessable by the ordinary interpretive apparatus of logic.

In some sense, defining truth in a frame model introduces an extra step of abstraction between language and the world. This is why we still call the objects in the frame model "representations." In theory, conventional models always leave us options like assigning the verb *walk* the actual set of walkers as their denotation, options that in effect reduce truth in a model to truth in the world. But we showed above how that denotation for *walk* was inadequate. That inadequacy led logicians like Montague to make use of the more elaborate ontologies of intensional logic. But such ontologies themselves require a step of abstraction. Unless one adopts the radical "realist" view of possible worlds espoused by David Lewis, one must think of models of Montague's intensional logic as formal objects mediating between language and the world. What I have proposed is replacing the ontology of possible worlds in such objects with the ontology of frames.

We now have a theoretical construct with the following components:

(1) A "grammar" consisting of a set of phrase structure rules with associated semantic rules, which associates with each node of a phrase structure tree a (dispensable) logical representation.

(2) An interpretation procedure (not dispensable) which tells us the denotation of any meaningful expression (any string of English analyzed by one of our phrase structure rules) in a frame model.

(3) A core English frame representation which defines possible domains for English frame models.

(4) A lexicon. This gives three kinds of information about lexical items, first a phonological representation, presumably a feature matrix, second, a morphosyntactic representation, presumably also a feature matrix, and third, the correct denotation of that lexical item under the *In* for English.

1.9 Core Participants and Adjuncts

I want to begin this section creating some new terminology to express some old ideas. Consider what we need to do to capture a notion like *argument* in the system of representation just sketched. By *argument* I mean here the intuition of argument, but not the formal concept of predicate logic. That is, arguments are something that lexical heads have; they are the central participants in the scene that the head presents, and thus in the situations the head is instantiated by. If we are speaking of verbs then subject and direct object will certainly be chosen from among the arguments, though everyone, as far as I know, allows other grammatical roles to be arguments. Often the term *argument* is used to mean something like the semantic correlate of subcategorization. That is, anything that is subcategorized for by a verb is an argument, and vice versa. In systems that have recourse to a level of logical representation, argument has a strict formal sense; the argument of a lexical head is semantically interpreted as "in" the "relation" that translates the head, where "in" and "relation" have the usual set theoretically defined senses. This formal sense of argument will not do for the following discussion, since I have chosen a logical representation in which only subjects and direct objects are formally "arguments" . It is a non-logical, intuitive notion of argument I wish to discuss here. Rather than using the term *argument*, which has the wrong meaning in the logic, I will adopt the term *core participant*.

What I will claim is that the intuition underlying the notion of *core participant* is one about lexical semantic structure, and that it can be represented in the present system, with a few simple modifications.

It will be helpful to approach the right theory of core participants by way of a couple of false starts, which will define the intuition a little, and raise a few basic issues of representation.

1.9.1 Preposition meanings

Consider the sentence "Beatrice longed for a Buick on Tuesday." A natural formulation of the necessary underlying lexical representation of *on* is as a very general scene called a TEMPORALLY_LOCATED_OBJECT with one participant.

```
(TEMPORALLY_LOCATED_OBJECT
(AKO (THING))
(TIME))
```

We can now capture the compatibility of the verb *long* with the preposition *on* very simply. The LONGING scene will be AKO TEMPORALLY_LOCATED_OBJECT:

```
(LONGING
 (AKO (THING) (TEMPORALLY_LOCATED_OBJECT))
 (KARMAN)
 (LONGER ))

(EXISTS* SIGMA (EXISTS X (AND (LONGING SIGMA BEATRICE)
                              (FOR SIGMA X)
                              (BUICK X)
                              (ON SIGMA TUESDAY))))
```

Since there will be a *time* slot in LONGING, the logical representation makes sense as well. The denotation of ON will presumably be <TEMPORALLY_LOCATED_OBJECT, TIME>, and an appropriate LONGING scene that satisfies the requirements of the logical representation will be one with Tuesday as the value of its *time* slot. To have a sort called TEMPORALLY_LOCATED_OBJECT is to claim that not all heads are compatible with temporal adjuncts. Examples like "The book on Tuesday" support this view.

Note that there is something special about the TEMPORALLY_LOCATED_OBJECT frame; unlike the others we have considered, it has only one participant, a *time*. Call scenes with only one participant entity-modifiers, because they can be thought of as involving a relationship between an entity (the frame itself) with their single participant (in the example above, a *time*). To take another example a SPATIALLY_LOCATED_OBJECT relates an entity to a location ("the fish on the boat," or "they fished on the boat"). Call preposition scenes with multiple participants participant-modifiers because they relate a participant in some scene with one or more other participants in that same scene (a longer with a karman). This seems a very natural way of describing the relevant situations, and it corresponds to what has often been proposed as a natural distinction between core participants and adjuncts. Adjuncts modify entire VP's; core participants are core participants (that is, the participants enter into a relation with other participants). We might then propose the following semantic characterization of "core participant," dubbed Hypothesis A:

(1) Nuclear terms are always core participants.

(2) If a complement is a PP, it is an core participant if the Preposition meaning is a participant-modifier, an adjunct if it is an entity-modifier.

What is particularly appealing about this hypothesis is that in the framework proposed here, it suggests that adjuncts should be more abstract in meaning, and compatible with a large class of situations. This is because if a scene A is AKO another scene B, then A must have at least the participants that B does. Without this, the characterization of semantic compatibility via AKO would not be fully general; it would be possible for a verb scene to be AKO a preposition scene, yet lack the slot that the preposition marks. Thus the more specific a scene, the more participants it will tend to have; conversely, scenes with one participant will tend to be more general. This seems to be a correct, if very rough, generalization about adjuncts.

I will not be adopting Hypothesis A in this dissertation. There is, I think, good reason for seeking some way of reconstructing the core participant/adjunct distinction in our lexical representations. However, it is doubtful that there is one class of preposition meanings that must always be adjuncts and another that must always be core participants. Rather, it is the meanings of the verbs that decides the issue. Thus, prepositions occur in what appear to be the same meanings both as obligatory and highly optional complements.

(56) The Campanile towers above Berkeley

(57) *The Campanile towers.

(58) The Red Army crossed the Danube above the Main.

I thus pass Hypothesis A by, not without recognizing in it a certain merit. Undeniably, there are certain preposition meanings which are more adverbial or "adjunctlike" than others. Location and time are rarely, if ever, obligatory complements, and those cases where one of them may appear to be (the verb *put*) will be shown in Chapter 5 to fall under the very special case of predicative PP's. We may tentatively conclude that location and time are rarely subcategorized-for. Another, less typical, example of a preposition that is rarely subcategorized for is *without*. This distinction among prepositional meanings has its analogue in case-marking languages in the distinction between concrete and abstract cases; although that distinction, too, is not without its problems, it does capture certain tendencies observable among the various functions of a morphological case. Thus, it is rare, though not unheard of, for a verb to govern the locative case in a Slavic language (Nichols 1983).

In the next section, I will modify the system proposed thus far in a different way to reconstruct the distinction between core participants and adjuncts, replacing Hypothesis A with one that does the necessary work on the basis of individual lexical properties.

1.9.2 Direct Inheritance

We can open the discussion by examining a more fully specified version of a lexical entry, with a pair of auxiliary slots displayed:

```
(LONGING
   (AKO (SPATIALLY_LOCATED_OBJECT)
        (TEMPORALLY_LOCATED_OBJECT))
   (LONGER)
   (KARMAN)
   (TIME)
   (PLACE))
```

The question is now: what does it mean for a lexical entry to bear a slot? In principle, all slots are candidates for grammatical realization; some procedure, perhaps a Fillmorian subject selection hierarchy, choses from among them those that will be nuclear terms. What now choses from among the obliques?

This can be put another way: How do we state the fact that a participant is obligatorily realized, if it is oblique? This could be an extra task of the procedure selecting nuclear terms, or it could be an arbitrary stipulation beyond that task. But the second alternative creates the unsettling possibility that a verb meaning "long" could have its locative participant chosen as the obligatory complement. So it seems that we would be best off by having, minimally, a procedure that picked the top two or three salient participants, those that are "possible" candidates for a core participant of *wish*. The procedure for selecting the top two or three candidates might even be independent of the procedure for determining which of them will be nuclear.

How might such a procedure work? The most obvious tactic would be to say that the participants inherited via the shortest path up the sort hierarchy are core participants. Call this Hypothesis B. Under this hypothesis, LONGER and KARMAN would win for any of the verbs of LONGING, because they would be introduced directly in the LONGING frame, which is the scene which each of their lexical scenes immediately instantiates. This procedure would entail a very strong prediction about the relationship of core participants to participant roles: if the core participants of two verbs are inherited from a common scene, then those verbs will exhibit exactly the same possibilities of complementation for all complements, including adjuncts. To give an example: since *wish*, *ask*, and *hope* all share the *karman* and *longer* roles inherited from the LONGING scene, none of them is compatible with an adjunct that the others are incompatible with. For that to happen, given our definition of compatibility, one of them would have to be AKO to some scene that the others weren't AKO to; but then the participant inherited from that scene would be more directly inherited than either *karman* or *longer*, and that participant should have been the core participant.

With respect to the representations given thus far, this claim appears to be too strong:

(59) John prayed for rain by dancing the old dances.

(60) John searched for the Buick by flying repeatedly over the city.

(61) John wished for a fellowship by throwing salt over his shoulder.

(62) John wanted a Buick by making himself yearn.

(63) John desired a Buick by longing hard enough.

(64) *John yearned for a Buick by working on his attitude.

Here a test for distinguishing stative predicates, originally proposed by G. Lakoff, partitions the verbs of longing into two sets. Call the *by* that has a participial VP controlled by the subject *participial by*. Note that while it seems to be true that no stative verbs allow *by* in this use, it is not true that all non-statives do. Consider some verbs like *notice*, *mention*, and *stipulate*. In general, what Vendler 1957 calls accomplishments and activities seem to allow it, but acheivements split. So *reach* allows it, although *notice*, *mention*, and *stipulate* do not. I will not try to define exactly the semantic class we are concerned with here, but I will assume that it IS semantically definable, and will call the relevant scene a PURSUIT (to suggest that it involves activities which can be pursued to some conclusion); I will also assume it involves two participants, a *pursuer*, and a *means*.

Returning now to the split in the verbs of longing over the distribution of this adjunct. One could, of course, save Hypothesis B, by claiming that different participants, and thus different scenes, are responsible for the occurrences of *for* with the stative and active verbs. But now what of the participant introduced by the preposition *by*, the *means*. Then, by Hypothesis B, means will be as good candidate for core participanthood as *karman* or *longer*. This is a counterintuitive result. Of course, we might then rely on the procedure for selecting nuclear terms for ruling *means* out, but that looks like a long shot because *means*, or something very like it, does sometimes become subject: "Landing the Barnes deal earned John his promotion."

There is a separate, purely representional reason for ruling out this approach. In our effort to save Hypothesis B, we will make the notion of a participant shared by different verbs responsible purely to distributional facts. A scene immediately instantiated by a group of lexical scenes will really be a definition of a form class: the heads that can be followed by some class of complements. The ontology of scenes will be cluttered by objects that really introduce no semantic information.

This point deserves some clarification, since it brings out a central representational heuristic we will be appealing to again. Consider two alternative representations of the verbs of longing, both of which make the necessary distinction between active and stative verbs:

```
(PURSUIT_LONGING
   (AKO (SPATIALLY_LOCATED_EVENT)
        (TEMPORALLY_LOCATED_EVENT)
        (PURSUIT))
   (LONGER)
   (KARMAN)
   (TIME)
   (PLACE))

(STATIVE_LONGING
   (AKO (SPATIALLY_LOCATED_EVENT)
        (TEMPORALLY_LOCATED_EVENT)
        (STATE))
   (STATIVELONGER)
   (STATIVEKARMAN)
   (TIME)
   (PLACE))
```

Note that in this representation, the structure of the longing scene is really being stated twice, for example, the facts about its being spatially and temporally located. More importantly, whatever procedural information we need to intrepret the relation between *karman* and *longer* will need to be repeated. Note, that we do not have the alternative of factoring this information out into a higher frame (a LONGING frame with STATIVE and PURSUIT subtypes), because then under hypothesis B, *means* would be the only possible core participant for the PURSUIT verbs of longing. Alternatively, we can abandon Hypothesis B and simply represent verbs like *wish, search,* and *pray* as AKO both LONGING and PURSUIT.

This still leaves us with the problem of selecting core participants from among all the possibilities. The treatment adopted for the rest of this dissertation will be proposed in the next section.

1.7.3 The Right Theory

The example that we primarily concentrated on in the last section was that of the verbs of longing, and their compatibility with the *karman* meaning of the preposition *for*. What was striking about that case was that the scene shared by a group of verbs, the "longing" scene, was at the same time the lexical scene of a preposition meaning. If the representations always worked out that way, that would make a very strong claim about the preposition meanings of English: each group of verbs that forms a natural semantic class compatible with some preposition licenses a preposition meaning. However we have already seen a case where that course looks dubious:

(65) Lucy spoke against disarmament.
him

We want to associate the preposition *against* with a kind of situation we called a CAMPAIGN; it is rather unsatisfying to call *speak* a verb of campaigning, because it is quite unlike the verbs of campaigning in its relation to the role *contended-force*. The alternative would be to declare a new meaning of *against*, suitable, say, for verbs of communication, and claim that this was the meaning realized with *speak*.

This, too, seems to miss the boat. Rather what seems to be going on is what we called semantic narrowing. A speaking situation may or may not be an act of campaigning. We could represent that by having two verbs *speak*, one of which is an act of campaigning and one which is not, but much of the semantic information for these two verbs would be the same. Both, for example, are compatible with an *auditor* marked with the preposition *to*.

The solution I prefer is to reverse the direction of semantic selection. Up until now, we have implicitly treated all selection as being made by the head; that is, the marking that crucially determined whether a verb and a preposition could combine occurred on the frame associated with the verb. Suppose instead we let some preposition meanings select possible head meanings. The easiest case to illustrate this with seems to be *time*; suppose we recast our view of time a bit, and associate it a scene with two participants:

```
(LOCATION_IN_TIME
 (AKO (THING))
 (FIGURE)
 (TIME))
```

Given that something like this is the base of our represesentation for temporal *on*, this frame takes a slightly different angle on sentences like "John wished for a Buick on Tuesday." Before, "Tuesday" filled the *time* slot in the WISHING frame, inherited in virtue of the fact that every WISHING situation was also a TEMPORALLY_LOCATED_OBJECT. Under the new proposal, TIME would no longer ever be a slot in the WISHING frame. Instead, the whole WISHING situation would fill the *figure* slot in a LOCATION_IN_TIME frame, and TIME would be a slot in that frame. The differences can be illustrated by picking some particular states of affairs that would satisfy the truth conditions of the sentence "John wished for a Buick on Tuesday," and displaying the different representations under the different proposals.

Old proposal:

```
(WISHING-1
 (AKO (WISHING) (TEMPORALLY_LOCATED_OBJECT))
 (LONGER (JOHN))
 (KARMAN (BUICK-1))
 (TIME (TUESDAY)))
```

New proposal:

```
(LOCATION_IN_TIME-1
 (AKO (LOCATION_IN_TIME))
 (TIME (TUESDAY))
 (FIGURE (WISHING-1
          (AKO (WISHING))
          (LONGER (JOHN))
          (KARMAN (BUICK-1)))))
```

What our representation of LOCATION_IN_TIME is missing is some specification of what sorts of scenes can be located in time. This happened automatically under the old proposal, because the LONGING scene was AKO TEMPORALLY_LOCATED_OBJECT, and it was precisely those objects that had *times*. There is no reason why we should rule such specifications out under the new proposal, but they will have to be included as extra procedural information on the *figure* slot. Recall that a slot can do more than just specify a value (in fact, *scene* slots will rarely specify a value); it can also specify a collection of procedures defining constraints on the value, among which are relations to the values of other slots. Suppose among those constraints we include some that specify what KIND of of object the value of a slot can be.

FRL distinguishes among the procedures attached to a slot by giving a slot some structure. A slot has facets, just as a frame has slots. Among those facets one special case is the *value* facet, the one to which we thus far devoted our exclusive attention. Let us define one other kind of facet, called a *require* facet; this facet specifies tests that the value of a slot must meet. When we write generic frames, the things we will want to say about particular slots will be procedures constraining the value of that slot, rather than values per se. Thus when we write something in parentheses after a slot name in a generic frame that will be interpreted as a name for a procedure in the *require* facet of a frame. We might,for example, wish to constrain the value of the *figure* slot in the TEMPORALLY_LOCATED_OBJECT frame in the following way:

```
(LOCATION_IN_TIME
 (AKO(THING))
 (LOCATION)
 (FIGURE(REQUIRE (TEMPORALLY_LOCATED_OBJECT))))

(TEMPORALLY_LOCATED_OBJECT
 (AKO(THING)))
```

The annotation to the *figure* slot should be read as an abbreviation for a procedure that says the value of that slot must be AKO TEMPORALLY_LOCATED_OBJECT. Note that the particular "abbreviation" I have chosen in this case is simply to write the name of the TEMPORALLY_LOCATED_OBJECT frame. This merits a slight digression.

In doing this bit of abbreviating I am exploiting a slightly different interpretation of generic frames which has not officially been incorporated into the formalism. Any generic frame G can be thought of as a body of rules which individual frames must meet in order to qualify as frames of type G (this, indeed, is how frames can be thought of as intensional descriptions). Consider, for example, the LONGING frame we started with:

```
(LONGING
 (LONGER)
 (KARMAN))
```

Suppose now that this is really the whole story,[1] as exhaustive a description of LONGING situations as we need to give for the theoretical

---

1. As an intensional description of LONGING, the LONGING frame says, "Any object satisfying the folloing structure will do, and we can proceed to do LONGING business with it." Now obviously, as a description of LONGING able to orient, say, a Martian intent on studying human epistemology, the above frame is less than a perfect attempt. But, for another standard of innocence, the computer, it may do for a while. The difference between the Martian and the computer is that the Martian is open to arbitrarily complex input. Obviously a creature who moves about involving itself in arbitrarily complex situations will soon find the above description of LONGING inadequate to its needs. However, a creature whose perceptual contacts are limited to frames written in a certain syntax, with a limited array of structures, and a single way of storing and accessing those structures, may do quite well with our somewhat impoverished picture of LONGING. For the duration of the dissertation, we shall have to imagine ourselves dealing with some such highly underendowed perceiver.

needs at hand. Then as a test on LONGING objects, the generic LONGING frame makes only two requirements:

(1) A frame for a LONGING situation has a LONGER slot.

(2) A frame for a LONGING situation has a KARMAN slot.

Although we will not, in general, be interpreting generic frames as objects in this way, let us adopt the convention that any generic frame written in the *require* facet of some slot in another frame is interpreted as a procedural test which any value for that slot must meet. In this dissertation we will mostly be writing generic frames, and in generic frames, annotations to slots will generally be procedures constraining values rather than actual values. Given that, let us stipulate that the default facet in generic frames will be *require*, rather than *value*, so that we can dispense with actually specifying it. When we need to distinguish *value* facets from *require*, we will write things as follows:

```
(FOO
 (AKO (INDEX))
 (NUMBER (REQUIRE (INTEGER))
         (VALUE (337337))))
```

Very soon we will be encountering constraints on the values of slots which we will state not just as frame names, but as entire frame descriptions; thus the conventions just outlined will license:

```
(PERSON
   (AKO (THING))
   (MOTHER (PERSON
                  (SEX (VALUE (FEMALE)))
                  (SPOUSE (PERSON
                                (SEX (VALUE (MALE)))))))))
```

The above frame should be interpreted as stipulating that the value of a person's *mother* slot should be a PERSON frame such that the value of its *sex* slot must be FEMALE and the value of its *spouse* slot must be a PERSON frame such that the value of its sex slot is MALE.

Returning to LOCATION_IN_TIME, we now have a representation which says only certain kinds of objects can be located in time; we are thus able to make the same distinctions we could make under the old proposal, between heads like *book* and heads like *wish*.

If all things were equal, of course, we would choose the old proposal over the new one, on general grounds of ontological parsimony. The new proposal does the work of selection with two frames where the old proposal used one. But various considerations suggest that things are not, in fact, equal. Consider the problem of "speaking against disarmament" once more. In that case, it was counterintuitive to say that SPEAKING, a COMMUNICATION-ACT, was AKO CAMPAIGN. A CAMPAIGN implies a *contended-force*, and SPEAKING may or may not involve such a participant. Under the old proposal, we would have had SPEAKING, the generic frame, inherit a great deal of structure that really applied to only a sub-class of speaking events. Under the new proposal, there is a way to tidy things up. Here are the relevant frames, along with a frame that satisfies the truthconditions of "Lucy spoke against disarmament."

```
(CAMPAIGN
 (CONTENDED-FORCE)
 (SOCIAL-EVENT (SOCIAL-EVENT)))

(SOCIAL-EVENT
 (AKO (THING)))

(COMMUNICATION-ACT
 (AKO (SOCIAL-EVENT)))

(SPEAKING
 (AKO (COMMUNICATION-ACT))
 (SPEAKER))

(CAMPAIGN-1
 (CONTENDED-FORCE (DISARMAMENT))
 (SOCIAL-EVENT (SPEAKING-1
                    (SPEAKER (LUCY)))))
```

As given, the CAMPAIGN frame requires a SOCIAL-EVENT in its SOCIAL-EVENT slot; I have represented CAMPAIGN as itself AKO a SOCIAL-EVENT. Some of the sort structure SOCIAL-EVENT fits into is given in the next two frames. A COMMUNICATION-ACT a kind of SOCIAL-EVENT, and SPEAKING a kind of COMMUNICATION-ACT. The verb *speaking* is thus linked with a frame which is AKO SOCIAL-EVENT. SOCIAL-EVENT is intended as a rather general scene that includes among its instances scenes like COMMUNICATION-ACT, CAMPAIGN, and LEGAL-ACT.

The exact status of SOCIAL-EVENT here is rather problematic.

In particular, Fillmore (personal communication) has pointed out that there are verbs which might be called verbs of communication which do not allow the *contended-force* meaning of *against*:

(66) *John whispered against Fran.

Perhaps what distinguishes *whisper* from *speak* is that *speak* can be used to describe an act that "goes on the record." It is not just communication, but communication that counts, taking voice with some social end in view. None of the verbs of communication which take actual propositional complements (and *whisper* is among them) allows *contended-force against*. Both *speak* and *talk* do. It is hard to imagine a category as broad as SOCIAL-EVENT which makes this fine a distinction among communication acts, and yet still admits some of the other verbs compatible with *contended-force against*, for example, *fight*, *play*, and *legislate*. It may be that the right requirement to put on the *contended-force* slot will be a disjunction. I will continue, however, to use the term SOCIAL-EVENT merely as a label for the right semantic class. The important point is that even when SPEAKING is viewed as an act of going on record, it need not involve any participant that that record is *for* or *against*. This is in marked contrast to our intuitions about the FIGHTING scene.

Thus far we have assumed that having a slot is something that can be exploited when we need it. Under the old proposal a scene like the LONGING scene inherited PLACE and TIME slots in virtue of being

AKO TEMPORALLY_LOCATED_OBJECT and SPATIALLY_LOCATED_-OBJECT, although clearly the lexical scenes instantiating LONGING belong to verbs for which temporal and locative adjuncts are optional. This meant that in general a slot could be unoccupied, and we found no way of distinguishing core participants from adjuncts.

Suppose instead that we made the default convention the following: if an entity is AKO a sort, in general it must have values for all the slots supplied by that sort. And the occupants of those slots will be core participants. This still means something needs to be said about optional core participants, but let us defer that problem until chapter 4. Under the new proposal, the optionality of slots like *time* and *place* and *contended-force* is represented by making the preposition scenes select the head scenes, and saying that those slots do not belong to the head scenes. When we do get around to optional core participants, we will represent those in a different way.

So far, the new proposal resembles the first one we considered, Hypothesis A, which said that adjunct meanings were a special class of meanings, distinguishable because they had only one participant. Under the new proposal adjuncts have a special status, too; they take entire scenes as a participant. Thus we need to make sure that the new proposal doesn't run into the same snag Hypothesis A did, erroneously predicting that same preposition meaning couldn't be both an adjunct and subcategorized-for.

The obvious example to turn to is the verbs of CAMPAIGNING (roughly, verbs semantically requiring an *against* role). For verbs like *fight, battle, defend,* and *attack,* we would obviously like *contended-force* to be one of the defining participants of the lexical scene. We can arrange that by making the scene common to all these verbs be a slighly more specified version of CAMPAIGN, call it STRIFE:

```
(STRIFE
 (AKO (CAMPAIGN))
 (BATTLER)
 (CONTENDED-FORCE)
 (SOCIAL-EVENT(:frame)))
```

Here the slots of the CAMPAIGN frame have all been inherited by the more specific STRIFE frame (to which *fight, battle, defend* and *attack* will be AK0-linked), and a new participant, the *battler,* has been added. Also, a special requirement has been put on the *social-event* slot. The annotation ":FRAME" should be read as stipulating that the value of that slot must always be the current frame. That is, for any particular STRIFE situation the value of the *social-event* slot must be that particular situation. For example, a frame satisfying the truth-conditions for "John battled against a grizzly," would be:

```
(BATTLE-1
 (AKO (STRIFE))
 (BATTLER (JOHN))
 (CONTENDED-FORCE (GRIZZLY-1))
 (SOCIAL-EVENT (BATTLE-1)))
```

Thus, the event directed against the grizzly is the very battle we are in.

Here we may take the CAMPAIGN scene as the lexical representation of the relevant meaning of *against*. The compatibility facts for the verbs of STRIFE are captured in the same way as they were for the verbs of LONGING and the preposition *for*. The lexical heads have scenes which are AKO the preposition scene.

Note that for the above treatment of the verbs of STRIFE to work, it was crucial that the requirement on the *social-event* slot be one that verbs of STRIFE could themselves meet. In this case meeting the requirement SOCIAL-EVENT was automatic for anything AKO CAMPAIGN.

Will all prepositions that are both adjuncts and subcategorized-for have to be treated this way? We have made the assumption that any preposition scene that can be an adjunct has a slot that takes situations as its values, and that compatible head scenes fill the requirements imposed on these slots. Call such slots situation slots. Will all verb scenes that inherit such situation slots have to fill them with self-referential pointers? In the next chapter, we will turn to some slightly more complex verb scenes, and formulate some mechanisms by which a scene can "inherit" slots from a subscene. With that apparatus available, there will be a more natural representation for CAMPAIGN. We will return to this example in 2.3

Some more examples may serve to show that the current proposal avoids some of the problems we have encountered in our search for a way of representing the notion core participant. Let us return to the case of the verbs of LONGING and the compatibility of some of those scenes with a particular meaning of *by*. Under the new proposal, the differences among the verbs of longing could be represented as follows:

```
(LONGING
 (AKO (THING)
      (TEMPORALLY_LOCATED_OBJECT)
      (SPATIALLY_LOCATED_OBJECT)
 (KARMAN)
 (LONGER))

(MEANS_TO_AN_END
 (AKO (THING))
 (PURSUIT (PURSUIT))
 (MEANS(ACTION)))

(PURSUIT
 (AKO (THING)))

(WISHING
 (AKO (LONGING)(PURSUIT)))
```

Here MEANS_TO_AN_END is the meaning of *by* in sentences like "John spoiled the party by talking too much." The class of situations that fit into its scene slot is has been called PURSUIT, and among the scenes of LONGING, WISHING (the scene associated with *wish*) has been defined as AKO PURSUIT. A constraint has also been placed on the class of situations that can be *means*. As a first approximation, these are called ACTION, intuitively, scenes with Agents in them. This is the simplest account along the lines we have been discussing that makes *by* in the relevant meaning an adjunct of *wish*.

To sum up the proposed treatment of adjuncts; I have proposed that adjuncts be distinguished from core participants by saying that the direction of compatibility is reversed. For core participant prepositional phrases, the heads select the prepositions (they are AKO the preposition meaning). For adjunct prepositional phrases, the preposition meanings take whole situations as participants, and put selectional constraints on the situation slot. This is in accord with an intuition that adjuncts are VP modifiers. Nevertheless, such adjunct meanings are allowed to make reference to particular participants in the scenes they "modify". At the same time, I have allowed the same preposition meaning to be both core participant and adjunct.

Perhaps the strongest argument for such a move is that, in the end, some such notion of situation-modifying adjuncts will be needed anyway. It is not possible to predict adjunct distribution strictly on the basis of the lexical semantics of the head and preposition, as some facts first noted in Vendler 1957 show:

(67) John read the book in an hour.

(68) *John read books in an hour.

Clearly this sort of semantic compatibility cannot be stated simply as a lexical relationship between *read* and a particular meaning of *in*. It needs to be expressed in terms of the selection by *in* of certain non-lexical situation categories. Some reading situations are what Vendler calls activities (here "reading books"), some what he calls accomplishments (here "reading the book"). and only the first is the kind of thing that can be done "in" a time period.

To sum up, the new proposal has done two things:

> (1) Allowed us a convenient way of specifying as a lexical property which participants are core participants, namely, all those inherited along AKO links. For the verbs of longing, this isolates a particular scene in which the core participant roles are defined, the LONGING scene. For the moment, I have made the general convention be that all core participants are obligatory.
>
> (2) I have set things up so that the lexical description of the verb *wish* simply lacks a LOCATION slot, even one that may be optionally filled.

This second result raises some interesting questions.

First, it is always plausible to separate matters of linguistics from matters of physics. Although the act of running always involves a time and a place, that does not mean the verb always does.

(69) John runs

This sentence has a preferred habitual reading which does not involve any particular spatial or temporal reference points. The present indicative morphology can be intrepreted not as telling us something about the activity, but something about John, namely that he is a current, actual entity. The past version of the same sentence, on the generic reading, entails that he was an actual entity at some point in the past. What about the non-generic readings? Surely one could say that they entail some reference points. This is probably true, but the existence of the generic reading is sufficient to show that temporal and spatial reference points ought not to be treated as a necessary lexical property of the verb *run*.

In the final analysis, the appeal of this approach to the notion core participant lies in the following consequence: verbs that are semantically alike will have like core participant structures. *Wish, want* and *long* all have two core participants BECAUSE they are all AKO the LONGING scene. Moreover those core participant pairs all share a common relation, the relation of *karman* to *longer*, and it it is this structural fact which explains why the realizations of those core participants are often marked with the same formal means.

1.8 Revising semantic compatibility

Our new treatment of adjuncts requires a slightly different notion of semantic compatibility. Since, we never explicitly stated how compatibility fits into the logic, I want to precede a reformulation with a brief sketch of how semantic properties of frames are turned into properties of predicates.

It will be easiest to illustrate what we mean when we say two scenes are semantically compatible in terms of a specific example. Consider the translation of "Beatrice longed for a Buick:"

```
(EXISTS* SIGMA (EXISTS X (AND (LONGING SIGMA BEATRICE)
                              (FOR SIGMA X)
                              (BUICK X))))
```

Sigma is what we have been calling a situation variable. Intuitively, what it means to say that two predicates are semantically compatible is that they can be predicated of the same situation; in terms of the syntax of the logical representation, it means they can share the same situation variable. When two predicates share a situation variable, what it means in the frame model is that that their other core participants are values of different slots in the same frame.

Consider one frame in a frame model that would satisfy the above logical formula:

```
(LONGING-1
 (LONGER (BEATRICE))
```

(KARMAN (BUICK-1)))

If this is a frame in our domain *A*, then the above logical expression denotes a non-empty set of properties with respect to the world state the frame model describes. Consider now what we have to know to know that this is a satisfying instance. We have to be able to reverse the mapping from lexical scenes to logical predicates, to know which core participant positions correspond to which pieces of structure:

(LONGING SIGMA BEATRICE) (FOR SIGMA BUICK-1)

```
(LONGING
 (KARMAN)
 (LONGER))
```

Suppose that in addition to the *for*-phrase in the above sentence we had the prepositional phrase *to Dan*. We would have map (TO SIGMA DAN) onto the LONGING frame, but if the lexical represention for *to* does not license such a mapping, then there can BE no such satisfying instance in any state of affairs.

In fact *to* does not appear to be appropriate with *wish*. We could capture this fact by saying that the predicate TO is not defined when the denotation of its first argument is a LONGING instancen that our core frame representation defines a "sortal" restriction on the predicate TO; that is, TO is defined only when its first argument (corresponding to the "sigma" position) belongs to some class of objects C. If TO picks out no slot in any LONGING frame, then the class of LONGING objects is disjoint from C.

Our first definition of semantic compatibility was stated simply in terms of scenes. We said that two scenes were semantically compatible if one was AKO the other.

Let us consider how this compatibility would be transferred to two- and three- place predicates. The denotation of a two-place predicate is a pair consisting of a frame and a slot, and the denotation of a three-place predicate a triple consisting of a frame and two slots: the result we want is that two predicates be compatible if the frame parts of their denotations are, that is, if one frame is AKO the other. Let A' and B' be two predicates and A and B the frames in their denotations. If A is AKO B, then any slot in the denotation of B' (we will say any slot *accessed* by B') will also be a slot in A.

By convention the first argument of a two-place predicate is the "sigma" argument, or situation argument. Call that argument position the frame position. Then our first kind of semantic compatibility, call it AKO compatibility, can be stated just in terms of frame positions. In fact, our truth definition for a two-place predicate does that work now — almost. Here it is again.

Definition A:

(*In* (R T1 T2)) is defined iff (*In* T1) is AKO (*In'* R);

and, if defined,

(*In* (R T1 T2)) = 1 iff
(get (*In* T1) (*In''* R)) = (*In* T2)

(*In* (R T1 T2)) = 0 otherwise.

The thing to focus on here is the first clause, which states a precondition which an interpretation must meet in order for the predicate to be well-defined, namely that the particular situation denoted by T1 be AKO the frame associated with frame position. Consider the logical representation of "John wished to a Buick:"

(69)

```
(EXISTS* SIGMA (AND (WISHING SIGMA JOHN)
                    (BUICK X)
                    (TO SIGMA X)))
```

Assume the following:

(*In* wishing) = <WISHING LONGER>
(*In* to)   = <TO GOAL>

The sentence will be true just in case there is some situation which is AKO both WISHING and TO, whose LONGER is JOHN and whose GOAL is a BUICK. This means the sentence will be defined just in case there is some assignment of object o to x, such that o is AKO both WISHING and TO, If in our frame model, the class of objects that is AKO WISHING is disjoint from the class of objects which is AKO TO, then this logical expression is undefined. This may or may not be a desirable stipulation to make about TO situations and WISHING situations; however, as the formalism stands now, there are frame models for which this sentence is not only defined, but true. This is not the result we want. We could guarantee there were no such frame models with a meaning postulate, but the thrust of the current enterprise is to avoid lexical meaning postulates by doing the work they did in the frame representations. A better solution is to slightly modify the first clause of the truth definition for two-place predicates. To begin with, let the above definition stand for preposition predicates. But for predicates associated with heads (verbs, adjectives, nouns), let the first clause be modified as follows:

Definition B:

(*In* (R T1 T2)) is defined iff (*In* T1) is not AKO anything not in the compatibility set C of (*In'* R)

By the compatibility set C of (*In'* R) I mean the set of frames with which (*In'* R) is compatible. Our compatibility definition for frames says a frame is compatible with any frames it is AKO; so WISHING has at least LONGING in its compatibility set. But as our definition for compatibility stands now, if WISHING is not AKO TO, then TO is not in its compatibility set. This means that no object o which is AKO TO can be the denotation of the first argument of WISHING. But the above logical representation is defined only if there is some object o which is:

(1) AKO TO (by the Definition A, now good only for preposition predicates).

(2) AKO some frame in the compatibility set of WISHING (by Definition B, since every frame except THING is AKO something), and not AKO anything not in the compatibility set of WISHING.

But if TO is not in the compatibility set of WISHING then there can be no such object, and the matrix of (69) will be undefined for every variable assignment, and thus (69) will be undefined.

The above definition extends straightforwardly to three-place head predicates. Taken together, the semantic definitions for atomic predicates will comprise the basic implementation of logical compatibility in force for the remainder of this dissertation. But two kinds of revisions will be necessary:

(1) We will need to generalize the notion of a compatibility set in the next chapter.

(2) We will need to complicate the mapping from grammatical categories to logical predicates.

The main reason (2) arises is because of our new treatment of adjuncts. Before revising the conventions linking logical predicates and grammatical categories, let us review the old ones.

(1) intransitive verbs: these always translate into two-place relations between a situation and a participant. Thus *run* is a two place relation between a running situation and a runner.

(2) transitive verbs: these are always three place relations between a situation and two participants, one the subject, one the object.

(3) prepositions: these are always two place relations between a situation and a participant; that participant is always grammatically realized as the object of the preposition.

What needs some immediate attention here is the prepositions. As it is actually worded, the above proposal can stand. Nevertheless there is a distinction that needs to be made between adjunct predicates and core participant predicates, corresponding to the distinction we have made in their frame representations. Let us take as our paradigm cases *for* in its *karman* meaning and *on* in its temporal meaning. The relevant frames are:

```
(ON
 (AKO(LOCATION_IN_TIME))
 (LOCATION)
 (FIGURE (TEMPORALLY_LOCATED_OBJECT)))

(LONGING
 (KARMAN)
 (LONGER))
```

A frame like LONGING will map to a two-place predicate, the first of whose arguments corresponds to an entire LONGING situation. We have called that argument position frame position. Adjunct prepositions will not have a frame position. Instead they will, intuitively, be a straightforward relation between the value of slots. So, there will be a predicate ON:

```
(ON' __ __)      (ON
                  (AKO(LOCATION_IN_TIME))
                  (LOCATION)
                  (FIGURE (TEMPORALLY_LOCATED_OBJECT)))
```

Note that the "sigma" position is still on the left, the argument corresponding to the "marked" slot (the object of the preposition), still on the right. The only difference between this predicate and FOR' (in its *karman* meaning) is that the first argument of FOR' corresponds to an entire LONGING frame. But note that the ON scene also places a sortal restriction on the first argument position of ON', namely that the objects filling it be TEMPORALLY_LOCATED_OBJECTS. It might seem that we could build these restrictions into the truth definition of adjunct preposition predicates in some way parallel to the technique used in Definition B, but in fact there are some technical problems with doing that. The current proposal for adjuncts allows them to select their VP's by some specification in their situation slots. Suppose we tried to define some notion of a Restriction set for a situation slot, that is, the set of generic frames whose instantiations satisfy the restrictions on that slot. One problem is that adjuncts can iterate, and different adjuncts will make different demands on the same heads, so we cannot have a clause demanding the head "not be AKO anything not in the restriction set". Giving up this negative form of statement, as we saw above, leaves us in a situation where a verb/preposition combination is undefined in some frame models, but not in others. Another problem is that, in general, there will no set of generic frames R, whose instances satisfy a situation slot. As we shall see in the following chapters, specifications on embedded frames can be arbitrarily complex. They will not always be simple requirements that the slotfiller be AKO some frame. As a simple example, consider:

```
(FOO
 (SLOT1 (BAR
        (SLOT2 (BAZ)))))
```

Here the restriction on *slot1* is that it be filled by frames which are AKO BAR and have the value BAZ in their *slot2* slot. Now if in general BAR frames can have arbitrary values in *slot2* there is no generic frame corresponding exactly to the restrictions on *slot1* in FOO.

What I propose to do about this problem is turn it into a feature of the theory. Suppose we say that in general adjunct predicates have no sortal restrictions associated with them, and that inappropriate uses of adjuncts, say, "The book at 3'o'clock," or "reading books in 3 hours," are not rejected in the logic, but in the frame representation; that is, they are not linguistically ruled out; rather they are ruled out because the situational structure required is impossible. This means that genuine semantic selection, and thus semantic compatibility, is the sort of business only conducted between heads and core participants.

This makes the truth definition for adjuncts simple. Suppose adjunct prepositions are associated with two-place predicates, but that their denotations are triples consisting of a frame (the preposition frame) and two slots (the slots that are being related in the predicate. Then we have:

(*In* (ADJ T1 T2)) = 1 iff
there is a frame F AKO (*In* ADJ)
such that
(get F (*In''* R)) = (*In* T2)
and
(get F (*In'''* R)) = (*In* T2)

(*In* (ADJ T1 T2)) = 0 otherwise.

Recall that we had good reason before to posit that certain preposition meanings could occur both as subcategorized for prepositions and adjuncts. An outstanding example was *against* in its *contended-force* meaning. This leads to an interesting result. Since we have different predicate definitions for core participant and adjunct prepositions, the same lexical frame will have to be associated with two different logical predicates. Yet this will not be a case of polysemy, because there is only one meaning representation. We will see more cases of this in the following chapters. In particular, the general case for Dative Movement will involve just that; one meaning with two different logico-grammatical realizations. Dative Movevment is notable in that it does involve any morphological apparatus. The same can be said for the two predicates associated with a preposition like *against*. They correlate with differences in grammatical function, but no morphology marks this difference. Such alternations in grammatical function are among the topics of chapter 4.

A final note on adjuncts is in order. The current treatment of all preposition meanings predicts logical equivalence if the prepositions are commuted, since in logical form everything is flattened into a single conjunction. Hans Uszkareit (personal communication) has pointed out to me that commutation of prepositions is not always meaning preserving:

(71) Bill made a sweater for Mary for John.

Commuting the *for*-phrases here suggests that a different person will end up with the sweater. The way to extend the current treatment to take such facts into account is to allow some prepositions to be three-place predicates and introduce their own situation variable. We could thus represent the above sentence with the following logical expression:

```
(EXISTS* SIGMA (EXISTS TAU (EXISTS XI (EXISTS X
   (AND (MAKE SIGMA BILL X)
        (SWEATER X)
        (FOR TAU MARY SIGMA)
        (FOR XI JOHN TAU))))))
```

This means we need new semantic rules for prepositional phrases of this new type in the syntax, namely:

```
<V1 -> V1 P2: (lambda tau
                 (lambda x (exists sigma
                              (and (P2 sigma tau)
                                   (V1 sigma x)))))>
```

We also need a new truth definition for such three-place preposition predicates, differing from the one for three-place head predicates (transitive verbs, for example) in that it lacks a clause stipulating when the predicate is defined.

1.9 Conclusion

In this chapter I have proposed a basic framework in which to undertake lexical description. I have argued that the ultimate goal of constructing a full set of lexical representations is that lexical representations are an integral part of a full-blown representation of cultural categories, and that such a culturally specific "knowledge representation" will be the foundation of a theory of discourse understanding.

I have assumed that adequate lexical representations must account for the phenomenon of *semantic compatibility*, the potential for different forms to combine in semantically sensible ways. As my paradigm example I have taken the compatibility of verbs and prepositions, and proposed a simple way of representing such compatibility in the scheme of lexical representations. I have also proposed a technique for mapping the semantic compatibility of lexical frames into their denotations.

Finally, I have proposed a lexical semantic analogue to the classical syntactic distinction between subcategorized-for complement and adjunct. This leads to different logical denotations for the adjunct and subcategorized-for versions of the same preposition meaning, but there is no polysemy, since both denotations are grounded in a single lexical representation. In the framework developed here, the logical denotations are really just encodings of grammtical function, so that it is quite natural that different functions should lead to different denotations. The real semantics remains in the frame.

In the next chapter we will enrich our definition of semantic compatibility as well as the representation scheme itself. We will take Fillmore's paradigm example of a scene, the COMMERCIAL-EVENT, and construct lexical representations that capture the relations of a number of verbs with different compatibility properties to a single situation-type. These different compatibilities will be used to define the particular "view" that a COMMERCIAL-EVENT verb takes on the COMMERCIAL-EVENT scene. In effect, we use the compatibility properties of a verb to construct its semantic profile, defining its place simultaneously in a number of intersecting paradigms.

2. Figure and Ground Scenes

2.1 Introduction

This chapter will propose some fairly major extensions of the theory outlined in the first chapter. In particular a distinction will be drawn between *figure* and *ground* scenes. BUYING will be a figure scene related to a particular verb; COMMERCIAL_EVENT will be a ground scene related to a class of verbs. A ground scene represents background material, a compendium of information about some situation type which is not found in the lexical (or figure) scenes related to that situation-type; either it is not found in the lexical scenes because there is no linguistic motivation for putting it there, or else it is it is information which cannot be fit into a single lexical scene, because of linguistic constraints. Among the constraints we will impose on lexical scenes in this chapter are uniqueness — the requirement that no role be assigned to to more than one participant — and completeness — the requirement that all participants be grammatically realized. Although lexical figure scenes will in effect be a special kind of figure scene, there is no reason why the relation between figure and ground should be limited in scope to lexical scenes. There may still be non-linguistic figure scenes.

2.2 A Commercial Event

Fillmore's canonical example of what a scene is is a commercial event. I will be focusing on lexical problems centering around events in this chapter because they involve us in a scene whose participant and situational structure is far more complex than that of the examples we have considered till now. In this section I will concentrate the business of buying and selling.

First, a commercial event involves one participant, a buyer, giving another, a seller, something called money for something else called the goods. This is a scene of transference of possession. More than that, it is a scene of two transferences of possession, The money starts out with the buyer and ends up with the seller. The goods goes the other way.

Let us first concentrate on the movement of the goods, beginning with the verb *sell*.

2.2.1 Selling and possessive to

The verb *sell* marks the role of the buyer with the preposition *to*, a marking which is clearly oriented towards the movement of the goods. We know this because there are a number of verbs in English which deal with possession transference which mark the new possessor with *to* and realize the new possession as direct object:

(1) John gave the book to charity.

(2) Reggie brought the rice to the children.

(3) Loretta handed the book to Alonzo.

(4) Trish assigned the task to a prelate.

(5) The enemy surrendered the candy to Bilbo.

(6) The seller transfers the goods to the buyer.

Thus, as a first pass we might make the meaning of *to* in such examples *acquirer*, with the emphasis here on *transferred* possession. Again, I am pursuing a strategy of narrow preposition meanings. There is, of course, always the appealing alternative of something like Goal to describe the preposition *to*, but "Goal" is usually taken to include both directional complements and possessional complements. An important motivation for distinguishing these complement-types is that only the latter undergo Dative Movement. A parallel distinction can be noted in case-marking languages which distinguish a "dative" case from one or more directional cases (in Slavic, directional complements most directly correlate with the accusative), or in a more analytic language like French, between those complements which cliticize as *lui* and those which cliticize as *y*.

If we say that English, too, has a distinction between directional *to* and possessive *to*, with the possibility of Dative Movement always indicating the latter, then we we will analyze verbs like *send* and *mail* as pure cases of possession transference. As far as the pure physics of the situation goes, acts of sending and mailing would seem to involve both transferences of possession and location. While we can imagine an act of giving in which the object given does not move ("I hereby give you my Kandinski"), it is hard to do the same for acts of sending ("I hereby send you a letter").

The right line to take here, I think, is that this a linguistic matter, not a matter of measurement. Although a complete description of a mailing situation would certainly entail "movement," it is not necessarily the case that the verb *mail* encodes this movement. Later in this chapter I will argue for a "split" system of representation, one that separates the lexical representation, which contains some limited, linguistically motivated semantic material, from a more complete representation with *all* the situational information. As far as our lexical description goes, the question is, should *mail* be classed with the transference of possession verbs or the transference of location verbs? The possibility of Dative Movement argues for the former.

More problematic are cases like *throw* and *roll*. The occurrence of a large number of locative prepositions with these verbs suggests they are directional; but Dative Movement, too, is possible:

```
(7a)Plonk threw the ball at Plink.
          rolled        to
                        under
                        past
                        behind
```

(7b)Plonk threw Plink the ball.
          rolled

Note however that Dative Movement precludes the possibility of a purely directional interpretation.

(8a)Plonk threw the ball to the floor.
(8b)*Plonk threw the floor the ball.

(9a) Plonk rolled the ball to the edge of the table.
(9b)*Plonk rolled the edge of the table the ball.

Probably the asterisks here are overly strict. If we imagine the floor and the edge of the table as cooperative entities able to enter into the spirit of a good game of catch, the (b) sentences are fine. The correct thing to say about verbs like *roll* and *throw* seems to be that they are both verbs of transference of location and of transference of possession.

Let us turn to the frame involving transference of possession, in an attempt to represent the common semantic component of verbs like *give, assign, transfer, hand, mail,* and *send.* The skeletal scene for possession transference might look like this:

```
(POS_TRANS
  (AKO (THING))
  (DONOR)
  (RECIPIENT)
  (PATIENT))
```

Here I have modified Roger Schank's name for a scene involving transference of physical location, PTRANS, to express a distinct notion of possession transference. Note that POS_TRANS is not AKO

PTRANS, or anything like it.

Returning now to commercial events, and in particular the verb *sell*. A natural treatment would be to regard the verb *sell* as a possession transference verb in the same class as *give*. Commercial events could be brought in by making COMMERCIAL_EVENT AKO POS_TRANS:

```
(COMMERCIAL_EVENT
  (AKO (POS_TRANS))
  (BUYER)
  (SELLER)
  (MONEY)
  (GOODS))

(BUYING
 (AKO (COMMERCIAL_EVENT)))
```

But now there is an obvious problem, and it is one the attentive reader will already have wondered about. How do we line up the roles? By the conventions thus far established, the BUYING scene will inherit the four slots introduced in the COMMERCIAL_EVENT scene, as well as four slots the COMMERCIAL_EVENTS inherits from the POS_TRANS scene. This gives us seven roles. How do we annotate the fact that what we MEAN is that the *buyer* is the *recipient* and the *seller* the *donor* and the *goods* the *patient?* That is, how do we represent the fact that the verb *buy* has a scene with only four participants?

What I propose here is to view each of the COMMERCIAL_EVENT participant roles as a more elaborated version of some slot in

POS_TRANS, that is, to view the *buyer* slot as a more elaborated version of *recipient*, and so on. We can represent this with a procedural attachment that constrains the *buyer* slot to be equal to the *recipient* slot:

```
(BUYER (= RECIPIENT))
```

With this notation in place, the COMMERCIAL_EVENT is:

```
(COMMERCIAL_EVENT
  (AKO (POS_TRANS))
  (BUYER (= RECIPIENT))
  (SELLER (= DONOR))
  (MONEY)
  (GOODS (= PATIENT)))
```

Now this may seem a rather curious sort of stipulation. Why couldn't it have been otherwise? Why isn't there a commercial events scene in which the *seller* is the *patient* and the *buyer* the *recipient* and the *goods* the *donor*? Or one where *donor, recipient,* and *patient* all equal the *goods?*

The answer is that viewing the *buyer* as a specification of the *recipient* is a way of defining what it means to be a buyer. A *buyer* is just a special kind of *recipient* in a special kind of POS_TRANS scene. Similarly, for the other roles.

This point might be clarified a bit, if we sharpen our initial characterization of what a frame is. What we have been looking at mid all these pairs of parentheses is skeletal structures which still need to be filled in with some specifications that express the relations among the parts. We will think of such specifications as procedures. In presenting the "unpacked" version of the COMMERCIAL_EVENT frame, I have taken the first step towards making those procedures explicit. That is, the relations among the participants in the COMMERCIAL_EVENT scene can be partially defined by "calling" the procedures that define the relations among the participants in the POS_TRANS scene. Thus the COMMERCIAL_EVENT frame is more than just AKO the POS_TRANS frame; it introduces new slots that are in the same relation. This is a kind of semantic decomposition, but a decomposition into structures rather than features. Additionally, the notation I have chosen allows us to defer the unpleasant business of choosing semantic primitives; it is a path that is likely to net us rather a large bag of primitives, but it helps us be clear on just what we will expect those primitives to do at each step.

The easiest comparison here is to the task of writing a large program. Often the general procedures and control structures of a large program are written first, so that the tasks of the bottom level procedures are completely defined by the time they need to be written. The direction is top-down, in contrast to the bottom-up direction that would be imposed on a semantic-primitives first approach.

To make predictions about the semantic compatibility of a COMMERCIAL_EVENTS verbs like *sell* with *to*, we shall also need a representation of the lexical scene for the preposition. I propose:

```
(POSSESSION
 (AKO (THING))
 (POSSESSOR)
 (PATIENT))
```

Now this does not represent an event involving *change* of possession; what suggests that that component is introduced by the POS_TRANS scene rather than being a part of the meaning of *to* is a verb like *belong*, which takes *to* in a possessive sense, but does not involve any transfer of possession. We now want POS_TRANS to be compatible to POSSESSION. The simplest way would be:

```
(POS_TRANS
 (AKO (POSSESSION))
 (DONOR)
 (RECIPIENT (= POSSESSOR))
 (PATIENT))
```

If the COMMERCIAL_EVENT scene is now AKO POS_TRANS, and the lexical scene for *sell* is AKO COMMERCIAL_EVENT, then *sell* and *to* will be compatible.

2.2.2 Buying and source

We now turn to the verb *buy*. First note that the verb *buy*, like *sell*, focuses on the transference of the goods rather than the money; this is clear from the use of the preposition *from* to mark the *seller*. Thus, we might well associate *buy* with a POS_TRANS scene whose *Patient* was the *goods*. For the moment we can chalk up the occurrence of the preposition *from* to a very general meaning we'll call *source*, because there is no clear formal motivation for a distinction between Possession and Movement situations, as there was with *to*. Then there is an abstract TRANSFERENCE scene:

```
(TRANSFERENCE
 (AKO (THING))
 (FIGURE)
 (SOURCE))

(POS_TRANS
 (AKO (TRANSFERENCE) (POSSESSION))
 (DONOR (= SOURCE))
 (PATIENT)
 (RECIPIENT (= POSSESSOR)))
```

The TRANSFERENCE scene would here be the lexical scene for *from*. And given that *buy* is associated with the POS_TRANS scene through the COMMERCIAL_EVENT scene, the semantic compatibility of *buy* and *from* would follow.

Previously the verbs we thought of as POS_TRANS verbs were verbs like *bring, give, hand, assign, surrender,* and *transfer*. With the TRANSFERENCE scene incorporated into POS_TRANS we can also think of verbs like *take, receive, get, acquire,* and *obtain* as POS_TRANS verbs. Their compatibility with the preposition *from* is predicted because POS_TRANS is AKO TRANSFERENCE.

There is, of course, an important difference between these sets of verbs. With the first set *donor* has become subject; with the second set, *recipient* has. The fact that the *receive* type verbs will not mark their *recipient* with *to* will follow from the syntactic fact that nuclear terms do not take complement marking in English; but we have said nothing yet about why these two sets of verbs choose different POS_TRANS participants as subject. That sort of question will be deferred until chapter 3. In fact, independently of the semantics of nuclear terms, it will be necessary to posit certain differences between verbs like *buy* and *sell* to account for differences in their behaviors with complements. From those differences in representations the differences in subject choice will eventually follow.

2.3 Revisions to POS_TRANS: a New Definition of Semantic Compatibility

Now there is something a little peculiar in the above version of POS_TRANS as a representation of an event of possession transference. That, of course, is that it misses the temporal and causal structure of the event. What happens is that there an event of transference, as a result of which the *recipient* possesses the *patient*. It is not really that there is one event which is both a sort of transference and a sort of possession. What we intuitively would like to call a POS_TRANS is a scene that involves two other scenes in some special relationship we might tentatively represent with a scene called CAUSAL-SEQUENCE:

```
(CAUSAL-SEQUENCE
 (AKO (THING))
 (ANTECEDENT)
 (CONSEQUENT))
```

Now suppose POS_TRANS is AKO CAUSAL-SEQUENCE. And suppose that it takes in its ANTECEDENT slot a TRANSFERENCE and in its CONSEQUENT slot a POSSESSION. Then we have:

```
(POS_TRANS
 (AKO (CAUSAL-SEQUENCE))
 (ANTECEDENT(TRANSFERENCE
                (SOURCE)
                (FIGURE)))
 (CONSEQUENT(POSSESSION
                (POSSESSOR)
                (PATIENT)))
 (DONOR (=SOURCE))
 (RECIPIENT(=POSSESSOR)))
 (PATIENT (=PATIENT)(= FIGURE)))
```

The notation here has some shortcomings which will be rectified in a moment, but first consider the intuition that is this representation tries to capture. What the new POS_TRANS frame says is that the *recipient* of the POS_TRANS scene is the same as the *possessor* of the POSSESSION scene that is the value of the *consequent* slot; and the *patient* of the POS_TRANS is the *patient* of that POSSESSION scene, as well as the *figure* of the TRANSFERENCE scene in the *antecedent* slot; finally the *donor* is the *source* of the TRANSFERENCE scene. One problem that immediately arises if we accept this representation is that the definition of semantic compatibility we have used till now no longer applies, since the proposed POS_TRANS scene is neither AKO the TRANSFERENCE and POSSESSION scenes nor selected by them. This means no POS_TRANS verbs will be semantically compatible with *to* and *from*.

What is required is a new extension of our definition of semantic compatibility, but in order to make that extension we shall have to make the above notation a bit more precise. To simplify what will ultimately be our new definition of semantic compatibility, it will be useful to copy all of the "embedded" slots in the above representation into the top level frame. What we will need is a procedure that allows a frame to inherit "horizontally", that is, inherit a slot from a frame which is a value of one of its own slots. We want to be able to "flatten out" frame structure.

(10)

```
(POS_TRANS
 (AKO (CAUSAL-SEQUENCE))
 (ANTECENDENT  (TRANSFERENCE))
 (CONSEQUENT (POSSESSION))
 (FIGURE (METONYMY 'antecedent))
 (SOURCE (METONYMY 'antecedent))
 (POSSESSOR (METONYMY 'consequent))
 (PATIENT (METONYMY 'consequent)(= figure))
 (DONOR (= source))
 (RECIPIENT(= possessor)))
```

Here we have simply declared slots called "possessor," "figure," "source," and "patient" in the POS_TRANS frame, but attached a procedure called METONYMY which accesses whichever slot has the embedded frame with the slot we want to copy.

The name "metonymy" is to suggest that the larger frame inherits the values of the appropriate TRANSFERENCE and POSSESSION scenes through its "close association." To recall a classic example, conventional uses of the phrase "The throne of England" involve metonymy because the throne, an object associated with the authority of the king, is used to stand for the abstract notion of kingship. Thus it "inherits" the properties of that authority, and we may say "The throne of England was secure," when we mean the kingship was secure. As a Lisp procedure, metonymy could be written:

```
(defun metonymy (associated-object)
  (get (get :frame associated-object) :slot))
```

Defun here is simply the Lisp function for defining functions. The above function definition works as follows: For the frame above, in the *patient* slot, (metonymy 'consequent) would be equivalent to:

```
(get (get :frame 'consequent) 'patient)
```

Here, as in Chapter 1, *:frame* means the current frame, and *:slot* is an extension of the same convention, meaning, the current slot. Consider a particular POS_TRANS situation, POS_TRANS-1:

```
(POS_TRANS-1
 (AKO (POS_TRANS))
 (ANTECENDENT  (TRANSFERENCE-1
               (SOURCE (HARRY))
               (FIGURE (BOOK-1))))
 (CONSEQUENT (POSSESSION-1
             (POSSESSOR-1(MARY))
             (PATIENT (BOOK-1))))
 (FIGURE (METONYMY 'antecedent))
 (SOURCE (METONYMY 'antecedent))
 (POSSESSOR (METONYMY 'consequent))
 (PATIENT (METONYMY 'consequent)(= figure))
 (DONOR (= source))
 (RECIPIENT(= possessor)))
```

The value of (metonymy 'consequent) in the *patient* slot would be:

```
(get (get 'POS_TRANS-1 'consequent)  'patient)
```

Evaluating the innermost set of parentheses, we have:

```
(get 'POSSESSION-1 'patient)
```

And the *patient* of POSSESSION-1 is BOOK-1. So the value of the *patient* slot in the frame POS_TRANS-1 is thus BOOK-1. Furthermore, the other requirement on that value is that it be equal to the value of the *figure* slot in POS_TRANS-1 (proof left as an exercise).

We are now ready to give an improved definition of semantic

compatibility.

When a frame A has a slot that requires a frame that is AKO B as its value, and when it accesses all the slots of the frame except the AKO slot through "metonymy," we shall say that A has B as a *component*. We don't want component scenes to have their AKO slots accessed by metonymy, because that would reduce "having as a component" to a special case of AKO. Thus the POS_TRANS frame defined above has the POSSESSION frame and the TRANSFERENCE frame as components. Let us further make the relation "being a component of" transitive. If A is a component of B and B is a component of C, then A is a component of C. Thus if the POSSESSION scene had slots which took scenes as their values, the scenes required for those slots would be components of the POS_TRANS scene. It will also be useful to have a general term covering two special cases where one frame A "uses" the definition of another B in its definition. One case is where A is AKO B, since, in effect, A is then defined with reference to the procedures of B. Case two is where A has B as a component. In either case we will say that A is an *extension* of B. Note that since both "being a component of" and "AKO-ness" are transitive, then "being an extension of" is also transitive.

Let us say furthermore that every frame is AKO itself, so that "extension of" will also be a reflexive relation.

It is now easy to give a new definition of semantic compatibility. A scene A is semantically compatible with a scene B if A is an extension of B. In terms of lexical scenes for heads and complements, this covers two cases that we have seen thus far:

(1) The head scene is AKO the complement scene. (The scenes for the verbs of longing and the LONGING scene itself.)

(2) The head scene has the complement scene or some extension of it as a component. (The scene for any POS_TRANS verbs and the POSSESSION scene).

This does not cover the case of adjuncts, as dealt with in chapter 1. There MEANS-TO-AN-END had a slot which required a PURSUIT, but it did not access the slots of a PURSUIT by *metonymy;* so PURSUIT is not a component of MEANS-TO-AN-END, and MEANS-TO-AN-END is not an extension of PURSUIT.

The new definition of semantic compatibility has not changed our truth definition for lexical predicates; it has only only changed the notion "compatibililty set" referred to there. Here is the definition for three-place lexical heads, as a reminder:

Truth Definition:

(*In* (R T1 T2)) is defined iff (*In* T1) is not AKO anything not in the compatibility set C of (*In'* R)

and, if defined,

(*In* (R T1 T2)) = 1 iff
(get (*In* T1) (*In''* R)) = (*In* T2)
(get (*In* T1) (*In'''* R)) = (*In* T3)

(*In* (R T1 T2)) = 0 otherwise.

The effect of the change can be illustrated with the new POS_TRANS scene and our interpretation of its predicate TO. Consider the following logical formula, corresponding to the sentence "John gave a book to Mary," with "gave" translated simply as POS_TRANS:

```
(EXISTS* SIGMA (EXISTS X (AND (POS_TRANS SIGMA JOHN X)
                              (BOOK X)
                              (TO SIGMA MARY))))
```

Suppose first of all that we retained the old notion of a compatibility set. Then POS_TRANS would be a predicate whose first position required objects that were AKO POS_TRANS. The above sentence would then have an undefined interpretation. This is because TO and POS_TRANS both place requirements on the interpretation of *sigma*. *Sigma* must be AKO POSSESSION, AKO POS_TRANS, and not AKO anything that POS_TRANS is not AKO. But POS_TRANS is not AKO POSSESSION. Therefore no assignment to sigma is defined and the existential quantification over sigma is undefined. Under the new definition of semantic compatibility, the compatibility set of POS_TRANS is broader and includes all frames which are components of POS_TRANS, including POSSESSION. Thus the requirements on sigma can be met and the sentence is defined.

The intuitive content of the compatibililty definition is this: TO is a relation which picks out the filler of the *possessor* slot for every frame that is AKO some extension of POSSESSION. Every frame that is either a POSSESSION or has a POSSESSION scene as a component will have a *possessor* slot.

We shall henceforth be making much more extensive use of scenes that take other scenes as components. To say this is simply to concede that the relationships among lexical structures are more complex than can be represented by a notion like "AKO-ness". It will thus be convenient to have an alternative graphic representation of frames, one in which it is easier to read off facts about the internal structures of slots. Since the representations we were just looking at involved slots that took frames as their values, a representation with a clearer "constituent structure" is in order:

(11)

```
(POS_TRANS: CAUSAL-SEQUENCE
  (ANTECEDENT
   (TRANSFERENCE
    (FIGURE <↑ PATIENT> <^ FIGURE>)
    (SOURCE <↑ DONOR>) <^SOURCE>)
  (CONSEQUENT
   (POSSESSION
    (POSSESSOR <↑ RECIPIENT> <^POSSESSOR>)
    (PATIENT <↑ PATIENT>)))
  (RECIPIENT)
  (DONOR)
  (PATIENT)))
```

Call the version of POS_TRANS in (10) the "flat" version. Call this version the "multi-tiered" version. This multi-tiered frame in fact represents exactly the same information as the flat version above. Here, the colon after the frame name is just an abbreviation for

AKO-ness. Items enclosed in angle brackets should be read not as slots which take further structures as their values but as "paths" (following a convention in Kay 1979), used as convenient names for the values found at the end of the paths. In a frame, an arbitrary path is named by starting from the top and indicating successive slot names. So for example the path <Abbot Partner Idol Admirer> names the value "Chaplin" in first of the following representations:

```
(ABBOT
 (PARTNER (COSTELLO
           (IDOL (LAUREL
                  (PARTNER (HARDY))
                  (ADMIRER (CHAPLIN)))))))

(ABBOT
 (PARTNER (COSTELLO
           (ADMIRER (HARDY))
           (IDOL (LAUREL
                  (PARTNER <↑ ADMIRER>)))))))
```

In fact, a path is a sequence of paths, so that <Abbot Partner Idol Admirer> could also be written, <<Abbot <<Partner> Idol>> Admirer>. It will be easier on the eyes to avoid the extra angle-brackets whenever possible; however, it will be useful to remember that a path is a sequence of paths sometimes when naming new paths in terms of old ones. Thus if

<Abbot Partner Idol> = P
then:
<P Admirer> = <Abbot Partner Idol Admirer>

The symbol " ↑ " in a path should be read as an abbreviation for the frame immediately dominating the position in which the " ↑ " is found.

Thus in the second example frame above the path "<↑ ADMIRER>" picks out the value Hardy, so that Hardy is both the value of the *partner* slot in the embedded COSTELLO frame and the *Admirer* slot in the embedded LAUREL frame. In the proposed representation of POS_TRANS the path <↑ PATIENT> simply names the value of the *Patient* slot in the top level frame. Although <↑ PATIENT> occurs twice in the POS_TRANS frame, its repetition is due only to the limitations of a two-dimensional page. The above representation says that the same piece of structure is:

(1) the value of the *patient* slot of the *possession* scene in the *consequence* slot;

(2) the value of the *figure* slot of the *transference* scene in the *antecedent* slot.

(3) the value of the *patient* slot in the top level frame.

Similarly the value of the *donor* slot of the top level frame is the same piece of structure as the value of the *possessor* slot of the embedded POSSESSION frame; the value of the *recipient* slot of the toplevel frame is the same as the *possessor* slot of the embedded POSSESSION frame. We can abbreviate our representations of POS_TRANS further with two conventions: first, our definition of component is stated so that when a slot contains a component, all the slots in the embedded frame are accessed by metonymy from a slot in the top level frame which has the same name. Thus, if we simply annotate a slot with the label "component", we can omit stipulating those automatic procedures for each slots. Let us think of slots that introduce components as "a kind of" slot, and place the annotation "component" after a colon following the slot name, parallel to the way the AKO value of an entire frame is represented. Second, when we mean to identify the value of a top level slot with the value of an embedded slot, we will not bother to copy the slot over in the top level frame. So instead of the above we will have:

```
(POS_TRANS: CAUSAL-SEQUENCE
  (ANTECEDENT: COMPONENT
   (TRANSFERENCE
    (FIGURE <↑ PATIENT>)
    (SOURCE <↑ DONOR>))
  (CONSEQUENT: COMPONENT
   (POSSESSION
    (POSSESSOR <↑ RECIPIENT>)
    (PATIENT)))))
```

Note that the angle brackets are only meant to identify the *values* of the embedded slots and the toplevel slots, not the slots themselves. So the slots may still have different procedures associated with them and place different *constraints* on the value. Even though we are identifying the value of the *donor* slot with the value of a *source* slot, there may still be more to being a *donor* than just being a *source*. This means that the *donor* and *source* roles are still distinct, even though they belong to a single participant.

The new style of displaying frames reveals their formal kinship with the functional descriptions of Kay 1979 and the F-structures of Kaplan and Bresnan 1982. Like the formal objects in those works, the

POS_TRANS scene can be interpreted as a directed-acyclic graph. This is not really surprising since my goal here is the representation of a kind of predicational structure, and capturing predicational structure is one of the chief motivations of functional representation as well. The general translation from "frame" to "graph" is fairly straightforward. There is always a root node that stands for a given frame. The slots become arc labels; the values become nodes. If we wish to decompose slots into procedures, then the picture becomes messier, but no more conceptually complicated. Arguments and values of procedures will be nodes. A given procedure with *n* arguments will turn into *n+1* labeled arcs, with the last arc terminating at a value. This picture allows there to be nodes that are not the values of slots. If we wish to capture the notion of slot and value in our graph, we can have special labeled arcs labeled SLOT, which are always rooted in the node that stands for the whole frame, and which always lead to nodes labeled with slot names. The slot nodes can in turn have labeled arcs called VALUE leading to their values.

In so far as the game here is a form of lexical decomposition, some resemblances to the representations of the more decompositional generative semanticists are also evident. I will not enter into a discussion of the similarities and differences of the relevant formalisms here; suffice it to say that it has been noticed before that the same formal devices that represent syntactic and grammatical structures can also be used to represent lexical structures. The problem has always been what to make of this fact. I have offered two equivalent representations of the POS_TRANS frames. Both the flat and the "functional" representation give us the information we need to determine what the core participants of the POS_TRANS scene are, as well as some information about semantic compatibility. The advantage of the "flat" representation is that it made it easier to state the definition of semantic compatibility. The advantage of the "functional" representation is that it is easier to look at, and for now I will use that as my only justification for representing complex scenes in a tiered format. The question of whether a unity among the representational devices of different "levels" of grammar is in itself desirable will be put aside.

One technical reason one might want to put aside the comparison with functional structure is that I have already countenanced some representations which are a bit more than a directed acyclic graph. Consider our representation of the the STRIFE scene (for verbs like *fight*) from chapter 1:

```
(STRIFE
 (AKO (CAMPAIGN))
 (BATTLER)
 (CONTENDED-FORCE)
 (SOCIAL-EVENT(:frame)))
```

What is intended here is that the value of a particular slot be the frame the slot is in. This means that our graphs have loops, which means they are not acyclic.

Ruling out such representations is of course advisable on general formal grounds; in this case simple semantic intuitions seem to argue for revision as well. Given the sentences, "John spoke against disarmament," and "John battled against the Huns," do we really want to make an analogy with the following terms: speech-1 : disarmament :: battle-1 : Huns? Speech-1 is some situation with John as a core participant, Battle-1 has both John and the Huns as the participant. Do we really want to say that the battle between John and Huns is directed against the Huns? Why not equally well against John? What would be more precise is to say that John is engaged in some kind of activity, not fully specified, and that activity is directed against the Huns. The situation relating both the Huns and that John-waged activity constitutes the battle. The new analogy is: speech-1 : disarmament :: activity-1 : Huns. A frame that could represent this intuition is possible, given our new notation:

```
(STRIFE
  (SOCIAL-EVENT: SUBSCENE
    (DIRECTED-ACTION: ACTION
      (ACTOR <↑ BATTLER>)
      (PATIENT <↑ CONTENDED-FORCE>))))
```

Here we have elected to impose some constraints on what we called the "unspecified action," namely that it be an action involving two participants, an *actor* and a *patient*, where that *actor* is also the *battler*, and the *patient* is also the *contended-force*, both roles in the top level frame. DIRECTED-ACTION is defined in terms of ACTION (is AKO ACTION) and both are new on the scene. We shall be seeing quite a bit more of ACTIONS and DIRECTED-ACTIONS. For the time being I give only an intuitive definition. An ACTION is a situation involving an *actor* (most often called *agent*); a DIRECTED-ACTION (the term is taken from Halliday 1967) is a kind of ACTION involving one more participant, intuitively, the one acted against.

One technical point worth noting. The *social-event* slot in the STRIFE frame has been called a subscene rather than a component, even though all the slots in its embedded frame have been accessed by the toplevel frame (both have attached paths beginning "<↑ ...>."). Why not call such a slot a component? The reason is that the notion component is specifically used in defining semantic compatibility; it involves a toplevel frame having all the same slots as an embedded frame so that prepositions marking those slots can modify heads associated with the toplevel frame. By definition, a frame A that has B as a component has all the slots that B has, and accesses those slots via metonymy. The above STRIFE frame accesses all the slots in its embedded DIRECTED-ACTION as well, but the annotation "subscene" means that that accessing need not be done by metonymy. That is, the toplevel frame need not actually contain the slots *actor* and *patient*. Instead it contains a slot *battler*, whose value is constrained to be the same as the value of *actor* in the embedded scene, and a slot *contended-force* equal to the *patient*. As the procedure for insuring this constraint we can simply use "=." That is, we can imagine the above frame abbreviating:

```
(STRIFE
  (BATTLER (= <SOCIAL-EVENT ACTOR>))
  (CONTENDED-FORCE (= <SOCIAL-EVENT PATIENT>))
  (SOCIAL-EVENT: SUBSCENE
     (DIRECTED-ACTION: ACTION
        (ACTOR)
        (PATIENT))))
```

When a toplevel frame accesses *all* of the slots in an embedded frame in this way, rather than through metonymy, we shall say the embedded frame is a subscene. The notion subscene will be important in chapter 3, when we begin to worry in a more precise way about the grammatical realizations of participants. Critically, subscenes will not count as participants, and will require no grammatical realization.

The new STRIFE frame is more satisfying semantically; and it avoids having any slots that point to itself, so that it can still be thought of as a directed acyclic graph. Thus, the extended notation has been put to good use.

In this section we have introduced separate but equivalent tiered and "flat" representations for the POS_TRANS frame, using devices already motivated in the treatment of adjuncts in chapter 1. The chief problem that this more elaborate frame solved was one of offended intuitions; it seemed peculiar to view the POS_TRANS scene, as we did in the last section, as a "kind of" POSSESSION. Instead it is an event which involves a POSSESSION scene as one of its components. Note that the new POS_TRANS scene has top level slots called *donor, recipient,* and *patient*, just as the old one did. In the rest of this dissertation, when representing a POS_TRANS scene, we will show only these three slots, unless the discussion calls for more of the frame's internal structure to be shown.

After making some of the devices in our new representation of POS_TRANS explicit, we were able to present a new, generalized definition of semantic compatibility between heads and complements.

2.3.1 Commercial events revisited

We have given rough accounts of two verbs, *buy* and *sell*, and two prepositions, *from* and *to*, by relating the verbs to a single scene involving the transference of the goods. In this section we will tackle two questions:

> (1) What is the difference in *meaning*, if any, between *buy* and *sell?*
>
> (2) How do we talk about the other POS_TRANS event going on in the COMMERCIAL_EVENTS scene, the transference of the goods.

Taking first the question of difference of meaning. The lexical scenes of both *buy* and *sell* will be AKO a COMMERCIAL_EVENT. But what will distinguish them? In fact, does anything need to distinguish them? Couldn't we simply say that here are two verbs that share the same conceptual structure, but which have taken different options in their logical realizations, and hence, in their grammatical realizations? This approach, appealing at first blush, fails to account for a number of semantic differences between the verbs:

(12a) Samantha bought a Porsche with her poker winnings.
(12b)*Tom sold his Porsche with Samantha's poker winnings.

(13a) Twenty K buys a pretty underendowed Porsche.
(13b)*Twenty K sells just about any Porsche.

(14a) You can't buy a Porsche on an academic salary.
(14b)*You can't sell a Porsche on an academic salary.

The contrasts here are all contrasts in interpreting a particular complement. My claim is that these contrasts point to semantic, rather than purely grammatical, differences between *buy* and *sell*. To put it simply, *buying* and *selling* just aren't the same actions, and something about their semantic representations must show that. Such a finding is good news for those who believe that the the semantics of a head determines the choice of subject and object.

In this section I will argue that the contrasts in (12) and (13) may be described in terms which of the participants is viewed as actor. The third contrast will involve giving BUYING a different situational structure.

In chapter 1, we assumed that *instruments* always involved a situation type called a MANIPULATION, and that the situation slot of that scene called for an ACTION, whose *actor* was always viewed as the manipulator of the *instrument*. Here is the representation for that scene in our new notation:

```
(MANIPULATION
 (AKO (THING))
 (USER)
 (INSTRUMENT)
 (ACTION
   (ACTOR <↑ USER>))
```

The extension of this account to *buy* and *sell* is fairly straightforward, if we assume that for BUYING the *buyer* is an *actor* and for SELLING, the *seller* is. (12) then becomes simple; for an act of buying, money can be viewed as instrumental, because the buyer is actor, and it is the buyer who uses the money for some end. (13) follows from a very general pattern that "promotes" instruments to subjecthood when the actor is missing ("John hit the stick with the fence," "The stick hit the fence,").

The proposed interpretation of the instrumental would also be appealed to to account for the following contrasts:

(15) John sold the car with his witty patter

(16) John's witty patter sold the car.

(17) *John bought the car with his witty patter.

(18) *John's witty patter bought the car.

The difference between *buy* and *sell* in instrument selection is on this account attributed to their difference in actors. For *sell* the *actor* is the *seller*. Witty patter is the sort of thing the *seller* can manipulate to sell, but not the *buyer*.

(14) must be accounted for by recognizing that BUYING has a somewhat different AKO structure than SELLING. What is involved is a very specialized use of *on* that we haven't seen yet. Let us provisionally call this new meaning of *on resource*. It is the *on* of the following examples:

(19) You can't live on rice and goat's milk.

(20) We went to Thailand on my Educational Loan.

(21) You can't get to Yosemite on 10 gallons of gas.

(22) Yusef's car runs on vodka.

Let's call the scene associated with the preposition *on* in this meaning RESOURCE-USE and the participants *consumption* and *resource*:

```
(RESOURCE_USE
      (RESOURCE)
      (CONSUMPTION (CONSUMPTION
                         (RESOURCE_USER)))
```

This is an adjunct meaning which takes something called a CONSUMPTION in its situation slot. The CONSUMPTION is simply defined here as having one slot, a *resource user*. BUYING will have to be AKO CONSUMPTION to be modifiable by the adjunct RESOURCE_USE. We can now represent the difference between BUYING and SELLING as follows:

```
(BUYING
 (AKO (COMMERCIAL_EVENT) (ACTION) (CONSUMPTION))
 (SELLER)
 (MONEY)
 (GOODS)
 (ACTOR <↑ BUYER>)
 (RESOURCE_USER <↑ BUYER>))

(SELLING
 (AKO (COMMERCIAL_EVENT) (ACTION))
 (BUYER)
 (MONEY)
 (GOODS)
 (ACTOR <↑ SELLER>))
```

This treatment parallels the one suggested in Jackendoff 1972, where what I call *buyer* here is Goal and Agent with *buy*, and what I call *seller* is Source and Agent with *sell*. But the payoff in the distinction here is in explaining the difference in the interpretation of adjuncts. The *actor* in both frames is identified with manipulator of the *instrument*, but in BUYING that *actor* is *buyer* and in SELLING it is *seller*.

Let me now turn to other question of this section. What of the other transference involved in a commercial event, the transference of the money? First, some motivation; there is at least one commercial event verb where the transference of the money is highlighted; this is *pay*. The most direct evidence for this would be for the seller to be realized with the preposition *to*. This seems to be possible, though not particularly highly favored:

(23) I paid half the money on Monday to an old lady wearing knickers, and the other half the next day to a sandy-haired gentleman with a noticeable limp.

Pay is much more commonly encountered in double-object constructions:

(24) He paid Pierre half-a-C-note for the recipe.

We noted before that there are a number of verbs appearing both in construction with *to* and in double-object constructions that can be plausibly be associated with a POS_TRANS scene; these are the "Dative Movement" verbs(see Chapter 4). *Pay* would fit into this class quite comfortably, with, possibly, the proviso that it strongly favors the double-object option.

If *pay* is a POS_TRANS verb, it is one where the transfer of the money is highlighted, since the *seller* must be a *recipient* (being marked with *to*), and the only thing the *seller* receives in a COMMERCIAL_EVENT is money.

The problem at hand now is that a COMMERCIAL_EVENT seems to involve two distinct POS_TRANS scenes; since our AKO mechanism as currently formulated leaves us no way to be AKO the same thing in two different ways, the easiest solution seems to be return to the sort of two-tiered scene we used in redefining POS_TRANS. Let us suppose that there is a scene called SIMULTANEOUS-SCENES with two slots, *first-scene* and *second-scene.*, understood as mutually "necessary" and together composing the top level scene.

```
(EXCHANGE: SIMULTANEOUS SCENES
                   (FIRST_SCENE1:COMPONENT
                    (POS_TRANS
                     (DONOR)
                     (RECIPIENT)
                     (PATIENT)
                     )))
                   (SECOND_SCENE:COMPONENT
                    (POS_TRANS
                     (DONOR <↑ FIRST_SCENE RECIPIENT>)
                     (RECIPIENT <↑ FIRST_SCENE DONOR>)
                     (PATIENT )
                     ))))
```

COMMERCIAL_EVENT will be AKO EXCHANGE, as will the scenes associated with verbs like *trade* and *exchange*. BUYING and SELLING are of course AKO COMMERCIAL_EVENT. Under the extended definition of semantic compatibility proposed in the last section, any verb that is AKO the COMMERCIAL_EVENT scene will have POS_TRANS as a component in either of two possible ways. This will give us the range of semantic compatibility we need to handle all three verbs discussed thus far, *buy*, *sell*, and *pay*.

This is certainly cheering; however, there remains a rather glaring inadequacy in this representation of COMMERCIAL_EVENT. As things stand now, a verb like *buy* is equally likely to realize the *seller* with the preposition *to* or the preposition *from*, since either of the two POS_TRANS scenes can be accessed. This is a rather peculiar result for what purports to be a semantic account of complement selection. Somehow, if the selection of *from* is a semantically motivated fact at all, it is because the verb *buy* is about a scene in which the goods are transferred from the *seller* to the *buyer*. Under the current representation of COMMERCIAL_EVENTS, the verb *buy* has a bit too much to be about. Yet any appropriate simplification of that representation will lose the connection between the scene for *buy* and the scene for *pay*.

This is the wrong redressed in the next section.

2.4 Lexical Representations and Knowledge Representations

We have tried till now to make our lexical representations directly out of the materials at hand in our knowledge representations. Representational objects were thus called on to perform two tasks at once, to capture the structures of salient situation types, and to capture the semantic structure of English verbs and prepositions, where semantic structure was taken to be revealed by compatibility facts. What I want to propose now is that those two tasks be separated.

This may seem a reversal of my earlier position that the knowledge representation as such is not a purely linguistic construct, and that those scenes within it which have linguistic status are not in any way distinguished. How do I maintain that linguistic objects have no special place if I accord a special status to scenes that capture a "semantic structure?" The answer is that the notion of "semantic structure" I have in mind is not exclusively a linguistic one. What we need are structures to represent culturally salient categories, whether or not those categories are associated with words. It seems to me perfectly plausible that some culture might conduct rational discourse involving a distinction between buying and selling without necessarily having words for that distinction. And in our description of such a culture, we will still want to say that buying and selling are things that mutually imply one another; that is, they occur in the same larger situational contexts.

I propose that scenes in general may be said to take a point of view on events. That is, they are based on certain regularities in the flow of things, and sometimes they will be underinformed about the event-types they describe. The BUYING scene will not directly encode the information that the scene it describes always co-occurs with a SELLING scene. This will be the job of a special kind of scene called a ground scene, which coordinates the views of one or more scenes into a single new scene that is neutral as to point of view. Looking ahead a bit, we will say the BUYING scene views the *buyer* as *actor*, and the SELLING scene views the *seller* as *actor*; the the ground scene relating these two scenes will be the COMMERCIAL_EVENT scene proper. In that scene, both *buyer* and *seller* will be *actors*.

2.4.1 Are there COMMERCIAL_EVENTS?

In the last section I was unhappy with my representations for *buy, sell,* and *pay* because the complexity of the COMMERCIAL_EVENT scene licensed some implausible semantic compatibilites. I want to consider two stronger examples of this before proposing an alternative account that seems to offer a solution. The cases in point are the verbs *cost* and *spend*. The first thing to notice is that neither of these verbs takes either *to* or *from*, so that considerations of compatibility would not bring us to represent either with a POS_TRANS scene. More striking, as Fillmore 1977b points out, neither allows the *seller* to be realized in ANY form. That is, the *seller* may not appear in the same clause; to bring this participant into the picture at all, some intervening predication is required:

(25) That old grammophone cost Johann 2K, payed in twenty installments to his uncle in Jersey.

On the one hand, one might look at this as par for the course. We have all along talked about facts of compatibility that are not rules; as such we are allowed to claim that lexical idiosyncrasy has once again intervened, and that it is just an arbitrary fact about a pair of highly arbitrary verbs, that they do not provide any means for realizing an expected participant.

But to say that is to put this fact about *spend* and *cost* on a par with the facts about idiosyncrasies of preposition selection that we saw before. Beside *decide on* we have *opt for* — despite the fact that these verb-preposition pairs express roughly the same meanings; whatever difference there may be in meaning is not likely to be one that we can ascribe precisely to a difference in the relevant meanings of *on* and *for*. Thus, the selection of *on* with *decide* is in some sense arbitrary given the meaning of *decide*. But the impossibility of *seller* with *cost* is a very different kind of arbitraryness. Somehow the choice of this lexical item reflects a choice to leave the *seller* out of the accounting. Indeed, it may even describe a situation in which the *seller*, in any conventional sense, is absent.

(26) Parking on High Street cost me twenty dollars.

This fact about *cost* is indeed an arbitrary fact, but it is an arbitrary fact about its meaning; it is a fact which ought to be reflected in our choice of lexical semantic representation, instead of being included among the "syntactic afterthoughts" that mark the actual complementation possibilities. This is a conclusive consideration, it seems to me, which rules out a syntactic recourse, even without entering into the technical difficulties of devising a form of syntactic marking that would rule out the realization of some core participant, in any of its possible forms.

I want to tackle this problem by first considering in some detail what I consider to be the wrong solution, which is to attempt to extend the same techniques we have used till now. Pointing out the inadequacies of this course will go a long way towards motivating the special status lexical representations will have in the "right" account.

Suppose we try the following solution: *cost* and *spend* will be distinguished from the other commercial event verbs by having them reference a situation different from the COMMERCIAL_EVENT situation. The outlines of a fairly plausible account are clear. We could call the new scene a MONEY-TRANSACTION; it would have only three participants, *buyer*, *money*, and *goods*. We could preserve our intuitions of lexical relatedness by saying the COMMERCIAL_EVENTS scene we have already presented is AKO this scene, and that it introduces the participant *seller*. The MONEY-TRANSACTION scene would not reference the POS_TRANS scene, and we will not expect verbs like *pay* and *spend* to be compatible with *to* and *from*.

So far nothing we have said addresses the problem that troubled us in the last section, namely that *buy* and *sell* exhibited too many semantic compatibilities. A simple extension of what we have already done will solve that problem, too. Suppose that we split our COMMERCIAL_EVENT scene into its two component POS_TRANS scenes, and made each of these separately AKO the MONEY-TRANSACTION scene. The AKO links would look like this:

MONEY-TRANSACTION

POS_TRANS ("Cost" "Spend") POS_TRANS

GOODS-POS_TRANS MONEY-POS_TRANS

ACTION ACTION ("Pay")

BUYER-ACTION ("Buy") SELLER-ACTION ("Sell")

A drawback to this scheme is that it predicts that *buy, sell,* and *pay* are semantically compatible with all the same complements as *cost* and *spend*. The most obvious problem with that claim is the double object construction. Although *cost* takes a double object construction it does so with the *buyer* and *money* following the verb. Neither *sell* nor *buy* allows that configuration, so that their double object construction must be semantically founded on a different frame structure than that of *cost*. As the framework stands, a lexical frame is not just compatible with a particular subcategorization; it is compatible with a particular assignment of roles to the complements in that subcategorization. The non-occurence of *buy* and *sell* with the *cost*-type double-object construction could, of course, be called a syntactic accident, but a more plausible representation would be:

MONEY-TRANSACTION

? ?

COST ("Cost") SPEND ("Spend")

POS_TRANS POS_TRANS

GOODS-POS_TRANS MONEY-POS_TRANS

ACTION ACTION ("Pay")

BUYER-ACTION ("Buy") SELLER-ACTION ("Sell")

In the alternative sketched here, a MONEY-TRANSACTION is still the root of the COMMERCIAL_EVENT "tree", but the COST and SPEND scenes are not inherited by the other verbs. The question marks represent other scenes that distinguish COST and SPEND from a simple MONEY-TRANSACTION, thus allowing *cost* and *spend* to be semantically compatible with complements that the other verbs do not take. On the face of it, then, we have solved all our problems about semantic compatibility simply by complicating our "sort tree" for COMMERCIAL_EVENTs. The COMMERCIAL_EVENT scene as such with its four participants has ceased to exist; but the same information has been distributed out over separate scenes.

I now want to argue that this solution is inadequate, chiefly on the basis of entailments among some of the commercial event verbs.

This point can be made most clearly if we look at our MONEY-TRANSACTION scene and ask just what information it must encode. It must satisfy the two needs of all our representations; it must adequately describe a certain type of situation, and it must adequately represent the semantics shared by a group of verbs.

A general pattern for making statements about compatibility begins to emerge. A verb is related to a class of verbs by being AKO the abstract object that unites the the class; its differences from the other members of the class, if any, can be represented either by the idiosyncrasies of its particular lexical frame or by making it AKO some new object or objects, No constraint is placed on the nature of this new object. So, in principle a MONEY-TRANSACTION verb could be AKO INTENTIONAL ATTITUDE, and we could have a lexical item specifically about intentional attitudes connected with sales.

We now come to the crucial question. We have been examining a group of verbs Fillmore has dubbed Commercial Event verbs. The question is: should there BE any constraint on what sort of object a commercial event verb can be? The intuitive answer is yes: at least if we return to our naive pre-theoretic notion of what a commercial event is. Why should there be a verb *buy* that presents a situation in which the buyer is actor, and another verb *sell* which presents the seller as actor. Because, intuitively, in a real life commerical event, both the buyer and seller act. What the set of representations above lacks is a single description of what a real-life commercial event is like. Instead the description has been scattered over a number of different frames. If we believe that the commercial event is an important kind of structure that ought to be a unit in our knowledge representation, then, in our eagerness to capture the lexical facts, we have failed to capture a representational fact.

The scheme offered above makes lexical scenes highly specified, with the MONEY-TRANSACTION scene an underspecifed object compatible with with all the COMMERCIAL_EVENT verbs. It is thus not particularly clear what it actually represents, apart from an abstraction of what a group of verbs has in common. If we believe that the COMMERCIAL_EVENT scene as such is an important structure, this is really backwards. The unifying scene of a lexical class should be highly specified, and particular verbs should pick aspects of that scene to highlight. They should be underspecified versions of that scene. So SELLING is a POS_TRANS scene with the *seller* as actor because it is a COMMERCIAL_EVENT verb, and a COMMERCIAL_EVENT involves just that kind of POS_TRANS scene. But a COMMERCIAL_EVENT verb can not represent an INTENTIONAL ATTITUDE because there is no intentional attitude involved in a COMMERCIAL_EVENT.

The important claim here is that a COMMERCIAL_EVENT should be a scene in which *both buyer* and *seller* are *actor*. That is, we should modify our COMMERCIAL_EVENT scene to look like this:

```
(COMMERCIAL_EVENT: SIMULTANEOUS SCENES
                   (FIRST_SCENE:COMPONENT
                    (ACTION_POS_TRANS
                     (ACTOR_DONOR <↑ SELLER>)
                     (ACTOR_RECIPIENT <↑ BUYER>)
                     (PATIENT <↑ GOODS>)))
                   (SECOND_SCENE:COMPONENT
                    (POS_TRANS
                     (DONOR <↑ BUYER>)
                     (RECIPIENT <↑ SELLER>)
                     (PATIENT <↑ MONEY>))))
```

Here ACTION_POS_TRANS is a scene derived by the following AKO chain:

```
               POS_TRANS
   ACTION                     ACTION

   RECIPIENT_ACTION  DONOR_ACTION

            ACTION_POS_TRANS
```

RECIPIENT_ACTION is a POS_TRANS scene in which the *recipient* is an *actor*, symbolized with a new slot name, ACTOR_RECIPIENT; DONOR_ACTION a POS_TRANS scene in which the *donor* is an *actor*, given the slot-name ACTOR_DONOR. An ACTION_POS_TRANS will have two ACTORS.

The nature of the ACTION-POS-TRANS frame deserves a bit of comment, since it is a frame which must inherit an *actor* slot from two different parents, one slot identified with *donor*, one with *recipient*. Let us say that when a frame inherits the same slot from two different sources, there are two possible things that can happen. First, the constraints on the slot are merged and the resulting slot is one for which all defined values must meet both sets of constraints. If we followed this course for ACTION_POS_TRANS we would get one *actor* slot whose value would have to be both *donor* and *recipient*. In other words, we would have described a scene in which some *actor* gives something to himself. Obviously, this is not quite what we had in mind.

Let us define another possibility as follows: when a frame inherits the same slot from two different sources, we may chose to interpret the resulting slot as taking an ordered-pair as its value; each member of the ordered-pair satisfies a separate inherited set of constraints on the slot. This is what we want in the case of ACTION_POS_TRANS.

```
(DONOR_ACTION
 (AKO (POS_TRANS)(ACTION))
 (PATIENT)
 (RECIPIENT)
 (ACTOR_DONOR <DONOR> <ACTOR>))

(RECIPIENT_ACTION
 (AKO (POS_TRANS)(ACTION))
 (DONOR)
 (PATIENT)
 (ACTOR_RECIPIENT <RECIPIENT> <ACTOR>))

(ACTION_POS_TRANS
 (AKO (DONOR_ACTION)(RECIPIENT_ACTION))
 (PATIENT)
 (ACTOR1 <ACTOR_DONOR>)
 (ACTOR2 <ACTOR_RECIPIENT>)
 (ACTOR_DONOR <DONOR> <ACTOR1>)
 (ACTOR_RECIPIENT <RECIPIENT> <ACTOR2>))
```

The ACTION_POS_TRANS frame illustrates both of the options possible when a slot has been inherited from two sources. In the case of the *donor, recipient, patient* slots, the constraints have been simply been merged and interpreted as simultaneous requirements on any value. Since the constraints from both sources are the same (neither DONOR_ACTION nor RECIPIENT_ACTION adds anything to those slots except the specifications *donor_actor* and *recipient_actor*, respectively), the merging is trivial. Let us call this option the default case and use no notation to mark it. In the case of the *actor* slot, however, the other option is taken: this is notated as if there were two slots ACTOR1, and ACTOR2, but this is merely a typographically convenient way of representing a single slot that takes an ordered pair as its value; it gives us an easy way to refer to the members of the pair separately using our path notation. The path <ACTOR1> points to the first member of the pair in the *actor* slot, the path <ACTOR2> to the second member. In RECIPIENT_ACTION, the slot *actor-recipient* is really just a convenience, a label with which to refer to something that is really a new participant role; and the same applies to the slot *actor-donor* in DONOR_ACTION.

Returning to the main topic. I have claimed that it is important to include commercial events among our knowledge representations. But what criteria determine the "importance" of a knowledge representional object? Why should we be losing a semiotic fact when we miss describing COMMERCIAL_EVENT? To lose generalizations about objects that can be cranked out at will is not very alarming, since there is always another generalization just around the corner.

The question, then, is one of evidence. What constitutes good evidence that something should be an object in our knowledge representation? I think the primary sort of evidence is linguistic, since a primary source for information about the knowledge structures a culture recognizes must be our language. To argue that there in fact ought to be some single situational object called a commercial event, I submit we examine the following set of entailments:

(a) x bought y from z
(b) z sold y to x
(c) x spent some money for y
(d) x paid z for y
(e) z cost x some money
(f) x owned y
(g) z owned y before x owned y

My claim is that (a) entails (b) through (g). (b) ,(c), and (d) also entail (a). (e) - (g) do not. A simple way to represent this is to say that (a) - (c) all reference the same situation, and that (e) - (g) reference more general situations. On this account of representation, entailment facts become one important criterion for mapping out the situational entities that structure lexical heads. They help us decide what entities to put into our ontology. Note that the scheme in () with MONEY-TRANSACTION at its root does not offer any easy route to the desired entailments. *Buy* and *sell*, for example, represent BUYER-ACTIONS and SELLER-ACTIONS respectively. To say that there was a GOODS-POS_TRANS with a *seller* as *actor* does not directly entail that there was a GOODS-POS_TRANS with *buyer* as actor. The problem is that these verbs have been associated with different kinds of situations in order to accomodate their different semantic compatibilities. Although they have been ultimately linked in the abstract situation MONEY-TRANSACTION, this only buys us entailments like "There was a MONEY-TRANSACTION", where what we want is entailments involving real lexical items.

2.4.2 The new Proposal

What we need, then, is a mechanism for characterizing the relation of different scenes with different compatibilities to a single grounding situation-type. I propose we distinguish among certain representations a special slot called *reference.* The value of the reference slot will be constrained to be an instance of a special kind of scene we will call a ground scene. For uniformity, we will require that all lexical frames have a reference slot; this does not mean that only lexical frames will have reference slots; as noted in the last section, we wish to leave open the possibility of describing a culture that has a salient distinction between BUYING and SELLING, but no words for that distinction.

It will simplify the following discussion considerably if we make the assumption that all lexical scenes have only one value in their AKO slot. This will not hamper our descriptive powers, because if we find for some reason that a lexical scene L ought to be AKO both A and B, we can always declare a new scene AB which is AKO both A and B, and say that L is AKO AB. For reasons which will become clearer below, we will call any scene that is the value of the AKO slot of a lexical frame the template scene. The following convention will hold

(1) Rule of Reference:

(2) If a scene A with a template B references a scene C, then C must be an extension of B.

This guarantees that A will have only slots that can be found in C. Thus, to return to the example discussed in the last section, a lexical item which references the COMMERCIAL_EVENT scene may not be AKO INTENTIONAL-ATTITUDE, because a COMMERCIAL_EVENT is not an extension of INTENTIONAL-ATTITUDE. We also want a lexical scene A to be more than just an ordinary B-type object: it must acquire some more specific slots from the scene it references. To do this, we shall first need to define the notion *elaboration of a slot*.

(1) Elaboration of a Slot

(2) A slot SLOT1 in a frame FrameA is an elaboration of a slot SLOT2 in FrameB if one of the following three conditions holds:

    (1) SLOT1 = SLOT2 and FrameA = FrameB. That is, a slot is an elaboration of itself.

(2) the value of SLOT1 is constrained by metonymy (which entails that SLOT1 = SLOT2), and the slot accessed by metonymy is constrained to contain only instances of FrameB.

```
(FRAMEA
 (SLOT1 (METONYMY 'SLOT3))
 (SLOT3 (FRAMEB
        (SLOT2))))
```

Thus, in the schematized instance, SLOT1 IN A is an elaboration of SLOT2 in B (and the slots, again, must have the same slot name). In our graphically convenient notation this is represented:

```
(FRAMEA
 (SLOT3 (FRAMEB
        (SLOT2 <↑ SLOT1>)))
```

Thus, if B is a component of A, all of B's slots have elaborations in A. An example we have already seen is the *possessor* slot in the POS_TRANS scene as an elaboration of the *possessor* slot in POSSESSION scene.

(3) FrameA = FrameB and the value of SLOT1 is constrained to be equal to the value of SLOT2. In the full-notation, the pattern is:

```
(FRAMEA
 (SLOT2)
 (SLOT1 (= SLOT2)))
```

In the other notation, this is:

```
(FRAMEA
 (SLOT1 <SLOT2>))
```

One example we have already seen is the *recipient* slot in POS_TRANS as an elaboration of the *possessor* slot in POS_TRANS.

(4) there is some SLOT3, such that SLOT1 is an elaboration of SLOT3 and SLOT3 is an alaboration of SLOT2. This condition imposes transitivity. By this clause, the examples in

> (1) and (2) entail that the *recipient* slot in POS_TRANS is an elaboration of the *possessor* slot in POSSESSION.

If SLOT1 is an elaboration of SLOT2 in virtue of conditions (1), (2), or (3), but not condition (4), we shall say that SLOT1 is a direct elaboration of SLOT2.

Because of the way that elaboration has been defined there will always exist a sequence of slots in F1 linking the elaborated slot SLOT1 with its source slot SLOT2, which justifies calling SLOT1 an elaboration of SLOT2. We shall call the sequence of paths which picks out these slots the elaboration sequence. A few examples will help make this notion clear.

```
(FRAME1
  (SLOT1))

(FRAME2
  (AKO (FRAME1))
  (SLOT2 <SLOT1>))

(FRAME3
 (AKO (FRAME3))
 (SLOT3 <SLOT2>))
```

First, SLOT2 is a direct elaboration of itself. The elaboration sequence is <SLOT2>. SLOT2 is also a direct elaboration of SLOT1. The elaboration sequence is <SLOT2, SLOT1>. In FRAME3 SLOT3 is an elaboration of SLOT2, with elaboration sequence <SLOT2, SLOT3>. But SLOT3 is also an elaboration of SLOT1 (which is inherited, though not shown), though not a direct one. The rule for forming extended elaboration sequences is to form the sequence of elaboration sequences in the chain of direct elaboration sequences, and omit the overlapping ends. Putting the two elaboration sequences linking S1 and S3 together we have: <SLOT1, SLOT2, SLOT2, SLOT3>. Omitting the overlap we have <SLOT1, SLOT2, SLOT3>.

Next, consider a case involving a component frame and METONYMY.

```
(FRAMEA
 (SLOT1)
 (SLOT2 (FRAMEB
         (SLOT3 <* SLOT1>)))
 (SLOT4 <SLOT1>))
```

Here SLOT1 is a direct elaboration of SLOT3. The elaboration sequence is <<SLOT2 SLOT3>, <SLOT SLOT1>>. SLOT1 in FRAMEA is an elaboration of SLOT1 in FRAMEB. The elaboration sequence is <<SLOT2 SLOT1>, SLOT1>. SLOT4 is a direct elaboration of SLOT1 in FRAMEA, and is therefore an indirect elaboration of SLOT3. The sequence, not suprisingly, is <<SLOT3 SLOT2>, <SLOT2 SLOT1>, SLOT1, SLOT4>.

We are now ready to define the way in which a lexical frame references the "structure" in a reference frame.

(1) Rule of Referenced Structure

(1) Suppose we have a lexical template scene T and a lexical scene L that references a scene R. Reference is always defined with respect to a path P in R; the value of P is constrained to be some frame K such that K is AKO T. That there will always exist such a path in R follows from the fact that R must be an extension of T, provided that we handle the trivial cases as follows: We may think of a frame as "constrained to be" AKO itself, and we may think of the nullpath in any frame as giving that frame. Thus, if L references R with the null path in R (written "<>"), R must be AKO T.

(2) There will be slots in K that are elaborations of slots in T (since K is AKO T). Furthermore, there may be other slots in R that are elaborations of those K slots, and thus elaborations of slots in T. We now construct all pairs <S1, S2>, such that S1 is a slot in T and S2 is an elaboration of that slot in R, and such that the first member of the elaboration sequence linking S1 and S2 begins with the path <P S1> (all the elaborations of T slots in R whose elaboration sequences are rooted in K). Then, for each such <S1,S2> the Rule of Referenced Structure makes the following stipulation: the lexical scene L will have S2 as a slot and S1 will be constrained to equal S2:

(S1 <S2>)

All of this preparation is so that we can talk about a lexical scene accessing only *some* of the structure in a reference scene. When a lexical scene acquires a slot because of the rule of reference, we will speak of it as "referencing" that slot.

The introduction of the notion elaboration sequence into the Rule of Referenced Structure is to allow for the possibility that a slot in R is an elaboration of the same slot in L in more than one way. As we shall see shortly, this is crucial precisely in the case of COMMERCIAL_EVENTS,

All of this is best illustrated by example. Let us start with a trivial example as a preparation for the commercial event verbs. Suppose that the template scene for verbs of longing like *wish* is PURSUIT-LONGING, and that the lexical scene for *wish* in particular is WISHING, with a reference scene, WISHING-R.

```
(PURSUIT-LONGING
 (AKO (PURSUIT) (LONGING)
 (PURSUER (=longer))
 (PURSUIT (:frame))
 (LONGER)
 (KARMAN))

(WISHING
 (AKO (PURSUIT-LONGING))
 (REFERENCE (PATH <>)
            (WISHING-R)))
```

Then WISHING-R must be AKO PURSUIT-LONGING as well, by our trivial case in the Rule of Referenced-Structure. And we have:

```
(WISHING-R
 (AKO (PURSUIT-LONGING)))
```

This is a trivial case. The path is "<>", the reference scene equals the template scene. Since a slot is an elaboration of itself, all the slots in WISHING-R (that is, all the slots it inherits from PURSUIT-LONGING), are added to WISHING by the Rule of Referenced-Structure. But WISHING, which is also AKO PURSUIT-LONGING, already has those slots, and we already know for any slot that its value is equal to itself. So here the lexical frame acquires no new meaningful structure. However, this is not to say that even in a trivial case like this, there is no point in distinguishing lexical scene from reference scene. WISHING and WISHING-R are still two different frames, and they can carry different information. If we need it, WISHING-R stands as a record of which structural facts about situation have not been built into the lexical semantics of the verb *wish*. I do not insist that there be any such facts. In some cases, the ground scene may just be a formal device with no advantage but uniformity.[1]

Now let us turn to the vastly more complicated business of COMMERCIAL_EVENTS. We will use the verb *buy* as our example. Suppose the template scene for BUYING is AKO RECIPIENT_ACTION. That is, suppose the BUYING scene is AKO RECIPIENT_ACTION; recall that *RECIPIENT_ACTION is the POS_TRANS scene in which the recipient* is *actor*. Intuitively, this is the template we want for BUYING. We want the lexical scene to determine semantic compatibility requirements; being AKO RECIPIENT_ACTION will license marking of the *donor* with *from,* but not *to*; and the *recipient* will be interpreted as manipulating any *instrument*. Yet the notion of RECIPIENT_ACTION is hardly specific enough to characterize BUYING. Through

---

1. Another possibility is that in such trivial cases the ground scene equals the template scene.

referencing the COMMERCIAL_EVENT frame, we will build into BUYING all the necessary specifications. To begin with, here is the COMMERCIAL_EVENT scene once again:

```
(COMMERCIAL_EVENT: SIMULTANEOUS SCENES
                  (FIRST_SCENE:COMPONENT
                   (ACTION_POS_TRANS
                    (ACTOR_DONOR <↑ SELLER>)
                    (ACTOR_RECIPIENT <↑ BUYER>)
                    (PATIENT <↑ GOODS>)))
                  (SECOND_SCENE:COMPONENT
                   (POS_TRANS
                    (DONOR <↑ BUYER>)
                    (RECIPIENT <↑ SELLER>)
                    (PATIENT <↑ MONEY>))))
```

Here is BUYING:

```
(BUYING
 (AKO (ACTOR_RECIPIENT))
 (REFERENCE (PATH <FIRST_SCENE>)
         (COMMERCIAL_EVENT))
 (ACTOR_RECIPIENT)
 (DONOR)
 (PATIENT)
 (ACTOR <ACTOR_RECIPIENT>))
```

It is in this case that the notion of reference relative to a path will do some work. Here are the major frames and slots involved, together with the variables they instantiate in the Rule of Referenced-Structure:

```
BUYING = L
COMMERCIAL_EVENT = R
RECIPIENT_ACTION = T
<FIRST_SCENE> = P
ACTION_POS_TRANS = K
```

Note that K is AKO T, as required in the rule. Here, then, are the pairs <S1, S2>, and the elaboration sequences that justify them. Note: I have left out any vacuous sequences where BUYING would inherit a slot it already had:

Pair	Sequence
<ACTOR_RECIPIENT, BUYER>	<<FIRST_SCENE ACTOR_RECIPIIENT>, BUYER>
<DONOR, SELLER>	<<FIRST_SCENE DONOR>, SELLER>
<PATIENT, GOODS>	<<FIRST_SCENE PATIENT>, GOODS>

Note that all the elaboration sequences begin with a path of the form <FIRST_SCENE slot>, where "slot" is the slot whose elaboration is being traced. This is the <P S1> in the definition. Note also that "rooting" these sequences in a particular location in COMMERCIAL_EVENT was crucial. Although the template scene has only one *patient* slot, the reference scene has two, and they have different elaborations. If we had not specified *which* elaborations of each slot in the template scene were allowed, both a *money* slot and *goods* slot would have been declared in BUYING, and both would have been constrained to be equal to "patient". Similarly, there would be two *donors* and two *recipients*, and it would have been quite unclear who was giving what to whom.

Here, then, is BUYING "before" and "after" application of the Rule of Referenced-Structure.

```
(BUYING
 (AKO (ACTOR_RECIPIENT))
 (REFERENCE (COMMERCIAL_EVENT))
```

```
(ACTOR_RECIPIENT <RECIPIENT>)
(DONOR)
(PATIENT)
(ACTOR <ACTOR_RECIPIENT>))

                   Reference Inheritance
                   =====================>

(BUYING
 (AKO (ACTOR_RECIPIENT))
 (REFERENCE (COMMERCIAL_EVENT))
 (ACTOR_RECIPIENT <BUYER>)
 (DONOR <SELLER>)
 (PATIENT  <GOODS>))
```

Note that BUYING has lost its *money* slot under the new analysis. the status of money and the provenance of the preposition *for* will be treated in the next section.

Also dealt with in the next section will be some facts about argument structure, noteably the inability of the verb *spend* to realize a *buyer*. The entailment facts suggest that *spend* references COMMERCIAL_EVENT (at least when used with the preposition *for*); what we want to do is arrange for it to do so in such a way that it referenceially inherits only three slots, and the *seller* slot is not among them. *cost*, because it does not entail a true purchase, will not reference the COMMERCIAL_EVENT, but one that is more general, which will not include a *seller* slot.

Since our primary purpose in referencing is to establish that a certain kind of situation takes place, for purposes of correct entailments, we will want at least the following property:

(1) Rule Of Entailment

(2) If a scene A references a scene B then for every instance of A, there is an instance of B such that the filler of every slot in A that is an elaboration of a slot in B is the filler of the corresponding slot in B.

That is to say every for every BUYING situation (every instantiation of the BUYING scene) there is also an instantiation of the COMMERCIAL_EVENT scene such that the *buyer*, *seller*, *money*, and *goods* are the same.

To guarantee that we will need to put a rider on our Rule of Referenced-Structure. To each slot countenanced by the Rule of Reference we add "(metonymy 'reference)."

```
(S2 (metonymy 'reference))
```

So for example *buyer* in BUYING will be:

```
(BUYER  ( = actor_recipient)
        (metonymy 'reference))
```

The METONYMY procedure on *buyer* says that value of the *buyer* slot for any BUYING frame must be the same as the value of *buyer* slot in the frame that is the value of the *reference* slot (that is, in some COMMERCIAL_EVENT frame). As always, we interpret the appearance of a scene A in the slot of another scene as a constraint on possible values for that slot. All such values must be AKO A. Similarly, for all the other slots referenced by BUYING. Intuitively, we can think of the METONYMY procedures on all the slots as mapping a BUYING "subsituation" onto the total COMMERCIAL_EVENT situation it is part of.

To get entailments between lexical items. we will need a COMMERCIAL_EVENT to point to its lexicalized subsituations, just as they point to it. Thus far, we have guaranteed that for every BUYING situation there is a COMMERCIAL_EVENT situation with a superset of the BUYING situation's participants. To get an entailment from *buy* to *sell*, we also need a pointer from a COMMERCIAL_EVENT to SELLING situations, guranteeing that for every COMMERCIAL_EVENT, there is a SELLING situtaion with a subset of the COMMERCIAL_EVENT's participants. In fact, we will need pointers to all the lexical scenes that reference COMMERCIAL_EVENT, so that this may as well be considered part of the rule of referenced structure. Simultaneous with declaring the reference slots in the lexical scene, we declare a subsituation slot in the reference scene, of the form:

(subsituation: COMPONENT (subsituation))

Thus, for example, we declare in COMMERCIAL_EVENT a component slot, called *buying*, constrained to take BUYING scenes as its value. The fact that it is a component slot means that all its slots are accessed by metonymy, which guarantees the correct lining up of slots. Let us add a convention like the convention that a component scene does not have its AKO slot accessed: neither does it have its *reference* slot accessed. With all this apparatus granted, then, for every BUYING scene, there is a COMMERCIAL_EVENT scene with the same *buyer, seller,* and *goods*. And for that COMMERCIAL_EVENT scene, there is a SELLING scene with the same *buyer, seller,* and *goods*. Thus a BUYING scene entails a SELLING scene, just as we wanted.

The Law of Entailment can thus be made part of the Law of Referenced Structure. Most importantly, it is not left as an extra stipulation on the frame representation, but is built into the defining procedures of the frames associated with a reference slot.

The role of compatibility in this revised system will change somewhat. Our definition of compatibility will remain as it was, but will only apply to the templates of figure scenes. This is because verbs and prepositions will both have figure scenes. While we know that a figure scene is an extension of its template, and will thus be compatible with everything a template scene was compatible with, nothing in our definition of compatibility guarantees tnat figure scenes that are extensions of compatible template scenes will be compatible with one another. Thus, in the next section we will develop a figure scene for *for* in one meaning, and a new figure scene for *buy*; those two figure scenes will not in fact be compatible, but their templates will. The sortal constraints on linguistic predicates will thus be defined by template scenes. It is the template scenes that actually impose a semantic structure on the lexicon, since they define the properties of linguistic predicates that determine possibilities of combination with other predicates. If two lexical items share the same template scene, they are semantically compatible with all the same complements. This amounts to saying that the template scenes taken together constitute a significant level of linguistic representation, which we can call lexical structure.

We can close this section with a terminological proposal. We have essentially divided the world into two kinds of frames: one kind has a slot called *reference*; it takes a particular "view" of the scene in its reference slot defined by the structure it "acquires" from that scene. Call scenes with *reference* slots *figure* scenes. The other kind of scene appears in the *reference* slot of a figure scene; let us call it a ground scene. A ground scene represents a generalization over figure scenes. It collects the facts about a certain situation-type which in some sense underlies all the figure scenes. It is tempting to say that the *ground* scene represents the real world scene on which the figure scenes take different views, but to put it this way is to give the two kinds of scenes a different ontological status. I would rather say that the ground scene represents a recognition that the figure scenes are situationally-related, and as such defines a new more complex category.[1]

---

1. The terms figure and ground were suggested by Fillmore.

2.4.2 Some technical revisions and stipulations

Our current definition of extension plays two independent roles in the framework. It directs compatibility traffic, and it crucially constrains the Rule of Referenced Structure used to define figure and ground scenes.

In this last capacity, it is a little too restrictive. As things stand now, a frame A is an extension of another frame B if it fits one of three clauses in the following recursive definition:

(1) A is AKO B.

(2) B is a component of A.

(3) A is an extension of C and C is an extension of B.

This leads us into an undesirable situation with respect to figure and ground scenes, which can be illustrated with the following mock frames:

```
(FRAMEA
 (SLOT1))

(FRAMEB: FRAMEA
 (SLOT2)
 (SLOT3))

(FRAMEC: FRAMEA
 (SLOT1)
 (SLOT2))

(GF: FRAMEC
 (SLOT1)
 (SLOT2)
 (SLOT3))
```

As things stand, GF is an extension of FRAMEA and FRAMEC, but not of FRAMEB. Nevertheless, we may wish to think of SLOT3 in FRAMEB as being the same slot as SLOT3 in GF. This would make a difference if FRAMEB were the template of some verb scene V, because GF could not be a legal ground scene for V, even though, intuitively, its structure contains any structure defined in FRAMEB. One way to make GF an appropriate ground scene is to simply stipulate that it is also AKO FRAMEB. GF then inherits SLOT1 from two different places. Suppose that no new information is added to SLOT1 in either FRAMEB or FRAMEC. The generalization about SLOT1 is captured in FRAMEA; but we are losing it again in GF by having it inherited twice.

We can avoid this sort of redundant AKO stipulation by loosening our definition of extension. Let us define a new notion called *constituenthood*. A Frame A is a CONSTITUENT of a FRAME B if either:

(1) B is AKO A.

(2) We can construct a frame B' which is AKO both B and A, and B' has a structure identical to B.

Intuitively, what we are after here is this: A is a constituent of B if making B AKO A would make no difference in the structure of A, that is, if the structure of A contains the structure of B. AKOness is a special case of one frame containing the structure of another. Constituenthood generalizes this notion of contained structure to include cases where the structure is "incidental," rather than stipulated by

AKO links.

In our example with mock frames both FRAMEB and FRAMEC are constituents of GF, even though GF is not AKO FRAMEB. We now generalize our definition of extension:

(1) B is a constituent of A.

(2) B is a component of A.

(3) A is an extension of C and C is an extension of B.

Now since the Rule of Referenced Structure depends on the definition of extension, FRAMEB will be a legal template scene for GF. We will be making use of this revised definition of extension in our further encounters with the COMMERCIAL_EVENT verbs.[1]

One might wonder whether with the notion of constituenthood available, there is any use for AKOness at all. We could define "contained structure" in terms of sets of requirements on particular slots, and say that one frame contained the structure of another if it contained all of its slot requirements. Elsewhere, any appeal to AKOness could be discarded in favor of contituenthood. For example, our truth definition for one place predicates requires that denotation of

---

1. The Rule of Referenced Structure also makes use of the notion AKO at one point, where it requires that K, the frame rooting the reference path, be AKO T. In order for the trivial cases with an empty path to work, we must relax this requirement; T need only be a constituent of K.

a term be AKO the denotation of the predicate. We might just as well require that the denotation the predicate be a constituent of the denotation of the term. Thus, for "(DOG X)" to be true, X would have to have all the slots defined in DOG and satisfy all the constraints on them defined in DOG, but it would not need to be AKO DOG.

The trouble with switching over to this way of looking at things is that it gives us no way of stating generalizations about shared structure. Without stipulated AKOness, there is no way for one frame to make use of structure already defined in another. Since lexical structure is our chief concern, we will thus continue to use the idea of AKOness. However, the idea of extension, and thus both the Rule of Referenced Structure and the definition of semantic compatibility, will make use of the more general notion of constituenthood.

Two more formal points need to be made before we continue with the COMMERCIAL_EVENT verbs.

First, we will be making the assumption that no lexical scene assigns the same role to two different participants. Call this constraint *uniqueness*, after the LFG principle of the same name which constrains each grammatical function to have only one realization (see Kaplan and Bresnan 1982). Uniqueness is not only a standard assumption common to many varieties of case grammar; it is also technically necessary to make our semantics work in the general case. The mapping from prepositions to participants must be determinate; if a preposition marked some role R, and the governing head assigned two participants to that role, how would we know which participant was being marked?

Uniqueness will rule out scenes like ACTION_POS_TRANS as lexical scenes, because in an ACTION_POS_TRANS scene, both the *donor* and the *recipient* have the *actor* role. This is of course a special stipulation that distinguishes lexical representations from others, but it is a stipulation that can be confined to the grammar, and need not be expressed in the frame representation as such. We can think of it instead as a requirement imposed on the mapping from lexical items to their denotations as defined in the lexicon. Any scene which assigns the same role to two participants is simply not suitable for inclusion in a lexical denotation. We will be discussing the mapping from scenes to denotations in greater detail in chapter 3.

The relevance of uniqueness at this juncture is that it will help us decide which material belongs in a figure scene and which material must be in a ground scene. For example, the COMMERCIAL_EVENT scene will have two *actors*, but no COMMERCIAL_EVENT verb will.

The second formal point also concerns separating figure scene material from ground scene material, and will lead to another constraint imposed on lexical scenes by the grammar. We assume that all of the participants in a lexical scene will be grammatically realized. Call this assumption *completeness*. To define completeness requires some sharpening of the notion *participant*.

First, certain kinds of slots will not count as participant slots. In particular, *ako* and *reference* slots will not; neither will *component* or *subscene* slots (see 2.3). Excluding these slots, a participant may be thought of as a maximal elaboratior set, where an elaboration set is a set of toplevel slots in some frame F such that for any two slots in the set, one is an elaboration of the other, and where a maximal elaboration set in F is an elaboration set of F that is not contained by any other elaboration set in F.

For a participant to be grammatically realized means that one of its slots is grammatically realized. We will specify in chapter 3 what it means for a slot to be grammatically realized. Intuitively, for a governing head it means the slot is either a subject, an object, or marked by a subcategorized-for complement. If a governing head grammatically realizes all its participants, then any subcategorized-for preposition must also, since the head is an extension of the preposition scene. A participant in an adjunct preposition is realized if it contains a slot that is either realized as object of the preposition, or is an elaboration of some slot contained in the situation slot.

In what follows, we will appeal to completeness to decide what material belongs in a figure scene and what belongs in a ground scene.

We have already seen an example of material that must, by this principle, be in the ground scene. The verb *spend* is a COMMERCIAL_EVENT verb, but does not realize the *seller*. Therefore, the *seller* must not be included in the lexical scene for *spend*.

2.5 the preposition *for* and more COMMERCIAL-EVENT verbs

2.5.1 Buy, sell, and pay

Throughout most of our discussion of COMMERCIAL-EVENT the participant *money* has played only a supporting role. We have analyzed one verb, *pay* as having a figure scene concerned with the POS_TRANS of the money, with *buyer* as *donor* and *seller* as *recipient*, but we have totally ignored the realization of *money* with the verbs *buy* and *sell*. To deal with this question we shall need to consider with some care various occurrences of the preposition *for*. Let us begin with two old standbys:

(27) John bought the Porsche from Mary for $200.

(28) John sold the Porsche to Mary for $200.

On the easiest readings, in one case John gives the money, in the other he gets it. It would be desirable, of course, to ascribe both these occurrences of *for* to the same meaning, one that in the COMMERCIAL-EVENT scene, picks out the *money*. Under the proposal concerning figure and ground scenes introduced in the last section, this would mean that the figure scenes for both *buy* and *sell* would have to be some variety of the POS_TRANS scene compatible with the relevant meaning of *for*. The following examples, all involving other POS_TRANS verbs, make this approach look promising:

(29) John gave Harry the book for a dollar.

(30) Trish assigned the task to a prelate for a small bribe.

(31) Trish acquired the old book for a very reasonable price.

(32) *Trish received the old book for a very reasonable price.

(33) The seller transfers the goods to the buyer for a good price.

Note the unsuitability of *for* with *receive*. A first hypothesis is that this meaning of *for* requires POS_TRANS verbs with an ACTOR. When the *actor* is *donor*, the object of *for* is interpreted as coming into the *actor's* possession (the *actor* is also a *recipient*); when the *actor* is *recipient*, the object is interpreted as leaving the actor's possession (the *actor* is also a *donor*). In what appears to be the relevant sense, *for* also occurs with non-POS_TRANS verbs.

(34) John vacationed in Sienna for under $300.

(35) Mary fixes computers for an outrageous salary.

(36) John made a film for 10K.

(36) appears to allow both a reading on which John got the money and one on which he spent it. We will pursue an account that grants *for* a meaning something like "exchange," and will assume that the apparent "ambiguity" of (36) is due to semantic vagueness. John may get or give the 10K; all that *for* means is that the 10K is one of the items in an exchange involving John's making of a film.

A slightly different class of examples that can be subsumed under the same meaning is discussed in O'Connor 1983:

(37) John rewarded Mary for her loyalty.

(38) Mary punished John for his disloyalty.

(39) Mary sent John to bed without his supper for marking up the walls.

(39) involves a participial clause controlled by an element in the main clause, but that element does not appear to be chosen either by syntactic function or by semantic role:

(40) The Italians turned the copy over to Mary for helping them recover the original.

(41) The fort commander turned Mathers over to the Indians for behaving so savagely.

We thus assume that this meaning of *for* combines with ACTIONS, but that no role within the modified ACTION is singled out as crucially involved in the EXCHANGE. This is in distinction to our account of MANIPULATION, where the *actor* in a modified action was always understood as manipulator of the *instrument*. Given the greater flexibility of *exchange for*, something like the following ground scene will do:

```
(EXCHANGE: CONDITIONED_SCENE
 (PRECONDITION (ACTION))
 (SCENE
  (POS_TRANS
   (DONOR)
   (PATIENT <^ EXCHANGED_OBJECT>)
   (RECIPIENT))))
```

Here we call EXCHANGE a CONDITIONED_SCENE. We draw a distinction between the notion of cause (appealed to in the CAUSAL-SEQUENCE scene), and the notion of a conditioning event. A conditioning event constrains the occurrence of some other event, but does not necessarily cause it. It may, for example, occur after the event it conditions. Often we pay for things before we get them, but we can still speak of the acquisition as a condition on the payment. Conversely, if John makes a film for a salary of 10K, he may be paid afterwards, but we still speak of his directing the film as a condition on the payment of his salary. The basic idea of the EXCHANGE scene, then, is that some ACTION conditions a POS_TRANS scene. No role in that ACTION scene is distinguished; there is not even the requirement that the *actor* must be in the POS_TRANS scene as either a *donor* or a *recipient*, although all the examples we've seen would satisfy such a requirement. We could impose some such restriction, but its disjunctive nature would require some new notation, and it would have little effect on what follows.

Now the above scene cannot be the immediate representation of *exchange for*, because of the completeness principle we adopted in 2.4.2. When *for* is an adjunct, the ACTION will correspond to the scene of the matrix verb, but the only part of the POS_TRANS scene that is consistently realized is the *exchanged object*, which is object of the preposition. Therefore, to have a grammatically feasible representation of *for*, we will need to construct a figure scene which is missing the unrealized elements. This is easy enough to do. We begin by constructing TRANSITION, a scene of which TRANSFERENCE will be an extension, and proposing that POSSESSION be constructed out of a single-participant scene called UNDERGOING:

```
(TRANSITION
 (FIGURE))

(TRANSFERENCE
 (FIGURE)
 (SOURCE))

(UNDERGOING:THING
 (PATIENT))

(POSSESSION: UNDERGOING
 (POSSESSOR)
 (PATIENT))
```

Note that the extended definition of extension given in 2.4.2 makes TRANSFERENCE an extension of TRANSITION, even though there is no AKO relation between them (TRANSITION is a constituent of TRANSFERENCE). By more conventional means, POSSESSION is an extension of UNDERGOING. Using the TRANSITION and UNDERGOING scenes, we can construct a bigger scene of which POS_TRANS is an extension. Call this scene CAUSED_TRANSITION:

```
(CAUSED_TRANSITION
        (ANTECEDENT:COMPONENT
                  (TRANSITION
                     (FIGURE <^PATIENT>)))
        (CONSEQUENT:COMPONENT
                   (UNDERGOING
                     (PATIENT))))
```

Since TRANSFERENCE is an extension of TRANSITION, and CAUSED_TRANSITION makes no requirements at all on the *consequent* slot, CAUSED_TRANSITION is a constituent of POS_TRANS. We have in effect an underspecified version of POS_TRANS with no *recipient* and no *donor*. We now have the necessary material for the template scene of *exchange for*.

```
(EXCHANGE_TEMPLATE: CONDITIONED_SCENE
 (CONDITION  (ACTION))
 (SCENE: COMPONENT
       (CAUSED_TRANSITION
        (ANTECEDENT:COMPONENT
                  (TRANSITION
                     (FIGURE <^PATIENT>)))
        (CONSEQUENT:COMPONENT
                   (UNDERGOING
                     (PATIENT))))))
```

The lexical scene for *exchange for* will be called EXCHANGE_FOR; it will reference EXCHANGE, and it will be AKO EXCHANGE_TEMPLATE.

```
(EXCHANGE_FOR: EXCHANGE_TEMPLATE
  (REFERENCE (EXCHANGE)))


  Rule of Referenced Structure
================================>

(EXCHANGE_FOR:EXCHANGE_TEMPLATE
   (REFERENCE (EXCHANGE))
   (CONDITION (ACTION))
```

```
(SCENE:COMPONENT
      (CAUSED_TRANSITION
        (ANTECEDENT:COMPONENT
          (TRANSITION
            (FIGURE <↑PATIENT><↑ EXCHANGED_OBJECT>)))
         (CONSEQUENT:COMPONENT
                (UNDERGOING
                  (PATIENT<↑ EXCHANGED_OBJECT>))))))
```

As desired, the lexical scene lacks botn *donor* and *recipient* slots.

Now let us turn specifically to COMMERCIAL_EVENT verbs. The first question is: do we wish to make the money a core participant with *buy* and *sell*? Given that we have an account of *exchange for* as an adjunct, it would be plausible to claim that this freely occurring meaning of *for* is sufficient to account for its interpretation as *money* with verbs like *buy* and *sell*. Selectional restrictions argue otherwise:

(42) John gave Mary his Buick for a grand.

(43) John sold Mary his Buick for a grand.

(44) John gave Mary his stamp collection for a bottle of Scotch.

(45) ?John sold Mary his stamp collection for a bottle of Scotch.

Sell seems to require real currency as its medium of exchange. Under the current proposal for adjuncts (which take matrix verb scenes as participants), there is no way for a matrix verb to impose such a selectional restriction on an adjunct. Therefore, *for* must be subcategorized for. This is a new criterion for core participanthood: given an independently motivated preposition meaning, involving some scene S, any occurrence of that preposition meaning which involves some new restriction on S must be subcategorized for; the participant marked by the preposition must be a core participant of its governing head.

Besides the selectional restriction that money be the medium of exchange, there is another restriction. We have seen that in general *exchange for* can mark either things that the *actor* gets, or things that the *actor* gives:

(46) John made the film for 10K.

When used with *buy* to mark the medium of exchange, *for* must mark something the *actor* gives. I am not claiming here that *for* can never occur as an adjunct with *buy*. Indeed, it is easy to construct examples in which *for* simply marks some object whose exchange takes a purchase as its condition:

(47) For a bottle of Chivas, John bought a Porsche.

This sentence has a special offer interpretation: at some Porsche dealership, every Porsche purchaser gets a bottle of Chivas. This generous offer inspires John to buy. In this case, *exchange for* marks something John gets, but it does not mark something which can be interpreted as the medium of exchange in a COMMERCIAL_EVENT. The claim I have made is that when *for* occurs with *buy* to mark the medium of exchange in a COMMERCIAL_EVENT, the medium must be money, and it must be money the *actor* surrenders. To get this result, we shall have to impose some extra structure on an EXCHANGE scene, and we can do this only by making the EXCHANGED_OBJECT a core participant.

Given that, the COMMERCIAL_EVENT scene will be quite different from what we proposed last section. First, let us assume there is a general scene involving exchange of goods which will be used in building up the ground scenes of verbs like *exchange* and *trade*:

```
(POS_TRANS_EXCHANGE: EXCHANGE
  (CONDITION (ACTION_POS_TRANS))
  (SCENE (POS_TRANS
         (DONOR)
         (PATIENT <↑ EXCHANGED_OBJECT>)
         (RECIPIENT))))
```

Essentially, this is just an exchange scene in which the ACTION has been constrained to be an ACTION_POS_TRANS scene; recall that an ACTION_POS_TRANS scene is just a POS_TRANS scene in which both the *donor* and the *recipient* are *actors*. Now let COMMERCIAL_EVENT be AKO POS_TRANS_EXCHANGE.

```
(COMMERCIAL_EVENT: POS_TRANS_EXCHANGE
  (CONDITION:COMPONENT
       (ACTION_POS_TRANS
             (ACTOR_RECIPIENT <↑ BUYER>)
             (ACTOR_DONOR <↑ SELLER>)
             (PATIENT <↑ GOODS>)))
  (SCENE:COMPONENT
       (POS_TRANS
         (DONOR <↑ CONDITION RECIPIENT>)
         (PATIENT <↑ EXCHANGED_OBJECT> <MONEY>)
         (RECIPIENT <↑ CONDITION DONOR>)))))
```

The BUYING template will be the RECIPIENT_EXCHANGE_TEMPLATE

scene, a scene which has POS_TRANS_EXCHANGE as an extension, and thus has COMMERCIAL_EVENT as an extension:

```
(RECIPIENT_EXCHANGE_TEMPLATE: EXCHANGE_TEMPLATE
  (CONDITION:COMPONENT
      (RECIPIENT_ACTION))
  (SCENE:SUBSCENE
      (CAUSED_TRANSITION
       (PATIENT <^ EXCHANGED_OBJECT>))))
```

Recall that a RECIPIENT_ACTION is a POS_TRANS scene in which only the *recipient* is an *actor*. RECIPIENT_ACTION is thus a constituent of ACTION_POS_TRANS, and thus RECIPIENT_EXCHANGE_TEMPLATE has POS_TRANS_EXCHANGE as an extension. The construction of BUYING is then:

```
(BUYING:RECIPIENT_EXCHANGE_TEMPLATE
  (REFERENCE (COMMERCIAL_EVENT)))


Rule of Referenced Structure
==============================>


(BUYING: RECIPIENT_EXCHANGE_TEMPLATE
  (BUYER <ACTOR_RECIPIENT>)
  (SELLER <DONOR>)
  (GOODS <PATIENT>)
  (MONEY <EXCHANGED_OBJECT>)
  (CONDITION:COMPONENT
         (RECIPIENT_ACTION
             (ACTOR_RECIPIENT)
             (DONOR)
             (PATIENT)))
  (SCENE: SUBSCENE
         (CAUSED_TRANSITION
          (PATIENT <^ EXCHANGED_OBJECT>))))
```

In fact, in this version of *buying*, the only explicit element of

COMMERCIAL_EVENT that has been left out is the assignment of the role *actor* to the *seller*. This is because the way ACTION_POS_TRANS was originally defined, *donor* is an elaboration of *actor* but not vice versa. The *actor* is not the elaboration of any slot, and thus can only become part of the figure scene if it already exists in the template scene.

SELLING will differ only in that its template scene will be DONOR_EXCHANGE_TEMPLATE, a scene just like POS_TRANS_EXCHANGE except that only the *donor* in the POS_TRANS scene is an *actor*. The Rule of Referenced Structure will operate just as it did with BUYING, with *donor* replacing *recipient* as the role that is an elaboration of *actor*.

Note that the above representation of COMMERCIAL_EVENT has two POS_TRANS scenes. However, it does not represent those POS_TRANS scenes symmetrically; one is a *condition*, one a *scene*. Given that representation, no COMMERCIAL_EVENT verb will be able to subcategorize for *exchange for* to mark the goods. However, *pay* is a COMMERCIAL_EVENT verb, and one of the criteria we used to argue that *buy* subcategorizes for *for* also applies to *pay*. Namely, the *actor* must be understood as *recipient* of the goods in examples like:

(48) John payed a grand for the Buick.

In order to allow *for* to mark the *goods*, we shall have to complicate our representation of a COMMERCIAL_EVENT.

What I propose is that we allow COMMERCIAL_EVENT to be composed of two different *views* of a situation, one of which views the *money* as the *exchanged_object*, one of which allows *goods* to be. This can be done with only minimal new apparatus, but before introducing it, let us separately compose the two views. Let COMMERCIAL_EVENT1 be roughly scene we already have, which views *money* as the *exchanged object*. COMMERCIAL_EVENT2 will have to be:

```
(COMMERCIAL_EVENT2: POS_TRANS_EXCHANGE
  (CONDITION:COMPONENT
       (DONOR_ACTION
         (ACTOR_DONOR <↑ CONDITION RECIPIENT>)
         (PATIENT <↑ EXCHANGED_OBJECT> <MONEY>)
         (RECIPIENT <↑ CONDITION DONOR>))))
  (SCENE:COMPONENT
       (ACTION_POS_TRANS
            (ACTOR_RECIPIENT <↑ BUYER>)
            (ACTOR_DONOR <↑ SELLER>)
            (PATIENT <↑ GOODS>))))
```

Two things have changed. First, the two POS_TRANS scenes have exchanged places. Second, the POS_TRANS scene involving the exchange of the *money* has been changed to a DONOR_ACTION scene, because the same considerations that led us to call the subject of *buy* and *sell* an *actor* argue that that subject of *pay* is an *actor* (namely the occurrence of *instruments*). We can merge these two COMMERCIAL_EVENT scene simply by having the two main slots be the sort that takes pairs of values. The resulting COMMERCIAL_EVENT scene is:

```
(COMMERCIAL_EVENT: POS_TRANS_EXCHANGE
  (CONDITION1:COMPONENT
       (ACTION_POS_TRANS
            (ACTOR_RECIPIENT <↑ BUYER>)
            (ACTOR_DONOR <↑ SELLER>)
            (PATIENT <↑ GOODS>))
       <↑ SCENE2>)
  (SCENE1:COMPONENT
       (DONOR_ACTION
         (ACTOR_DONOR <↑ CONDITION1 RECIPIENT>)
         (PATIENT <↑ EXCHANGED_OBJECT> <MONEY>)
         (RECIPIENT <↑ CONDITION1 DONOR>)))
       <↑ CONDITION2>))
```

The representation of a COMMERCIAL_EVENT is now absolutely symmetric, except that one POS_TRANS scene is an ACTION_POS_TRANS scene and the other is a DONOR_ACTION. I know of no verb which is focused on the exchange of the *money* and which views the *seller* as an *actor*. I have therefore let this minor asymmetry stand.

Note that in this new COMMERCIAL_EVENT scene one participant, the *buyer*, is an *actor* in two different scenes; intuitively, the *buyer* acts both in giving the *money*, and in taking the *goods*.

Given this change, we need to revise our representation of BUYING. In particular, we only want BUYING to perspectivalize one of the two views in COMMERCIAL_EVENT. We can do this by relativizing our path specifications to a particular view of ground scene. Where we have written (PATH <>) in the BUYING scene, we will simply write (PATH1 <>). This is intended to restrict the application of the Rule of Referenced Structure to only the first view in COMERCIAL_EVENT.

That is, the rule will only take into account the slots indexed "1" above. In particular, even though *scene1* is an elaboration of *condition2* by our definition of elaboration of a slot, BUYING will not inherit *condition2*. PAYING, on the other hand, will use PATH2.

There is still more structure that could be built into the COMERCIAL_EVENT scene, because there are valence possibilities built into COMMERCIAL_EVENT verbs that we have not yet accounted for. Consider, for example, *charge*.

I would like to suggest that all of the following examples are examples of the same semantic pattern:

(49) Sears charged Frieda a large sum for the lamp.

(50) The lamp cost Frieda a great deal of money.

(51) Sears billed Frieda several hundred dollars for the lamp.

(52) The IRS fined me several hundred dollars.

(53) That'll run you three-fifty. (ringing up cash register).

(54) The refs assessed Oakland a twenty yard penalty.

(55) The trip took Johann three days.

In all these examples there is a common semantic thread linking the verb and the two following NP'S. The first NP complement is the user of some resource, money, space, or time, and the second is a quantity of that resource. The verb always describes a situation in which said resource is lost. One might be tempted towards a more general characterization: perhaps this is a kind of inverse of the garden variety ditransitive construction, with dispossession in place of possession, and malefaction in place of benefit. But there seems to be little support from other verbs involving dispossession or unlucky events.

(56) *I took John three books. (on dispossession reading)

(57) *He ruined me three cars.

(58) *Frieda ate Bob all his food.

These examples suggests that this use of the ditransitive construction is limited to verbs which are really *about* the loss of a resource, that is, verbs whose figure scenes include some representation of resource loss semantics, as opposed to verbs whose ground scenes do. *Eat* may be one of the latter type. Eating of course always entails consumption of a resource, but it would be funny to define it as "the act of diminishing the food supply by ingestion;" on the other hand, it would not be so peculiar to define *fining* as "acting to take a sum of money from someone as compensation for a legal offense." To describe these facts, we would need a new scene, called, say RESOURCE_LOSS; if *charge* is to be a COMMERCIAL_EVENT verb, the RESOURCE_LOSS structure must also be built into the COMMERCIAL_EVENT, and CHARGING must reference the COMMERCIAL_EVENT scene so as to acquire that structure.

I will not pursue this exercise here, because I think that by now the general method of constructing ground scenes is clear. They will in general be very complex objects which encode a great deal of situational information. It is true that it is hard to know when you have finished specifying a ground scene; this is because a ground scene includes an arbitrary amount of background information; it includes all possible views of some object which, intuitively, is a single type of situation in the world.

2.5.2 A Note on Polysemy

Any theory of polysemy will prefer one meaning to two; but it is far from obvious that it will prefer three meanings to six. Three representations differing wildly in structure might very well be less perspicuous than six clustering together, or even six representations that were ordered by a transitive resemblance relation so that each successor was tolerably close to its predecessor, even though the ends of the chain were quite distant (this is the case of Wittgenstein's "family resemblances"). If the defineable relationships among our semantic representations are that complex, some decisions about individuating meanings can only be made after looking at all the uses for a particular form. But if deiiferent meanings for the same form share some non-trivial structure, that will count as evidence for them. If matters have gotten that far along, no decision about individuating meanings can be made without looking at all the uses for a particular form. Thus, we might derive encouragement for our account of *exchange for* by looking for other meanings of *for* built up out of the same components.

Along these lines, there is a well-known use of *for* that seems to be representable with a POS_TRANS skeleton:

```
(BENEFACTION
 (AKO (POS_TRANS))
 (DONOR)
 (BENEFICIARY <RECIPIENT>)
 (PATIENT (ACTION
          (ACTOR <^ DONOR>))))
```

This is the sense in which the *actor* is *donor* of an action, the classical benefactive:

(59) John made the sweater for Mary

(60) Mimi sang an aria for the audience

It is of interest that these sentences have paraphrases with double-object VP's, since we have already suggested that one use of the double object construction be related to the bare POS_TRANS frame. Note that any verb semantically compatible with the above frame would automatically be compatible with the POS_TRANS scene, and thus, with the double object construction related to POS_TRANS.

One more meaning of *for* deserves mention here, and this is our old friend, *karman*. Is it possible that we can decompose the LONGING scene as it stands into something a little more familiar? One obvious move is to reduce *karman for* to *exchange for*. Against that move we have the possibility of intensional readings with *karman for*, but not *exchange for*:

(61) John wished for a tootsie roll.

(62) John gave me an apple for a tootsie roll.

The question is, could we get this intensionality contrast with a single meaning of *for*, with the intensionality when it occurs always due to the meaning of the governing head?

The real answer to this question depends on an explicit account of intensionality, which I do not have. Yet I can offer some speculative considerations that argue for separate meanings in the present framework. First, whatever the correct treatment of intensionality, it will involve slots that take a very special kind of object. Here I mean "object" in the broadest sense. Obviously, *seek* is not a two-place relation between entities, but even on Montague's type-jacked possible-world account, it can be thought of as a two-place relation between peculiar objects, a relation which in one position demands as its "object" a function from possible worlds to sets of properties. Call the object type required to fill the "direct object slot" of *seek* a "peculiarity." Suppose that we assume that no elaboration of a entity slot can be a peculiarity slot, basing this on the convention in our system that information can be added to a slot, but never subtracted. Then a single meaning of *for* that covers all the cases would have to have a peculiarity slot; in the cases where *for* was extensional in use, the elaboration of *karman* in the head scene would have to be extensionalized. But then, this leaves no way to extensionalize the object of the preposition in the case of adjunct uses of *for*, because a head can have no "selectional" effect on the non-situation slots in an adjunct. A single meaning of *for* that is never an adjunct and takes only peculiarities solves this problem.

Nevertheless, there is enough similarity between *inducement* and *karman* so that something like this looks promising:

```
(LONGING: INTENTIONAL-STATE
   (LONGER <COGNIZER>)
   (KARMAN <O> (PECULIARITY <INTENDED PATIENT>))
   (INTENDED (POS_TRANS
              (RECIPIENT <↑ LONGER>)
              (DONOR)
              (PATIENT)))
```

This frame presupposes a general INTENTIONAL-STATE frame that will cover verbs like *believe, imagine,* and *expect*, assuming that the proposition connected with the state involves "coming to have," i.e. POS_TRANS, in the case of LONGING situations. Somehow, through a "black box" function I have called "peculiarity," the *karman* slot of the toplevel frame is associated with the *patient* slot in POS_TRANS. Although, the proposal is quite vague, I think it is quite plausible that a representation of *karman for* will include some POS_TRANS scene within it.

If so, we would have three different meanings of the multiply ambiguous preposition *for* which all use the POS_TRANS scene in their definition. While this hardly "motivates" the coincidence of these three meanings occurring with a single form, it at least suggests a connectedness of meaning which ought to be less costly than three utterly unrelated structures. That is, using the metaphor of acquisition, given two of these meanings of *for*, a third meaning with a POS_TRANS scene should be easier to learn than one with no shared structure at all.

2.5.3 Ex-spending the ontology

When philosophers discuss questions like "Are there qualities?" what they are trying to do is settle on a technical ontology, a collection of objects they must believe in in order to stay open for business. At times they have thought such questions are best settled by inspection of the world, at times by inspection of the language, and at times, it is hard to tell. It should be clear by now that ontological parsimony is not in the cards here, but this state of affairs is not necessarily offensive to parsimonious philosophers. Rarely, if ever, has the word "parsimony" been in used this connection to mean that there should be few objects. This would be curious restriction to impose on our disorderly universe. Rather, the term applies to positions in which the criteria for objecthood are few and stringent, so that only the things we are most likely to want to call objects can get by.

While I admit that I have already allowed some fairly curious creatures into the bestiary, I want to argue that the standards of admission are at least clear, if not particularly stringent. In this section, I want to briefly address some points of possible indeterminacy, and assist at the induction of a new member.

When we discussed the question of why one should believe that any such thing as a COMMERCIAL-EVENT was an individuable situation-type, I cited as evidence a few entailments among English verbs. We are thinking of an entailment between two verbs as showing that their use involves reference to the same situation type. Since our goal is the construction of a discourse ontology, this is sufficient grounds for admission. Curiously enough, it gives us no grounds for admitting ordinary unnamed objects like the keyboard this is being composed at, but this only reprises a point we have noted before in passing; a knowledge representational ontology is not a physicist's ontology. But when we get to specifics, a bit more has to be said.

Let us take as given that the very special relation between *buy* and *sell* licenses a scene we call COMMERCIAL-EVENT and a verb class we call COMMERCIAL-EVENT verbs. Then sentences like the following mutually entailing pair license adding *pay* to that class:

(63) John paid twenty bucks for a funny hat.

(64) John bought a funny hat for twenty bucks.

But, what now do we say about the following:

(65) John paid a thirty dollar fine for parking on Hyde Street.

(66) *John bought a thirty dollar fine for parking on Hyde Street.

That this is a different verb *pay* seems implausible. What appears more likely is that a single verb *pay* covers a wider range of situations than *buy*. One recourse, then, is to posit a scene slightly more general than COMMERCIAL-EVENT (call it TRANSACTION), and say that *pay* references TRANSACTION, rather than COMMERCIAL-EVENT. If COMMERCIAL-EVENT is AKO TRANSACTION, that will mean that every COMMERCIAL-EVENT is (entails) a TRANSACTION, and that will get us entailments from *buy* and *sell* to *pay*. The problem is that it will get us nothing going the other way; no sentence involving *pay* will entail a sentence involving *buy* or *sell*.

This presents difficulties for the proposed treatment of *pay*, but perhaps not insurmountable ones. Suppose that we think of scenes as structured sets of procedures that can test objects to determine whether they are a certain kind of thing. COMMERCIAL-EVENT is a single large procedure that returns yes or no depending on whether a particular object satisfies the COMMERCIAL-EVENT tests. Then it is possible that we can tell if some objects, specified by a verb as TRANSACTIONS, are further specified by the nature of its core participants to be COMMERCIAL-EVENTS. In particular, if the *goods* and *money* are suitable — if one is a merchandiseable item, and the other a real sum of money — then a TRANSACTION would invariably be a COMMERCIAL-EVENT.

I have no objection to such an account, exceptn that such test procedures are hard to formulate and somewhat of a departure from what we have done thus far. But it is clear that one needs to distinguish between scenes which are constrained to be COMMERCIAL-EVENTS with certain kinds of slotfillers, and those which are constrained only by a larger context, and not by their slotfillers. Consider *cost*:

(67) The printer breakdown cost me three hours.

(68) *I bought a printer breakdown for three hours.

Thus far, *cost* is parallel to *pay* in that it ranges beyond simple COMMERCIAL-EVENTS, but now consider the following pairs:

(69a) John bought that sweater for thirty dollars
(69b) John paid thirty dollars for that sweater.

(70a) John bought that sweater for thirty dollars.
(70b) That sweater cost John thirty dollars.

My claim is that the sentences in the first pair are mutually entailing. In (70), however, the sentence with *buy* entails the sentence with *cost*, but not vice versa. "That sweater cost John thirty dollars" is consistent with a situation in which John has paid for extensive repairs to his favorite cardigan.

One way to talk about these facts is the following: *buy*, *sell*, and *pay* all reference the same situation type, but *buy* and *sell* have extra selectional restrictions on their core participants, forcing the *money* to be real money and the *goods* to be what, for want of a better term, we will call "merchandise." On this account, it would be an accident for *buy* and *sell* to have the same selectional restrictions, and in fact, there seem to be some differences:

(71) Tom bought three hours of Willhelmina's time for a C-note.

(72) ?Willhelmina sold three hours of her time for a C-note.

(73) Jack sold his kidney to Menninger's.

(74) ?Menninger's bought Jack's kidney from him.

cost, on the other hand, references a more general scene, call it a COST, such that every COMMERCIAL-EVENT is a COST. This is consistent with the much broader range of contexts *cost* is appropriate with:

(75) Jack's coronary cost him a pint of blood.

(76) Phil's greasy comment cost him a million votes.

The account sketched makes a figure scene encode a bit more than we have imagined till now. Thus a ground scene encodes as much of the situational information as is consistent with all the verbs that access it; a figure scene is allowed to add selectional restrictions.

Furthermore, let us try the following constraints; a figure scene can add restrictions only to its core participant bearing slots (not to slots that take grammatically unrealized situations); and those restrictions must be entirely local to the slot. I mean by this to rule out statements of the following form: if slot1 is sortA, slot2 must be sortB. Such facts about lexical items must follow from the ground scene. The chief motivation for this constraint is to prevent figure scenes from bearing extra "relational" information, constraining the roles that that slotfillers play to one another; all that information should be found in the ground scene.

Let us now turn to the case of *spend*, which was one of the original motivations for introducing the figure/ground scene distinction, because it does not allow the *seller* to be realized. Now if *spend* is not a real COMMERCIAL-EVENT verb then the fact that it does not allow *seller* to be realized does not have to be represented as a difference between figure and ground scenes, and *spend* offers no motivation for the distinction. Consider:

(77) John spent thirty dollars for that sweater.

(78) John spent thirty dollars on that sweater.

Only the first sentence entails that John bought the sweater. The second, as with *cost*, is consistent with a heavy tailoring bill. This suggests the following: in one valence *spend* is a commercial-event verb; in another it is not. One entry is compatible with *on* and not *for*; and conversely for the other. To capture this fact, we will have to give *spend* two different figure scenes, and two different templates. Certainly lexical economy argues we should hang the differences on preposition meaning if we can. But pairs like this suggest different situation-types are involved:

(79) In the 1960's we spent billions of dollars on an unwinnable war.
?for

This pair seems to show that the *on* marks a different role from *goods*, not something that is owned after a transaction, but something that consumes a resource during it. A better name for this slot might be *liability*. Nor is *spend* with *on* limited to commercial transactions:

(80) I spent three days on that paper.
?for

Like *cost*, *spend on* seems to reference a more general situation type than COMMERCIAL-EVENT.

Since nothing more seems to stand in the way of *spend for*, let us propose a template scene:

```
(SPENDING-TEMPLATE: EXCHANGE_FOR
  (CONDITION
   (ACTION_DONATION:CAUSED-TRANSITION
    (DONOR)
    (PATIENT)))
  (SCENE
    (CAUSED-TRANSITION
      (PATIENT <^ EXCHANGED_OBJECT>))))
```

An ACTION_DONATION has an DONOR_ACTION as an extension; it

differs in that it lacks any participant corresponding to *recipient*. This template scene will thus have no slot whose elaboration is *seller* in the COMMERCIAL-EVENT scene, and thus *seller* will not be a core participant of SPENDING. The SPENDING scene will reference COMMERCIAL_EVENT with PATH2, because the *goods* are viewed as *exchanged_object*, just as they were with *pay*.

2.6 Other motivations for Figure and Ground

I have argued for a division of the information about lexical items primarily on the grounds of representational adequacy, where the criterion of adequacy was essentially capturing the right entailments, and semantic adequacy, where the criterion of adequacy was essentially semantic compatibility.

In this, the concluding section of the chapter, I will try to present some further arguments for the approach adopted.

To summarize the direction of the argument: first, an examination of a fairly complex interaction of compatibility facts led to some tentative lexical representations. In order to capture the full range of differences among situationally related predicates, we had to posit frames in a configuration that lost certain entailment facts. The alternative we then pursued was to have the COMMERCIAL_EVENT scene related to the various lexical scenes in a new way; we introduced a new kind of slot called a *reference* slot, which related scenes through a Rule of Referenced Structure, using mechanisms quite different from the inheritance machinery we have relied on till now.

Generalizing this to a method for the entire lexicon, we were left with two important frames for every verb, one the referenced situation, the other the lexical frame proper. We called the lexical scene the figure scene and the referenced scene the ground scene. The ground scene may in principle encode more information than is available in all the figure scenes that access it. It may encode more when there is situational information about a ground scene that was not a necessary part of any of the figure scenes. Fillmore points out, for example, that there is always some process of entering into an agreement that precedes the actual commercial transaction in any commercial event. This is part of its temporal and causal structure, part of the background assumptions we share in understanding any commercial event. Yet we have not discussed this aspect of a commercial event till now because we have no compatibility facts that depend on it. Yet, the "contract" nature of a COMMERCIAL_EVENT is arguably an intrinsic part of cultural significance; for example, discourse involving the legal consequences of a commerical event will nevessarily refer to the contract aspect. As such the "contract" implicit in any commercial event should be part of the fully expanded generic scene.

We posit scenes like BUYING and SELLING exclusively on the basis of linguistic evidence. Thus, the material in a lexical frame ought to be what is conveyed or asserted by the linguistic form, those aspects of the situation the predicate actually "presents" or "foregrounds." Most obviously, we can thus think of the slots in the template frame as chosing certain roles in the ground frame to foreground. The first figure representation we chose for *buy* "foregrounded" the role of the *buyer* as an *actor* and *recipient*, in a

RECIPIENT_ACTION scene, the *goods* as a *patient* in that scene, and the *seller* a *donor*; the modification proposed in the next section added to that the role of *money* as *payment*. It will be apparent to readers versed in case grammar and other theories of semantic roles that some of the roles "foregrounded" in the figure frame are more or less classical case roles like *actor* and possibly *recipient*," and some, such as *payment*, are definitely not. Note that all but the roles specific to COMMERCIAL_EVENT are in some way or another motivated by the compatibility facts of *buy*.

The roles in a template frame can be thought of as roughly analogous to the "deep" case roles of classical case grammar, with the following important differences:

(1) There are many more of them.

(2) As we shall see in the next chapter, only a subset of the of the roles in a figure frame will play a part in selecting nuclear terms from among the core participants.

(3) The role assignments are motivated by compatibility facts. In fact, one might say they are little more than an encoding of them. But this encoding induces some rather natural lexical semantic classes, such as the POS_TRANS verbs. As we shall see in the next chapter, it also defines at least a partial mapping onto lexical predicates, that is, a partial definition of the semantics of nuclear terms.

In the theory presented in this dissertation there will be three kinds of facts the figure frame is responsible to, compatibility facts, "-arity" facts (how many core participants a lexical head has), and facts about the realizations of particular core participants as nuclear terms. In addition to this, a lexical head may be associated with extra, derivative claims on the real world not revealed by its semantic compatibilities; capturing such claims is the function of the ground frame. The ground can be thought of as a projection made up out its figures, like the vision of the elephant constructed by the six blind men. The relation between a figure frame and a ground frame is mediated by the Rules of Reference and Referenced Structure. A figure frame must chose its structure from the available structure of the ground frame.

Entailments facts will follow from the structure of the ground scene and its linkage to lexical frames. This is in keeping with the "structural" view of lexical entailment adopted at the outset. Lexical entailments are not just scattered facts; they are consequences of the knowledge representational structure and should follow from correct lexical representations.

A structural view of entailment is intended as a replacement for an axiomatic approach, where the model theoretic interpretations of lexical items are constrained by "meaning postulates." On that sort of account, each lexical item would be associated with certain axioms, and certain groups of lexical items would share axioms, and be related by them. To give an example, one axiom might specifically state that every COMMERCIAL_EVENT is an ACTION, and thus yield an entailment relating, say, *buy* and *do*.

(81) John bought a VW.

(82) John did something.

Suppose the frame for *do* is simply the ACTION scene. In the framework adopted here, the entailment between *buy* and *do* would follow from the fact that BUYING has an RECIPIENT_ACTION as a component, and RECIPIENT_ACTION is AKO ACTION. Our interpretation of the AKO mechanism is already such that anything that is AKO RECIPIENT_ACTION is automatically AKO ACTION; our interpretation of component scenes is such that any BUYING scene must automatically involve a RECIPIENT_ACTION with *buyer* as *actor*.

On this view, lexical entailments are never specifically stated, as such. Methodologically, they are among the intuitions that guide our design of the procedures implemented in a frame representation. They are tests of the theory. They are not themselves the objects of our description.

Some comment ought to be made about the contrast between figure and ground representations and other classical semantic contrasts, in particular, the contrast between extension and intension. In an informal sense, both figure and ground frames are intensional descriptions; that is, they are descriptions of sets rather than sets. The "referenced" frame is not really referential in the model theoretic sense, since the COMMERCIAL_EVENT frame doesn't change even if the set of specific COMMERCIAL_EVENTS changes. Moreover, the intension/extension distinction is generally interpreted so that the intension gives you more information. That is, given the intension you have a procedure for determining the extension, but not conversely. In Montague's treatment, for example, intensions are functions from possible worlds to extensions; so given a world and intension, you have in hand an extension.

In the case of figure and ground scenes, it is the ground which is more fully specified (more informative) and the figure which is less specified. Similar comments apply to Frege's sense/reference distinction, in so far as I understand it. The distinction offered here is primarily one between the structure of the real world situation-type ("real" in the sense of culturally real) and the structure of a particular view of that situation-type.

On the other hand, this view of lexical description is quite compatible with others that have been advanced. First, of course, it seems to be a reasonably straightforward interpretation of Fillmore's dictum, "Meanings are relativized to scenes," where scenes in our terms are ground scenes, and "meanings" are figure scenes. There is also a good deal of conceptual similarity between Langacker's notion of "profile" and "base" (see Langacker 1983) and figure and ground scenes, respectively. Both these proposals differ from mine in that I have motivated figure scenes through considerations of semantic compatibility. But some of the same semantic intuitions can be captured.

Consider a simple case that was discussed in chapter 1, the notion of a "figure" as a preposition role:

(83) The ball is over the box

(84) The box is under the ball.

Intuitively, we can think of the prepositional phrase in both cases as predicated of the subject (this notion will be elaborated in chapter 5). We can also think of the subject in both cases as the object being located; in Talmy's work, figure, in Gruber's, theme, and the classical term, Patient. At the risk of confusion with the notion of figure and ground scenes, let us adopt Talmy's more specific term and call the role here *figure* (we have already made this terminogical choice in the TRANSFERENCE scene associated with *from*). Both *over* and *under* can be thought of as referencing the same real world situation, two objects vertically oriented in space. But the figure scenes differ in which participant they encode as *figure*. This is rather a simple case compared to COMMERCIAL_EVENTS. The relevant scenes are:

```
(ORIENTATION_IN_SPACE: THING
  (FIGURE)
  (GROUND))

(VERTICAL_ORIENTATION: SIMULTANEOUS_SCENES
  (FIRST_SCENE: COMPONENT
   (ORIENTATION_IN_SPACE
    (FIGURE <↑ INFERIOR>)
    (GROUND <↑ SUPERIOR>))
  (SECOND_SCENE: COMPONENT
   (ORIENTATION_IN_SPACE
    (FIGURE <↑ SUPERIOR>)
    (GROUND <↑ INFERIOR>)))

(OVER: ORIENTATION_IN_SPACE
  (REFERENT ((PATH <SECOND_SCENE>)
            VERTICAL_ORIENTATION)))
```

ORIENTATION_IN_SPACE simply defines an unspecified scene concerning two objects in space, one of which, the *figure*, may be thought of as being oriented with respect to the other. VERTICAL_ORIENTATION is a ground scene involving two objects and two orientation scenes. By referencing VERTICAL_ORIENTATION with the path <SECOND_SCENE>, the figure frame OVER makes the *superior* the *figure*. UNDER will reference VERTICAL_ORIENTATION with the path <FIRST_SCENE>, making the *inferior* the *figure*. Both frames reference the same situation, but assign different roles to the same ground participants. When we define the mapping to nuclear terms for prepositions, *figure* will outrank *ground* and will thus be mapped to the predicate position corresponding to subjects. Thus, the predicates UNDER and OVER will have the right entailment relation, but still have different nuclear term realizations.

Now the above representation of VERTICAL_ORIENTATION poses certain problems which were implicit in the representation of COMMERCIAL_EVENT, but which can be discussed a bit more clearly with this simpler example. What I seem to have done is to create a ground frame which is simply two preposition meanings welded together. That is, without the notions of figure and ground, one might very just take what I have in the *first-scene* slot as the meaning of *under*, and the *second-scene* slot as the meaning of *over*. In what sense is VERTICAL_ORIENTATION a description of a new situation-type, instead of just a cross-indexing of two related meanings?

To make my defense here, I will need to make a small digression into the domain of situation semantics (Barwise and Perry 1980), where some very similar issues have arisen in a different connection.

The starting point of the Barwise and Perry program seems to be this: a theory of how language carries information about the world must be founded on a theory of information. But information, and thus meaning, is in the world to begin with in the form of regularities across situations. Among these uniformities we find the traditional building blocks of logicians, objects, properties, and relations. Barwise and Perry thus propose a theory of meaning that focuses on the described world rather than on the mind that describes it. Mind enters the picture here: particular organisms individuate particular primitive uniformities. These primitives define the meaningful relationships for that organism. Naturally, those we are most interested in are the uniformities important to humans.

Two points are of interest here. The first will help us answer the charge that we have smuggled linguistic material into our description of situations. The Barwise and Perry line is that the salient regularities among situation types are part of the information available in situations; they are not imposed by language. They are exploited by it.

At the very beginning I said that the purpose of a knowledge representation was to explain discourse understanding, with discourse understood in the widest sense, including nonverbal interaction. The Barwise and Perry program might be taken as even more general, depending on how one wants to interpret the particulars. One of the objects of study of situation semantics is meaningful relationships among situations. Examples given by Barwise and Perry are the following:

> Smoke means fire.
> Kissing means touching.
> The ringing bell means class is over.
> "Cookie" means cookie.

Barwise and Perry treat the last of these examples, the most straightforwardly linguistic, as essentially similar to the rest (which is not to say identical); "means" in each case picks out a lawlike relationship, an essential uniformity, that humans are able to individuate among phenomena. The second example is of linguistic interest, as well, because it can be recast in a form we might call a lexical entailment ("Mary kissed Bill" entails "Mary touched Bill"). Of that case, they write:[1]

> Suppose the issue is whether Mary has ever touched Bill. If you learn somehow or other that Mary has kissed Bill, then you have the information available to conclude that Mary has touched Bill. This has nothing to do with language per se; kissing and touching are uniformities across situations recognized by human beings in this culture — relational activities. And it falls out of our recognition of these activities that kissings are touchings. Kissing is just a more fine-grained uniformity than touching.

The situation semantics view of a "meaningful relationship" is quite congenial to the view of lexical entailments adopted here. Lexical entailments ought to fall out from the structural relations of situation types; they are not linguistic statements. They are part of the uderstanding of the world imposed by our structuring of it (read, the uniformities we are attuned to). Of course language will be one of the chief sources of evidence in formulating hypotheses about such uniformities, but meaningful relationships are not constrained to be linguistic, and we should not expect all the regularities expressed in scenes to be reflected in lexical entailments.

Let us return now to figure and ground scenes. We have briefly sketched the situation semantics view that linguistic meaning can be viewed as a special kind of uniformity among situations, or perhaps better, a special kind of information available in situations. Both

---

1. Barwise and Perry 1982. p. 16.

ORIENTATION_IN_SPACE and VERTICAL_ORIENTATION are scenes, situation-types in Barwise and Perry's terminology. Both express a certain uniformity among situations, irrespective of the fact that one is directly associated with a particular lexical item. The claim made by the particular representation above is that ORIENTATION_IN_SPACE is a component of VERTICAL_ORIENTATION, that, in effect, it expresses a more primitive uniformity among situations. VERTICAL-_ORIENTATION situations can always be broken down into two subsituations, one in which the inferior object is "oriented" with respect to the superior, another in which the superior is oriented with respect to the inferior. Now it is clear that in this definition "oriented" conceals an appeal to a perceptual category; but that appeal may be made entirely independently of language.

At the risk of blundering into some rather well-traveled philosophical landscape, I want to argue that concealed perceptual categories are the rule rather than the exception in frame descriptions, as they must be in the Barwise and Perry program, where the *interesting* uniformities across situations are those happened on by human perceivers. One of the salient uniformities about squares for humans is that, viewed from most angles, they are parallelograms. It is no accident that much spatial vocabulary, cross linguistically, can encode implicit information about the location of a perceiver (*behind* and *in front of* are simple cases). If our task is to model the structure of the uniformities among situations, then it is quite reasonable to posit "orientation with respect to" as a more primitive uniformity than "absolute orientation," and to compose certain cases of the latter out of the former.

It is because I share the biases of situation semantics just outlined that I have chosen to make lexical frames proper (the figure frames) the same kinds of objects as all other frames. The BUYING scene is every bit as much a type of situation as the COMMERCIAL_EVENT scene. It is simply that they bear a very special relation to each other which is mediated by a special kind of slot. The reason the ground frame contains all the raw situational information is for economy of encoding; this is information shared by all the figure frames. All frames, in situation semantics terms, capture regularities among situations. A ground frame can be thought of as one step of abstraction higher, a regularity among certain of these regularities. In this light, there is no particular reason why a lexical scene needs to have a ground scene. If no other scenes share this lexical item's particular situational material, the ground scene is superfluous. Nevertheless, to facilitate the statement of our compatibility definitions, we will continue to assume all lexical items have ground scenes, allowing a figure scene to reference itself on occasion.

I now want turn back to the question of motivating two kinds of frames, figure and ground, and move the field of argument back to a linguistic plain. One of the chief payoffs in this kind of abstraction is in helping us maintain a useful distinction between ground participant and core participant. The simplest case of this was the verb *spend*, a COMMERCIAL_EVENT verb that simply didn't include the *seller* in its figure frame. Because of this, the question of that participant's realization as a complement simply doesn't arise.

A little reflection shows that such non-occurring participants will be far from rare in lexical description. Consider the word *alimony*, cited by Fillmore as one that presupposes quite a bit of background knowledge for felicitous use. Minimally, the necessary script for this word involves two once-married participants. Should the alimony payer be a core participant of *alimony*? Probably not, considering the unsavoriness of examples like these:

(85) The alimony from Chris arrived every third Thursday of the month.

(86) Chris's alimony came to two grand a month.

Results for the alimony recipient seem to be similar:

(87) Tracy's alimony came to two grand a month.

(88) The alimony to Tracy arrived every third Thursday of the month.

All of these examples improve drastically if *alimony* is replaced with *alimony payment*. We can describe this state of affairs as follows. Call the ground alimony frame ALIMONY; it includes two participants with the appropriate history. Call the figure frame ALIMONYP; it references ALIMONY and is itself AKO THING (giving it no compatibility privileges). But it has no participants, and thus by our definition of core participant, no core participants. Again we represent ground participants, important to the understanding of a lexical item, without calling them core participants.

In general, when we get to nouns the fairly robust intuitions we have about what constitutes a "participant in a situation" will leave us, and we shall have to get by with a much vaguer tag like "associated thing." Consider a noun phrase like *the father of our discipline.* Should the *child* be considered a core participant in the FATHER scene? Or perhaps our picture *fatherhood* as a condition is clear enough so that we can say, with some confidence, what sorts of participants enter into it. A word like *skill* may be more slippery. It seems fairly reasonable to claim that both the owner of a skill, and its domain are fairly important participants in defining the concept; and perhaps a noun phrase like "John's skill at plowing" will convince us that both participants belong in lexical frame as full-fledged core participants. In some cases, it seems clear, there will be participants important to the definition of a noun that we do not wish to grant a grammatical status.

The basic account here follows Fillmore's in this respect: core participants are chosen from among the participants of a scene.

Scenes, of course, are justified mainly in terms of the situational knowledge we extract from a lexical item, and if a participant in a scene is "left out," we'll know about it only because of our knowledge of the relevant ground scene. Until now the only motivation I have given for ground scenes has come from lexical entailments. Another kind of motivation, perhaps linguistically stronger, is the phenomenon of morphological derivation.

Consider the verb and noun *blame*:

(89) Bilbo blamed the mishap on Blaise.

(90) Bilbo blamed Blaise for the mishap.

(91) The blame for the mishap.

(92) *The blame on Blaise (for the mishap).

(93) *The blame of Blaise (for the mishap).

It appears to be the case that the noun does not allow the *culprit* in any realization, reminiscent of *spend* and the *seller*. A similar relationship, where one core participant is mysteriously excluded, seems to hold between the verbal and nominal forms of stems like *envy* and *credit*. We can even find such "exclusions" in the morphology of the semantic domain we have been discussing:

(94) A buyer of Chaldean pottery

(95) *A buyer of Chaldean pottery from Macy's

(96) A seller of antique books

(97) *A seller of antique books to children

All of the nouns in these examples are describeable in terms of figure scenes that import only some of the participants from the ground scene, where the corresponding verbs have inherited at least one participant more. There is a good deal more going on, of course, since presumably we want to represent some difference of meaning between the noun and the verb, but whatever account we choose will need to capture the difference in argument structure and the similarity in the situations evoked, a very common feature of different kinds of morphological derivation. Figure and ground scenes give us a mechanism for doing that.

2.7 Conclusion

In this chapter I have elaborated the bare bones apparatus for lexical description outlined in chapter 1. The elaboration has resulted in a basic split-up of the semantic information about a lexical item into what I have called figure and ground scenes.

The initial motivation for this split was to capture the differences in complementation possibilities among lexical items which can in some sense be linked with the same scenes. Linking verbs like *buy* and *sell* with a single COMMERCIAL_EVENT scene gives us the conventional entailments among these verbs, although it was argued that such entailments are facts about the way we individuate the world, not facts about language. This approach to entailment has been most clearly articulated by Barwise and Perry, although it is clearly implicit in much artificial intelligence research on reasoning and knowledge representation.

It was also argued that the distinction between figure and ground scene gives us a very handy way of representing the differences in argument structure among semantically related lexical items, in articular among items related by morphological derivation.

3. Where are the case theories of yesteryear?

The question I wish to address in this chapter has been very succinctly posed by Paul Kay (personal communication): "Why can't you say, 'Three o'clock ate the hamburger by John?'" Less succinctly, it is the question of how meanings are mapped into grammatical functions like subject and direct object. In the "case grammar" proposed in Fillmore 1968 the answer involved two major theoretical decisions:

> (1) an analysis of what sort of semantics can be fit into a single lexical item, stated in terms of a (hopefully small) number of semantic roles which the arguments of a head may play, and placing co-occurrence restrictions on these roles (prohibiting, for example, two occurences of the same case role with the same head);
>
> (2) a hierarchy determining which of the semantic participants of a head become subjects.

3.1 Why Case Grammar?

One of the central functions of case roles as formulated in Fillmore 1968 was to encode semantic information about how clauses are canonically organized, especially in terms of grammatical relations. This was the motivation for the subject hierachy, a fragment of which is:

Ag > I > Pa > Go > So

Things work very simply: if there is an Agent in a lexical entry it will become subject; if not the subject will be the next available member of the hierarchy. The possibility of an absolute hierarchy which decides the issue for every lexical item seems remote, because of pairs like *like* and *please*, but I will argue below that the basic premise of such a hierarchy, that there is a "semantics" behind subjecthood, is born out. Let us extend the idea of a case hierarchy as Fillmore does in later works to include direct object selection, and refer to the two grammatical functions, subject and direct object, as the nuclear terms of a clause. We can state the central hypothesis of this chapter as follows: nuclear terms are chosen in accordance with a partial ordering on semantic roles.

Early formulations of case hierarchies suffered because they failed to distinguish the situation-type a predicate references from the particular point of view the predicate takes on a situation. Two very simple examples, which we have already encountered, show the relevant problem.

(1a) The ball is in the box.
(1b) The box contains the ball.

(2a) The sphere is over the table.
(2b) The table is under the sphere.

No one would deny, I think, that the sentences in each of these pairs "mean" different things. The problem is that no description of the real world situations these sentences describe can ever capture the "meaning" difference, and therefore that no such account can capture any semantic factor motivating the difference in choice of subjects here. To speak simply of situations involving spatial location will never predict for us which of the objects in a location scene makes a good subject. What we need to talk about is which object is being located with respect to which. In (a) the sphere is being located with respect to the table; in (b) just the opposite has happened. In (a) the ball is being located with respect to the box; in (b) the communicative act is not one of locating one object with respect to another. What is being expressed is a property of the box which is, of course, independent of its location. Modifying some examples in Gruber 1976, one can show this with question-answer pairs:

(3) Where is the ball?
The ball is in the box.
?The box contains the ball.
?The ball is contained by the box.

(4) Where is the sphere?
The sphere is over the table.
?The table is under the sphere.

Only the first answer in each example functions as an appropriate answer to the locative question. The fact that the passivized version of the sentence with *contain* is also inappropriate shows that appropriate responses cannot simply be characterized by saying "the located object must be subject."

At the end of Chapter 2 we gave a semantics for *over* and *under* which assigned the two prepositions different figure scenes and the same ground scene. The mechanisms developed there for linking figure and ground guaranteed that sentences of the form "a is under b" and "b is over a" would entail each other. At the same time the figure scenes of the two prepositions differed: for *over*, the *superior* was the *figure*; for *under*, the *inferior* was the *figure*. Suppose now that the lexical representations consulted by something like the Fillmorian Case Hierarchy are figure scenes, and that the roles are interpreted simply as slot names. And suppose we made the following addition to Fillmore's Case Hierarchy:

Ag > I > Pa > Go > So > Figure

This would pick out the right participants as subject for *over* and *under*.

In this chapter I want to accomplish three things:

(1) Review some of the obvious right generalizations made by classical case hierarchies, and add a few new ones.

(2) Exploit the fact that the figure/ground distinction encodes the sort of "predicate point of view" displayed by *under* and *over*. I will also argue that there are still very strong constraints on what roles we assign to particular predicates. Those constraints are basically of two kinds, situation-type and semantic compatibility. Without some such constraints on role assignment, a theory of the semantics of nuclear terms is vacuous.

(3)

Present an "implementation" of the theory sketched: an algorithm that maps from figure scenes to logical predicates, where, in the grammar proposed in Chapter 1, predicate position corresponds to grammatical role. The algorithm will not be complete. That is, not every predicate will have its nuclear terms completely determined by the partial ordering on roles that the "Saliency" Hierarchy (to use the term in Fillmore 1977b) gives. As far as the theory goes, these cases are "pot luck."

I will begin these various tasks in the next section, where I briefly discuss some other examples of clear semantic constraints in choices of nuclear arguments. I will then discuss some more recent work of Fillmore's in which the case hierarchy as such (and with it cases) is discarded in favor of something called the Saliency Hierarchy, which does much the same work but is, for various reasons, more desireable.

3.2 Some Facts about the Semantics of Grammatical Relations

What kinds of semantic objects become subjects? What kinds become direct objects? What kinds become adjuncts? These are the kinds of questions linguists have, in one terminology or another, been asking ever since Panini. With over two millenia of the semantics of core participanthood behind us, we can with some confidence draw two conclusions: (1) there are some solid generalizations about the connections between semantic role and grammatical function; (2) there is no complete algorithm; that is, in some cases, it is best to say, either that the choice is arbitrary, or that only "grammatical meaning" is involved. This might, for example, be the most perspicuous way to talk about the difference between *like* and *please*.

In what follows, when I say subject or object, I shall mean, roughly, logical or underlying subject or object; I shall have nothing to say about "derived" grammatical functions like that of *the beans* in *The beans were overcooked.*

Let's begin by trying to back up conclusion (1), that there are some solid generalizations about the semantics of grammatical relations.

It will be useful to begin by selecting the roles which will be used in the informal statements of Fillmore's Saliency Hierarchy in the next section. In this preliminary discussion I am only concerned with describing the intuitive content of the roles; later we will look at the kinds of evidence that can justify their assignment.

The obvious role to start with is *actor*. An *actor* "does something." We will speak of *actors* as the primary source of an ACTION;, where only creatures capable of volition can be the primary source of an activity. Ultimately, the notions defined here must apply to the linguistic presentation of reality in clauses. In "John made Bill walk," John is active in the matrix clause, Bill inactive; but Bill is active in the downstairs clause. In "Henrietta moved the Book," both the book and Henrietta are most naturally viewed as moving, but only

Henrietta as primary source of that activity is *active*.

Along with this we use a closely related notion of *causer*, (although ultimately we will dispense with this category). Again, we are confined to single clauses; if "Bill hits the ball across the park," Bill causes the ball to move across the park. Bill's role can now be thought of as *causer* in addition to *actor* In "The key opened the door," the key is *causer* but not *actor*.

Finally, we shall need a notion of *changed*. If the vase breaks, it changes.

We can now get down to cases.

3.2.1 Active and Causal subjects

As conceived thus far, *actors* correspond exactly to the *agents* of Fillmore 1968 (although this understanding of *actors* will be revised later). Like Agents in Fillmore's system, they will be the paradigm examples of subjecthood in this one. What evidence is there, then, that something is an *actor*?

In this framework, all roles are defined with respect to scenes, and all scenes have their place in the lexical system as a whole. *actors* occur in ACTIONS, which are compatible with *instruments*, *exchanged objects*, and *beneficiaries*, all preposition frames we declared in Chapter 2. The first is a meaning of *with*, the next two meanings of *for*. Here they are:

```
(EXCHANGE_FOR:EXCHANGE_TEMPLATE
   (CONDITION (ACTION))
   (SCENE:COMPONENT
         (CAUSED_TRANSITION
           (PATIENT <↑ EXCHANGED_OBJECT>))))

(MANIPULATION: THING
 (INSTRUMENT)
 (ACTION
   (ACTOR <↑ USER>))

(BENEFACTION
 (AKO (POS_TRANS))
 (DONOR)
 (BENEFICIARY [recipient])
 (PATIENT (ACTION
         (ACTOR <DONOR>))))
```

Saying a verb has an *actor* entails that it combines with *with* and *for* with just the specified interpretations, For example, with *instrument with* , the *actor* is understood as manipulator of the *instrument*; with *benefactive for* the *actor* is understood as *donor* of the ACTION. And so on. In short, there are both distributional and semantic consequences to calling something an *actor*. We have concrete tests to determine if something fills that role, and therefore the claim that *actors* are subjects becomes testable.

Let us also identify a role *causer*, which will semantically be like the*actor* role, except that the requirement that the *actor* be capable of volition is dropped. *Actor* is thus a further specification of *causer*, and like *actors*, *causers* will make excellent subjects. The subjects of the following sentences will be *causers*:

(5a) The key opened the lock.

(5b) The magnet attracted the filings.

The status of *causer* is somewhat problematic, and we will dispense with this role later on; for the time being it is a useful repository for those participants called both *instruments* and *forces* (see Fillmore 1971) which are realized as nuclear terms.

3.2.2 Change and Effective Instrument

Before discussing roles other than *actor*, it will be useful to clarify the ultimate goal. What we desire is a partial ordering of semantic roles which constrains the choice of nuclear terms in a clause. We have begun by discussing the role *actor*; as it happens *actor* will be the nuclear term role par excellence, outranking all other roles; if a verb has an *actor* the *actor* becomes subject. *Causer* is similar but its status with respect to *actor* is unclear. As we move on to other roles, we will need to keep in mind that we are constructing a partial ordering. Given that some role plays a part in determining the semantics of nuclear termhood, we need to ask how it is ordered with respect to the other roles that also play a part — if it is. The fact that we are constructing a partial-ordering leaves open the possibility that any two roles may be unordered with respect to one another.

Our next example involves the notion *changed*. Consider as one special subcase of "changing" the property of "moving." Suppose we claim that moving objects make better subjects than non-moving objects. This predicts that no verbs will fit into the following sentence frames, with the indicated meanings:

(6) The store <Verb> the meteorite.
The meteorite approached the store.

(7) The store <Verb> <Preposition> the meteorite.
The meteorite approached the store.

(8) Zeus <Verb> the store <Preposition> the meteorite.
Zeus hurled the meteorite at the store.

(9) Zeus <Verb> the store the meteorite.
Zeus hurled the meteorite at the store.

Of course, the role *changed* needs to be located in the ordering of roles. It appears, for example, to rank lower than *actor*. In "John blew the filings across the table," John does not move, but John's role is still the subject role. We can get this effect by including in the ordering of roles the statement:

Actor > Changed

Thus any choice between the role *actor* and *changed* will be decided in favor of *actor*. *Causer* will also have to rank higher than *changed*, because a motionless object outranks a mover if it acts as a causer (for example, "the magnet attracted the filings.").

Consider a different kind of semantic generalization about grammatical functions, a negative one; effective instruments may not be nuclear terms/ By an effective instrument I mean an instrument that occurs in the same clause with an *actor* and a *changed* element. The following examples are from Fillmore 1977a:

(10a) He broke the vase with the hammer.
(10b) He broke the hammer against the vase.

(11a) I hit the fence with the stick.
(11b) I hit the stick against the fence.

Let us assume that the verb *break* has a figure scene in which its "breakee" necessarily changes. The hammer is then an effective instrument. Note that it can no longer be interpreted as an *instrument* when realized as a direct object. The direct object of *break* is always interpreted as the "breakee." This is not the case with *hit*. The fate of the fence and the stick remain the same in the (a) and (b) versions of (11). *Hit* does not take effective instruments; that is, it does not predicate any necessary change of its direct object in either syntactic valence. In classical case terms, we might call the "hittee" a Goal, where we would call the "breakee" Patient. In our terminology here, the "breakee" is *changed*.

The claim I made above was that effective instruments cannot be direct objects. How can we talk about this in terms of a ranking of roles? By definition effective instruments imply both an *actor* and a changed participant in the same clause. If both the *actor* and the changed participant always rank higher than the *instrument*,, then *instrument* is ineligible for either of the nuclear term positions. In particular, this prevents effective instruments from becoming direct objects, and rules out the following verb frames, with the indicated meanings:

(12) John <Verb> the needle the pillow.
John pierced the pillow with the needle.

(13) John <Verb> the needle <Preposition> the pillow.
John pierced the pillow with the needle

The examples here are chosen to evoke one of Gruber's (Gruber 1977), which seems to pose a possible counterexample. Here is the relevant sentence, along with one that differs minimally:

(14a) John pierced the needle through the pillow.
(14b) John poked the needle through the pillow.

I find (a) quite grating and (b) fine, so that I disagree with Gruber's judgements. I think that mine may be explained in terms of effective instruments. For me, the piercee is necessarily changed with the verb *pierce*, and therefore the *instrument* is not a happy candidate for direct objecthood; with *poke*, on the other hand, the state of the pokee may be utterly unchanged. I propose that for anyone who can use *pierce* in Gruber's fashion, *pierce y through x* means "force y through x;" change in x is of course implied, but not foregrounded. Even for such speakers, I suspect this use is rather marginal; (a) sounds grating to me; (14+1) is absolutely out.

(15) *The needle was pierced through the pillow.

Some further comments are in order about these claims. In making the case for effective instruments, I implicitly appealed to the distinction between a feature of the linguistic presentation, and a feature of the real world situation. Suppose that Gruber and I both have the same truth conditions for sentences with *pierce*, despite our differences in judgement about the appropriateness of some of them. I maintain that our differences in judgement reflect a difference in the semantics we have learned, and that for Gruber, *pierce* really means something different than it does for me.

This puts me in something of a methodological bind. Whenever someone's lexical judgements disagree with mine, I can claim they have learned a different lexicon. The move is quite parallel to the standard generative appeal to "different dialects." The dangers of both moves are obvious. On the one hand, something like this notion is obviously needed, especially at the lexical level; we all know words at the limit of our competence as speakers, words we can use in limited contexts, and then only with great uncertainty. Even better, we have all known words which later linguistic authority has shown us to know imperfectly or wrongly. The lexicon is the clearest place where the differences in our linguistic competence emerge. But even in describing the lexicon some hypothesis about a common body of knowledge shared by a community of speakers is essential, and appeals to differences of idiolect need to be backed up with some evidence for these differences in the assumed grammar. At present I have no independent justification to offer for my claims about Gruber's sense of *pierce*, but note that the difference I have ascribed to his lexicon is a difference involving one lexical item. I assume that in everyone's lexicon, in fact, in the lexicons of all languages, the role *changed* still plays an important role in determining nuclear terms.

How would we represent the meanings I have attributed to Gruber's lexicon and to mine? The hypothesized divergence in understandings can be described straightforwardly in terms of figure and ground scenes. Since we have assumed both speakers have roughly the same truth conditions for sentences involving *pierce*, we assume they have the same ground scenes. But now in my version of the figure scene of *pierce*, the "peircee" fills a slot called *changed*; in Gruber's it does not.

The claim I have made about effective instruments is that they cannot be direct objects. *Hit* and *poke* take non-effective instruments and thus allow the *instrument* to be become direct object. *Hit* also offers a further option, that of tacking on a Locative complement that gives us a sort of resultative location for the same participant. "John hit the ball across the park." Note that in this valence the *instrument* cannot become direct object. We do not have: "*John hit the bat against the ball across the park." We could explain this by noting that in this valence there clearly HAS been a change in the "hittee", a change of location. Then the *instrument* in this valence is effective. We shall return to these resultative locatives in Chapter 4.

3.2.3 Experiencers and Causers

Suppose we admit another semantic category often invoked in Fillmorian Case Grammar, that of the *experiencer*, taking this to be a necessary participant role for any verb involving perception, emotion, and cognition. We have already recognized the features *actor, causer,* and *changed* as playing an important role in the selection of subjects. Suppose we now add *experiencer* to the list.

Here are some examples:

(16) Mary sees Bilbo.

(17) Bilbo suprised Mary.

(18) Mary thought about Bilbo.

(19) Mary liked Bilbo.

(20) Bilbo pleased Mary.

(21) Bilbo seems funny to Mary.

(22) Bilbo's soup tastes funny to Mary.

If the various realizations of *experiencers* in these examples are to be accounted for, we will need to identify clearly the roles of those participants with verbs like *surprise* and *please* which outrabk the *experiencer*. One move in the right direction is made in Fillmore 1971.

Fillmore distinguishes those verbs where the "intentional object" (the content of the cognitive state, the perceived, or the target of the emotional state) can be thought of as causing the intensional state. If the intentional objects of these verbs are called *causers* and if *causer* outranks *experiencer* in the ordering of roles, then just those intensional objects which are *causers* should be selected over *experiencers* as subjects. Some of the relevant verbs: *surprise, astonish, disgust, thrill, amuse, excite, sadden, impress, please* and *stun*.

Note that these verbs allow complements with *by*:

(23) John amazed me by arriving on time.

(24) Bill pleased Roberta by arriving on time.

In contrast we have:

(25) *Tina liked Bill by focusing on his strong points.

(26) *John believed Slim by performing an act of faith.

In Chapter 1, we called the situations these *by* adjuncts selected PURSUITS. If we suppose that PURSUITS contain *causers*, then the fact that the *experiencers* aren't subjects with these verbs and the fact that they allow *by* adjuncts can be explained together.

Along with *causer* another high-ranking Saliency feature we noted was *actor*. Clearly, certain intentional attitude verbs involve participants we would like simply to call *actors*; these, too, outrank the *experiencers*:

(27) John persuaded Bill to use case grammar with several classical arguments.

(28) John persuaded Bill to use case grammar for his advisor.

Thus, *experiencer* seems to be involved in at least the following orderings:

Actor > Experiencer
Cuaser > Experiencer

Clearly problematic for this simplistic account are the verbs like *seem* and *taste*. Neither of the ordering statements appears to apply, yet *experiencer* rates only an oblique realization. Moreover, the behavior of these verbs is something more than a case of random lexical misfire. They appear to be examples of a phenomenon observable in a number of languages, both Indo-European and others (see Nichols 1977), which is sometimes called inversion. Loosely speaking, inversion involves verbs in a number of semantic domains, including possession, perception, and modality, with animate arguments that are realized obliquely, with the subject often a dummy or absent. Some typical examples from Polish:

(29)	Mnie	zimno	jest
	Me (Dat.)	cold (neuter)	is (3rd sg)
	I'm cold		

(30)	Nam	nie wolno	jesc	kapusty.
	Us (Dat.)	not permitted(3rd sg.)	eat (inf.)	cabbage (gen.)

We're not allowed to eat cabbage.

The term "inversion" is motivated by the fact that these oblique animate arguments exhibit a number of subject properties, including, as in the second of the Polish examples, control of infinitives. Another subject property is extensionality: note, for example, that with *seem* the subject position is not extensional, as is often the case with raising verbs ("A unicorn seems to be approaching."), but the *experiencer* argument (realized with *to*) is. Moreover that position strongly favors definiteness, another property typical of subjects:

(31) *?A unicorn seems to a centaur to be approaching.

(32) A unicorn seems to me to be approaching.

Perlmutter 1975 postulates that these arguments begin as subjects, but that there is a syntactic inversion rule causing them to be realized as surface Indirect Objects. A general problem for the GPSG framework to which I have hitched my wagon, and for the Dowty-style representation of grammatical relations which it adopts, is how to handle syntactic phenomena that give evidence for multiple levels of grammatical relations, particularly where obligatory processes have applied. Inversion is one such phenomenon. I have little to say about it here, except to note that it shows both syntactic and semantic symptoms, and that a general account of the semantics of nuclear terms must ultimately find an account for it.

What I propose to do with verbs like *seem* and *taste*, then, is class them among the mysteries. The only truly unsettling thing about the particular mystery of inversion is that it is not very clear, in English, just what its boundaries are. Are the following examples cases of inversion?

(33) It takes me four hours to drive to Eureka.

(34) It is amazing to her that you even came.

The *it* preceding *take* is presumably extraposition-it, so that the subject is the infinitive clause. Why does this clause win out over an *experiencer*? A parallel question arises for *amazing*. The appeal to a *causer* element is plausible in sentences like "John amazed Mary with his impudence," but (34) clearly has an adjectival head (only the present participle form of *amazing* takes the preposition *to*). The problem is that in 3.3, when we do consider hierarchical rankings for adjectives, we shall want *experiencers* at the top; even ignoring that point, it seems likely that adjectives never have *causers*, because they are stative. Why, then, does the *experiencer* occur obliquely here?

Let me now back up and summarize the current state of intentional attitude verbs. All of them by definition involve something we call an *experiencer*. If there is no *causer* or *actor* element in the same clause, the *experiencer* becomes subject. Complicating this simple picture, there is a special class of verbs called inversion verbs which seem to be immune to this rule. The class of exceptions (if the inversion verbs are indeed exceptions) shows some evidence of being semantically characterizable. Apart from these verbs, there is a large class of verbs whose subject arguments can be correctly characterized with the notions, *actor*, *causer*, and *experiencer*.

3.2.4 Summary

In this section, we have used the notions *actor*, *causer*, *changed*, and *experiencer* to make some fairly broad generalizations about what kinds of semantic features promote subject- and direct object-hood in English. Before that we noted that that the role *figure*, already invoked in Chapter 2, also played a role in some significant semantic observations about subjecthood. In the next section we will discuss Fillmore's proposal for a Saliency Hierarchy which uses notions like *actor*, *causer*, *experiencer* and *figure* to state facts about the semantics of nuclear terms.

3.3 The Hierarchy and its Function

One can distinguish among a number of different theories of deep case two function served by the cases. First, a paradigmatic classification of lexical heads according to the semantic roles played by their nominal arguments; this enterprise falls into the domain of lexical semantics. If successful, such a classification elucidates the lexical semantic structure by defining a useful kind of lexical relatedness; it can capture natural verb classes, predict entailment relations, and help reduce the number of lexical entries. But case theories were never meant to complete the task of lexical semantics. In a representation rich enough to show the detailed local relationships of verbs like, say, *buy* and *sell*, a good deal of extra and very specific semantic apparatus is needed. One of the goals of this dissertation is to show how having such specific semantic apparatus around helps us formulate the generalizations of case grammar in a testable way.

The second role of deep cases was our principal concern in the last section: to represent semantic generalizations about the realization of grammatical relations in clauses. This enterprise takes us away from the mere cataloguing of situation types and involves us in the problem of the possible linguistic encodings of those situations. A theory that concentrated primarily on this second function of case roles might well omit them entirely from specific lexical descriptions, and might constrain the use of classical case roles to its metalanguage.

This seems to be one reading of the theory presented in Fillmore 1977a and Fillmore 1977b. In Fillmore 1977b, a procedure for selecting nuclear arguments is formulated, and case roles as such play no part in it. Instead an assumption is made that there are semantic representations rich enough to encode the kinds of features discussed in the last section. Those features are ranked in a hierarchy which governs the selection of nuclear terms. Fillmore calls his hierarchy the Saliency Hierarchy:

(1) An active element outranks an inactive element.

(2) A causal element outranks a noncausal element.

(3) A human (or animate) experiencer outranks other elements.

(4) A changed element outranks a nonchanged element.

(5) A complete or individuated element outranks a part of an element.

(6) A 'figure' outranks a 'ground.'

(7) A 'definite' element outranks an 'indefinite' element.

These seven statements[1] are consulted in order and when one that fits is reached, the ranking element becomes nuclear if a nuclear slot is still available. If we think of this as a formal procedure, then of course everything depends on the particular choice of lexical representations, and how the necessary information is extracted from them. Fillmore does not make a commitment about the exact nature of those representations, but he does assume that lexical representations proper are *frames* linked with *schemata* that charaterize the structure of actions, institutions, and objects in the world. In sum, although Fillmore makes none of the notational choices subscribed to here, this venture in lexical representation is in very much in the spirit of the program outlined there.

It remains to talk a bit about the hierarchy itself. The seven

---

1. Fillmore 1977b, p. 102.

kinds of choices indicated by the hierarchy can be illustrated with some examples from the lore of case grammar (where NP's denoting elements relevant to each choice are italicized):

(1) *The man* hit *the fence*.

(2) *The duck* surprised John.

(3) *John* liked *the duck*.

(4) John loaded *the truck* with *hay*.

(5) Bill hit *the car* on *the bumper*.

(6) *The ball* is on top of *the table*

(7) Roman made *the log* into *a canoe*.

The hierarchy is doubtless incomplete, and some details of its formulation may be open to question, but it offers, I think, just the right sort of scaffolding on which to build.

There are a number of advantages to approaching the semantics of nuclear terms with a saliency hierarchy instead of a more classical case theory. The difference here is not simply in the choice of a more abstract set of features; It is in the kinds of decisions forced on the analyst. Rather than seeking an exhaustive taxonomy of verb argument relations, we are seeking subject-inducing semantics. When we finish listing the statements in a Saliency Hierarchy, there is no need to claim that we have defined some set of primitive semantic entities which must play a role in the semantics of every open class lexical item. It is perfectly consistent with the enterprise to have verbs that lack any semantic features mentioned by the hierarchy. For these verbs the Hierarchy simply has nothing to say. Indeed, the fact that Hierarchy does not completely determine subjects and objects for every verb will play an important role in our characterization of possible valences.

The inherent shift in the nature of the enterprise might perhaps be best illustrated with an example. The example will also provide with us a addition to Hierarchy to use in the revised Hierarchy in the next section. Fillmore tells the story of the early days of case grammar when a skeptical Paul Postal asked what deep cases he could conceivably assign to a verb like *outnumber*. In the then-current framework there was no easy answer. If, instead of a small inventory of semantic roles, one is only interested in the semantics of nuclear terms, that particular question does not arise. The relevant question is: what if anything is there about the semantics of *outnumber* gives it the particular choice of subject that it has?

The question could be rephrased: "Could there be a verb *blik* that means "is less than in number," whose subject was the lesser object and whose object was the greater one? If the answer is no, then this is a fact about the semantics of subjecthood, and needs to be represented in the Saliency Hierarchy.

The constraints imposed by the Hierarchy presumably apply to all verbs, both basic and derived. Hence we can find our data both among the ordinary verbs and the morphological processes, like prefixation, that apply to them. The verb *outnumber* is the output of a productive prefixation process in English. *Out-* roughly means "to exceed in," and occurs quite productively, in words like *outnumber, outshine, outplay,* and *outeat.* Bresnan 1980 argues that it is a transitivizing prefix which attaches only to intransitive verbs.[2] What is important here is that there is no corresponding prefix meaning "to do less well in." In general it seems that verbs whose content implies ranking on some scale, whether of quality or quantity, will take the superior element as their subject. We will capture such facts by adding to the Saliency Hierarchy the clause: The Superior outranks the Inferior.

The claim that the Saliency Hierarchy must also apply to the output of the morphology is quite important, considering the general unpredictability of the semantics of morphological processes. Despite the enormous range of semantic creativity discussed for denominal verbs in Clark and Clark 1979, it seems correct that one kind of use that *won't* occur for "The Duchess teapotted the dean is one in which the dean instigates some action with a teapot. The same kind of evidence

---

2. *outnumber* and *outweigh* may seem like counterexamples, but they can quite plausibly be called intransitive, since their complements are exclusively quantitative, and they do not passivize.

can be adduced for our proposed addition to the hierarchy. Note that *dwarf*, despite its meaning as a noun, takes the entity of greater magnitude as its subject. Compare *tower*.

3.4 Some Issues in the Semantics of Nuclear Terms

This section ties together a number of loose ends that need to be addressed before we present the actual procedure for assigning subcategorizations in the next section. We will begin by examining possible extensions of the Hierarchy to other categories besides verbs. We will then present a long-overdue discussion of optionality, taking as our paradigm example the case of the *instrumental*. Next, we will turn to a subcategorization puzzle raised in Kajita 1967 concerning the verb *serve*, and finally we will present a further decomposition of the POS_TRANS scene, crucial for developments in Chapter 4, which extends the current interpretation of the roles *figure* and *ground*.

3.4.1 Cross-Categorial Claims

Throughout this dissertation I have concentrated mainly on verbs, but have maintained that the same principles and methods would carry over to the other lexical heads, the adjectives and the nouns. In dealing with Saliency Hierarchy, however, I need to revise this position somewhat.

It has been fashionable, particularly among proponents of X-bar theory, to draw an analogy between subject noun-phrases in sentences and genitive noun-phrases in noun-phrases. Jackendoff 1977 formalizes the analogy by assigning both nouns and verbs the feature [+SUBJ], and defining subject as a noun phrase immediately dominated by

X3[+SUBJ]. This leaves as somewhat problematic the status of adjectives. One of the original motivations for drawing the noun/verb analogy in the first place goes all the way back to Chomsky 1970, where the problem of representing the relationshsip of such heads as *criticism* and *criticize* is addressed. Opting against a transformational account, Chomsky suggests that the lexicon contain entries unspecified for the features distinguishing nouns and verbs. In effect this provides a place to record the shared selectional restrictions of the two forms. Jackendoff's definition of subject provides the necessary syntactic account of which argument positions correspond in the fully specified versions.

Unfortunately for such a syntactic account, the very same problems arise in connection with adjectives. The adjective *perverse* corresponds to the noun *perversity*, and this time it becomes impossible within the system of projection rules Jackendoff adopts, to state the parallel:[1]

(1) John is perverse

(2) John's perversity

(3) I consider John perverse.

Jackendoff adopts a very different kind of account here, claiming that for adjectives the correspondence between noun and adjective arguments

---

1. Jackendoff 1974, p. 502.

must be stated at the level of thematic relations.

The same sorts of problems do not arise in the framework adopted here. I have assumed logical predicates with fixed mappings from argument positions to grammatical function. Therefore I am free to state correspondences on argument positions. Thus, I can define subject to be a particular argument position for nouns, verbs, and adjectives, or indeed, something more complicated, if needed. The point is that the intrusion of the verb *be* between an attributive adjective and its "subject" need not be reflected in the logic.

Nevertheless, there are some problems in pursuing this analogy down the line. First of all, if a genitive is to be an argument of the head noun. what are we to do with the head nouns which lack genitives? Either, "the destruction" and "the city's destruction" involve different lexical items as their heads, or the first has a missing argument, existentially quantified over or filled with a deictic variable. And do we strive for complete uniformity? Is "John" an argument of "lamp" in "John's lamp?"

One solution to these problems is to generate more than one logical predicate from a single figure scene. Thus the lexical semantic representation for *destruction* might yield two logical predicates, one for genitives, one not. Then "Tyre's destruction" and "the destruction" would involve different predicates, but would map to frame representations that were AKO the same lexical frame, DESTRUCTION. We have already had recourse to multiple logical predicates for the same lexical representation: this was the move taken for the argument and adjunct predicates of prepositions like *against*; we will take the same course with verbs when we turn to dative movement. I now recommend it wholesale for nouns. But what about nouns like *lamp*? I believe that the right answer is that the English genitive is ambiguous between a grammatical and a non-grammatical function. *lamp* should map to only one logical predicate because the lexical scene for LAMP countenances no extra argument positions. And whatever restrictions there are on what can occur as possessor of a lamp are determined by non-lexical factors.

The road thus seems open for a complete cross categorial definition of the notion "nuclear term." I will not, however, carry this enterprise out in all its gory detail, because of two complicating factors. First, there is good reason to believe that different categories require different saliency hierarchies, that this may even be an essential part of the "semantics" of syntactic categories. Second, an explicit semantic account of genitives as subject in the noun phrase is a major enterprise, involving problems in the semantics of control that would take us too far afield here.

The second point is just a plea for clemency. The first requires some evidence.

The relevant evidence is to be found in Amritavalli 1980; using a framework of Jackendoff-style thematic roles, Amritavalli argues that the privileges of subject selection are different for nouns and adjectives than for verbs.

(4a) John amused the children with his stories.
(4b) *John's amusement of the children with his stories.
(4c) The children's amusement at John's stories.
(4d) The children were amused at John's stories.

Once again the semantic class at issue is what we analyzed as the causal intentional attitudes in the last section. The problem is that example (b), where the noun's subject corresponds to the verb's subject in (a), is ungrammatical. Instead we have (c). If, with Wasow 1977, we call the head *amused* in (d) the output of an adjective formation rule, then the noun *amusement* and the adjective *amused* pattern together. If this were an isolated instance it would have little consequence for Amritavalli's theory or anyone's. However, she cites a large body of nouns and adjectives, all in the same semantic class, that behave identically. A sampling of her data:

(5) annoyance, astonishment, boredom, conviction, delight, disappointment, disgust, dismay, distress, elation, embarassment

(6) annoyed, astonished, bored, convinced, delighted, disappointed, dsigusted, dismayed, distressed, elated, embarassed.

In the account we have been pursuing, we could describe this data by having a different Saliency Hierarchy for nouns and adjectives. All we need do is move the statement involving *experiencers* to the top of the list, interpreting it as the highest ranked of the roles.

I think Amritavalli's data shows we can not have a category-independent Saliency Hierarchy. In the remainder of this section, I want to explore some possible consequences of this view in the domain of nouns, where Amritavalli's case is stronger (as noted before, it may be that we do not want our lexical representations for adjectives to ever include the roles *actor* or *causer*, if adjectives are stative). In particular, I want to explore the possibility that for some categories, not only is the Saliency Hierarchy different from that of verbs, but there are more ways of realizing a particular nuclear term. The obvious candidate with nouns is the grammatical function that can be realized in either of the following ways:

(7) John's arrival

(8) The arrival of John

Suppose that the Saliency Hierarchy for nouns was something like this:

(1) An Experiencer outranks a non-experiencer.

(2) A Changed element outranks a non-changed element.

(3) An Actor element outranks an Inactor element.

(4) A Causer element outranks an Non-Causer element.

The Hierarchy may or may not continue, but this is all we need for now. The most striking thing about it is that I have moved not only the statement about Experiencers, but also the statement about Changed elements.

Let us assume that the notion transitive may be carried over to from verbs to nouns, where a transitive noun realizes one of its arguments as a genitive and the other as object of the grammatical preposition *of*. I propose that nuclear terms in nouns be realized as follows: the grammatical possibilities of the top-ranked argument differ depending on whether the noun is transitive or intransitive. For intransitive nouns, the top-ranked noun may either be genitive or object of the case-marking preposition *of*. For transitive nouns, the genitive slot will be taken up by the second-ranking noun, and the top ranking noun will only have one possible realization, as object of case-marking *of*. In the examples we have considered, then, *of* always functions as a grammatical preposition marking the top-ranked noun (in Chapter 4, we will examine some cases where *of* has meaning). The obvious inspiration for such split marking convention is ergative languages. As we shall try to show below, this slight complication of the grammatical mapping simplifies the description of the numerous "valence" possibilities for nouns. Taking as our paradigm case, *destruction*, the hierarchy allows (a) - (c) as basic realizations of the noun, without any syntactic derivation. It blocks (d) on the reading that paraphrases the other examples:

(9a) Tyre's destruction by heaven
(9b) The destruction of Tyre by heaven
(9c) Heaven's destruction of Tyre.
(9d) *The destruction of heaven (<PREP> Tyre).

I am assuming that in (a) and (b), the option to have an intransitive noun has been taken, and that *by* in the noun phrase is a semantically contentful preposition marking an oblique argument. In (c) the transitive option is taken, and only one syntactic configuration is possible. The intransitive option (d) is blocked because the destroyer would have to outrank the destroyee. Note that any saliency hierarchy in which *actor* outranks the *changed* in nouns would have to resort to some extra mechanism to block (d); this is the chief pay-off in an ordering of the noun hierarchy which ranks *changed* elements above others.

The following examples would then seem to be problematic:

(10a) The shooting of the deer
(10b) The shooting of the hunters

(11a) The approval of the program
(11b) The approval of the deans

If *program* and *deer* are assigned the feature *changed* in these examples, then both the (b) examples are the sort that did not occur with *destruction*. If the role *changed* is not involved, then the examples are not problematic; let us for the sake of discussion assume they are. For *approval* and *shooting*, then, the *changed* element can be omitted while the other element is not. The way to handle these examples within the framework of the current proposal is to have the *changed* element be semantically optional for both these nouns. We will deal with the question of optionality in somewhat greater detail in the next section, but the relevant point here is this: when an element is marked as optional in a lexical representation, the grammar may treat that lexical item as if the element were not present at all. The Saliency Hierarchy may then safely ignore it. This move complicates things a little. Now in order to account for the non-occurrence of *the destruction of heaven* in the relevant reading we need to say that with *destruction* the *changed* element is semantically obligatory. This may seem a peculiar claim, given noun phrases like *the destruction*, but we will establish a general basis for making such claims in the next section when we draw a distinction between semantic and syntactic obligatoryness. The case of *destruction* will be taken up then.

In sum, what I am proposing is that the Saliency Hierarchy and the mapping into the syntax be arranged so as to give nouns more options than verbs. The result would be that the scene DESTRUCTION could gives rise to three separate logical predicates. Let us assume predicate conventions for nouns quite parallel to those for verbs: "intransitive" nouns map into two-place predicates, one of whose position is a frame-position; "transitive" nouns map into three-place predicates. Nouns also have an option which verbs do not have; they may have *all* of their core participants realized obliquely. Such non-argument-taking nouns map into one-place predicates. DESTRUCTION, for example, yields three predicates, one one-place, one three-place, and one two-place. Some examples:

(12a) The destruction was awful.
((THE X (DESTRUCTION1 X)) (AWFUL X))

(12b) The destruction of Tyre by heaven was awful.
((THE X (AND (DESTRUCTION2 X Tyre)
(BY x heaven))) (AWFUL X))

(12c) Tyre's destruction by heaven was awful.
((THE X (AND (DESTRUCTION2 X Tyre)
(BY x heaven))) (AWFUL X))

(12d) Heaven's destruction of Tyre was awful.
((THE X (AND (DESTRUCTION3 X Tyre Heaven))) (AWFUL X))

The most unconventional choice I have made above is to represent versions of *destruction* often assumed to be the output of passive as in some sense basic. That is, I posit no relation-changing rules that link these different predicates; they exist solely in virtue of the option in the grammar to "create" both intransitive and transitive nouns from the same semantic material. Again, I have taken the choice of creating several predicates from a single lexical representation, as I did with adjunct and argument prepositions like *against*. In doing this I am exploiting a possibility generally available to us once we recognize a level of lexical representation, the possibility that the grammar will leave us certain options in the mapping to grammatical form, and that sometimes multiple options may be taken. Thus, alternations that seem like rules need not in any formal sense be rules at all. They are simply areas of flexibility. This will be the account adopted for Dative Movement and promotion of Instruments to Objects as well. The strongest argument I know for placing these alternations on a different level from relation-changing rules like passive is the morphology. In particular, there is no morphological reflex for the "passive" in noun phrases, or Dative Movement in verbs.

The same case for instrument-promotion is more difficult (cross-linguistically) and will be discussed in a bit more detail in Chapter 4.

One of the chief advantages of this treatment is that, without a syntactic passive rule for nouns, we do not have to explain a semantically systematic class of "exceptions":

(13) *John's love by Mary

(14) *Kant's perception by John

(15) *physics's knowledge by John

These facts fall right out of the noun hierarchy as given.

A final point to be taken up about nominal passives is *by*. The analysis sketched above assumes that *by* in noun-phrases is as contentful a preposition as, say, *against* in verbs. It has been argued

(Bresnan 1976) that *by* can always be analyzed this way, on the basis of examples like:

(16) A symphony by Beethoven

The problem with this claim is that Passive affects a bewildering semantic variety of verbs, and the roles of the "demoted" subjects are simply too varied to be characterizable with anything but the vaguest meanings. To borrrow an example from Anderson 1977:

(17) The top of the hill was occupied by an obelisk.

I thus prefer to call *by* with verbal passives a grammatical preposition, and limit its active semantic life to marking *actor* or *causer* with nouns. That *by* occurs in this sense in nouns in other than passive contexts is shown by both the Beethoven example above and others like:

(18) The decision by IBM to go public

Note that if nominal *by* has no grammatical status, it should compete with other semantically appropriate prepositions to mark complements. This seems to be the case:

(19) The order by the general to leave.

(20) The order from the general to leave.

Note that in () and () the participant marked with *by* can also be marked with *of*. This can be accounted for by allowing the lexical representations of *decision* and *order* to be realized both as intransitive nouns and non-argument-taking nouns. The intransitive versions take grammatical *of*; the non-argument versions take *by*. *Decision* and *order* thus exhibit two of the three possibilities exhibited by *destruction* above.

If the distribution of *by* in nouns is semantically governed, then it ought to show a more restricted distribution in nouns than in verbs; the emotion nouns in () constitute an entire class whose verbal passives take *by* and whose nominal "passives" do not. Less systematically, there are nouns which exhibit passive-like valence alternations, neither of which has any grammatical claim to being more basic, and neither of which uses *by*:

(21a) John's gift to Deirdre
(21b) Deirdre's gift from John
(21c)*Deirdre's gift by John

(22a) Joan's interview with John
(22b) Joan's interview
(22c) *John's interview by Joan

By this point, I hope to have shown that the idea of different saliency hierarchies for different syntactic categories at least has some interesting possibilities. I have presented a case in some details for nouns, but Amritavalli's evidence argues that a similar case could be made for adjectives. If that is so, the treatment proposed for nominal passives could be extended to adjectival passives, including those cases discussed in Wasow 1977 as instances of a second "lexical" passive rule which creates adjectives.

There is an interesting complication in the Saliency Hierarchy for adjectives, though. If we followed a line somewhat like that which we followed with nouns, we would simply take the *Experiencer* statement in the Hierarchy, and move it to the head of the list, ahead of the statements involving *actors* and *causers*. But there is some question whether adjectives ever involve *actors* and *causers*, given their stative nature, and thus whether any substantive change to the verbal hierarchy is necessary for adjectives.

A final point to note in passing is that some such division among categories is necessary if our proposed addition to Saliency Hierarchy, "The Superior outranks the Inferior," is to stand. This is because there are both adjectives and nouns whose subjects can rank lower on some scale than an oblique argument.

(23) Two is less than three.

(24) The inferiority of object to subject

Thus the scope of this Saliency Statement must be limited to verbs.

3.4.2 Optionality and Instruments

One last piece of business needs to be transacted before we return to the hierarchy itself. This is to revise our treatment of *instruments*. Until now we have been treating *instruments* just like other adjuncts. The problem with this is that, as we have seen, they can sometimes become nuclear terms. We thus want to grant them genuine argument status so that we can manipulate them just along with other arguments in the hierarchy. We need to do this in a way that does not lose what we had captured in the previous account, the fact that the *actor* was understood as *manipulator*. Also, to get anywhere at all, we are finally going to have to say something about optional arguments.

That optionality exists is uncontroversial in anyone's theory. That there need to be two kinds of optionality is a point often overlooked. To make this point it will be useful to return to several of the verbs of LONGING we discussed in chapter one. I claim that *try*, *apply*, and *wish* cannot appear discourse initially without their complements. This point can be nicely illustrated with a test originally suggested in Panevova 1974 and elaborated in Peter Sgall 1980. The following exchange indicates that a misunderstanding or omission has occurred:

(25) -- John applied

(26) -- What did john apply for?

Compare:

(27) -- John read.

(28) -- What did John read?

The question in () can be read as a request for amplification on information the addressee may or may not have. The question in (), however, had better be answerable, or else the first speaker had no business *saying* that John applied in the first place.

Another "well-formed" example might serve to make the contrast clearer:

(29) -- John loaded the truck

(30) -- What did he load it with?

Here, it seems to me, the first speaker can felicitously reply: -- I don't know, but he had to do it all alone, because Mary wouldn't lift a finger. That is, the contents of the truck can be utterly irrelevant with *load*; the *karman* cannot be with *apply*.

Another sort of test involves negation:

(31a) John hasn't applied yet.

(31b) John hasn't loaded the truck yet.

I believe (a) can be uttered so that it commits the speaker only to a claim about a specific application. That is, if the speaker utters (a) in a context where applications for Florida trucking jobs are at issue, (a) will still be true even if John has applied for a Berkeley post-doc. In contrast, even if the last hour's conversation has revolved round a half ton of bananas stored in a nearby warehouse, (b) is literally false if John has packed the salient truck full of oranges.

The right way to talk about *apply* seems to be to say that it is possible to omit overt syntactic expression of the *karman*, but that the *karman* must always be semantically present. Fillmore (personal communication) has suggested calling such cases of purely syntactic optionality *omissibility*, and reserves the term *optionality* for semantically optional elements like the direct object of *read* and the locative complement of *load*.

Returning to our example from 3.4.1, *destruction*, a similar distinction can be made.

(32) -- The destruction was wanton and willful.

(33) -- The destruction of what?

Here, the first speaker must know of which carnage he speaks, or he is not engaged in cooperative communication. There is a related sense of *destruction* here which is not issue, meaning something like the substance resulting from the destruction, or perhaps, in some poetic sense, the effect itself: "The destruction went on for miles." One can imagine such a description uttered by a speaker confronted with miles of rubble, with no idea what structures once stood in its place. In this use *destruction* seems to be a mass noun denoting a substance (perhaps an abstract substance), and presumably the correct lexical representation would be one without any core participants. What concerns us here is *destruction* in the use where it denotes an event.

Having drawn this distinction between omissibility and optionality we return to *instruments* and ask, which are they? The Panevova test tells us they are truly optional. There is no misunderstanding or failed communication in the following exchange:

(34) -- Bill hit John.

(35) -- What did he hit him with?

I proposed that we represent such truly optional elements as optional slots in frames. Whereas elements that are merely syntactically optional, such as the *karman* of *apply*, will be represented at the frame level as ordinary slots; that is, every satisfactory instance of an *applying* situation will have to fill its *karman* slot. Sentences in which the *karman* is syntactically omitted will be treated as cases of null-anaphora. Thus, the missing syntactic material will have to be reconstituted in the semantic interpretation with objects of the appropriate type, just as it must be in resolving any of the cases of Anaphora Hankamer and Sag 1979 call Deep Anaphora.

In the case of *instruments* I propose to represent the optional material not just as an optional slot, but as an entire optional subscene of the frame. Consider the following ground scene:

```
(MANIPULATION: CAUSER-SEQUENCE
  [ANTECEDENT
   (DIRECTED-ACTION:ACTION;UNDERGOING
    (ACTOR <↑ACTOR>)
    (PATIENT<↑ INSTRUMENT>))]
  (CONSEQUENT
   (DIRECTED-ACTION:ACTION;UNDERGOING
    (ACTOR)
```

(PATIENT))))

When all the slots are filled this scene works as follows: it consists of a first ACTION scene in which an *actor* does something to an *instrument*; then there is a second ACTION scene in which the *actor* does something to a *patient*. When the first subscene is absent, matters reduce to a *actor* doing something to a *patient*.

The representation offered here is inspired by comments in Fillmore 1977a that suggest that thinking of *instrument* as a special kind of *patient* may help explain its occasional elevation to direct objecthood. Here I have represented *instrument* as the *patient* of an embedded scene, with the "ultimate" *patient* lodged in a resulting scene. Note that the *instrument* is not a participant in that resulting scene. This choice has made a number of technical details of the treatment that follows go smoother. But it is also supported by some crucial entailment facts:

(36a)John hit the fence with the stick.

(36b)John hit the fence.

(36c)The stick hit the fence.

It seems to me that (a) entails (b) much more naturally than it entails (c). (c) seems to have two readings, one "personification" reading, clearly not at issue, and another on which its strikes the fence not under any particular control; it may be flying through the air, some agent may be randomly swinging it about. Thus, on the true *instrument* reading of (c), the crucial feature of control is missing, while on the true *actor* reading of (a) it is required. John may hit the fence accidentally, but he must be controlling the stick when he does. We will return to this concept of control below.

We now need to articulate the figure scene for the instrumental meaning of *with*. The following would seem like a good candidate:

```
(MANIPULATION_T: CAUSED_EVENT
  (INSTRUMENT)
  (CONSEQUENT (DIRECTED-ACTION
               (ACTOR)
               (PATIENT))))
```

Here CAUSED_EVENT is a constituent of CAUSER_SEQUENCE and MANIPULATION_T is thus a constituent of MANIPULATION. The lexical scene for *instrumental with*, call it MANIPULATION-L, will simply be AKO this scene and will reference reference MANIPULATION, without acquiring any structure not in MANIPULATION_T.

Note that nothing in MANIPULATION_T has been designated as optional; this, in fact, is what we want for the preposition's figure scene. Let us adopt the convention that any particular figure scene may require optional material in its ground scene to be realized. This is, in effect, a lexical choice made with respect to a particular scene description.

The treatment of *instrumental with* is intended to allow it either to be subcategorized-for or to be an adjunct. As an adjunct *instrumental with* modifies only ACTIONS, and the *actors* of those ACTIONS must be understood as the manipulators of the *instrument* (because of the ground MANIPULATION scene). I assume that most ACTION verbs take *instrumental with* as an adjunct: *break, turn, destroy, fix, operate, write,* and on indefinitely.

I want to argue, however, that there is a special class of ACTION verbs which subcategorizes for *instrumental with*, namely those that take the kind of instruments we called non-effective in 3.2.2: *hit, touch, beat, slam,* and *beat*. Fillmore has called these verbs of impingement.

The principal thing distinguishing the impingement verbs from the other ACTION verbs is that the verbs of impingement allow the instrument to become direct object:

(37) John hit the stick against the fence

(38) Mary beat her fist on the door.

(39) Ila slammed her shoe against the table.

Presumably any participant that can be realized as a nuclear term is a core participant.

I assume then that the verbs of impingement have further specifications of MANIPULATION as their ground scenes, and have figure scenes, compatible with MANIPULATION_L, in which the *instrument* is optional.

But what about the fact that all ACTION verbs allow *instruments* to be realized as subjects in the absence of the *actor*? The following example is paradigmatic.

(40) The hammer broke the vase.

I suggest that because of examples like these the notion *actor* must be extended beyond animates to embrace any of the effective agents that can be subjects for these verbs. This means that nothing will block examples like this one, discussed in Fillmore 1971:

(41) ?The storm broke the window with a tree.

This will have a coherent frame interpretation, but it will be one in which the storm manipulates a tree and in so doing breaks a window. That is, it will amount to a personification of the storm.

This analysis amounts to collapsing *instrument* with *actor* in subject position, and claiming that other *instruments* can only be understood as objects manipulated by an *actor* in a complex event. The immediate consequence for the Saliency Hierarchy is that the distinction between *causer* and *actor* is no longer necessary, and we can get by with one less statement.

One of the problems with such an analysis that Fillmore has discussed is an ambiguity in the sentence, "He hit the window," disambiguated in the following two texts:

(42a) I shoved John hard. He hit the window. The glass shattered.

(42b) John was furious with me. He hit the window. The glass shattered.

In both cases I will call John an *actor*, but in one case the physical event is one of his body, not under his control, striking the window; in the other, some part of his body, or perhaps even an instrument, makes contact under his control. Let us call an *actor* in control of an event an *agent*. Note that I have described the notion *agent* without reference to volition. This is because volition, although often cited as a feature distinguishing *agents* from *instruments*, seems to be orthogonal: In fact, adverbs of volition typically apply only to *actors* in control. In "John accidentally hit the window," John is unquestionably an *agent*. Only in the case of an entity in control of some course of events does the question of some accidental result arise. This is why it is peculiar to have:

(43) I shoved John hard. He accidentally hit the window.

What I have to say about these example will apply only to the verbs of impingement. The right description of these facts can, I believe, be had in the current analysis if we take a particular interpretation of what it means for a constituent of a scene to be optional.

What it means linguistically has, hopefully, already been made clear. But what it means conceptually has not. What does it mean to say that a HITTING scene has an optional subscene in which an instrument is wielded? Does it mean that the actions described in sentences with and without instruments differ significantly? It had better not. Rather, what it ought to mean is that the instrument component may be unspecified and unindividuated in an actual HITTING situation. On the other hand, in an APPLYING situation, both the *applicant* and the *karman* must be fully individuated and specific. The natural physical difference here is that the *blunt instrument* in a HITTING scene may actually be an undetached part of one of the participants, a hand or an elbow, and an absolute line cleaving *actor* from *instrument* may be hard to draw.

Suppose we say that having an optional subscene means two things:

(1) The participants of that subscene may be unspecified.

(2) The procedures connecting that subscene with the rest of the scene are to be viewed as constraints on its individuation. That is, they only apply when the subscene is fully specified.

Given (2) and a MANIPULATION scene with an unspecified *antecedent*, we are free to imagine any prior scene we like. Consider "John hit the window," on the reading where John is not an agent. Here we may imagine a prior ACTION in which a distinct *actor* has done something to John, or alternatively, a simple UNDERGOING:

(44) John slipped. He hit the window.

On the reading in which John is an *agent*, he is the *actor* of the *antecedent* scene, and the *patient* will fall within the usual range of blunt instruments, hammer, stick, elbow, nose.

What I essentially propose, then, is that the notion *agent*, or *actor* in control, has no place in either the Saliency Hierarchy or the lexical description of these verbs. Whether it ever has a place in lexical description is an open question. What would help decide us is to find a verb that took *instruments* but would not allow those *instruments* in subject position. In fact there do appear to be such verbs:

(45) John passed Mel the sample with his forceps.

(46) *The forceps passed Mel the sample.

To talk about the interpretation of an unindividuated prior scene will not do, of course, for verbs which do not have such a prior scene. This will presumably be the case for verbs that do not subcategorize for instruments. What I would like to suggest is the relevant ambiguity are far more difficult to get with the other verbs, and that this is further support for an analysis which treats the *instruments* of ordinary ACTION verbs as adjuncts.

(47) ?I picked John up and threw him across the room. He broke the window.

(48) ?I picked the hammer up and threw it across the room. It broke the window.

A final point that needs to be touched on. The above

representation for the MANIPULATION scene would seem to require that *instruments* occur only with transitive verbs, since both an *actor* and *patient* are in evidence. This can be fixed by having a kind of ACTION called REFLEXIVE action:

```
(REFLEXIVE-ACTION:DIRECTED-ACTION
 (ACTOR)
 (PATIENT (=actor)))
```

This will let us handle examples like "Superman walks with a cane." At the same time, it provides a general account for the bizarreness of notional instruments as the subjects of intransitives:

(49) The cane walks

If the above frame is a constituent of WALKING, the interpretation of (34) would have to be that the cane, by acting on itself, engaged in walking.

3.4.3 Kajita's Quandary and Subcategorization features

It may be useful to consider an "application" of the theory of instruments offered in the last subsection to a small puzzle articulated in Kajita 1967. The problem is the verb *serve*, which Kajita claims subcategorizes for transitive complements.

(50) The ice served to chill the beer.

(51) *The ice served to chill.

To subcategorize complements for arbitrary syntactic properties like transitivity is an unpleasant extension of the account of subcategorization embodied in most generative theories. In particular it raises the question of just how non-local the syntactic requirements that a head makes on its complements can be. Structurally, we have gone from the requirement [__ VP] to [__ [V NP]]. The theory of strict subcategorization proposed in Chomsky 1965, for example, did not allow this kind of specification.

What alternative account can we offer, then, to cover his facts?

Suppose we propose the following structures to describe *serve*:

```
(ACTOR_IN_ACTION
 (ACTOR)
 (ACTION (ACTION
          (ACTOR <^ ACTOR>))))

(SERVING: ACTOR_IN_ACTION
  (ACTOR_NOT_IN_CONTROL <ACTOR>)
  (ACTION
   (EFFECTIVE_ACTION_WITHOUT_CONTROL:ACTION; CHANGE
    (ACTOR_NOT_IN_CONTROL <ACTOR> <^
    ACTOR_NOT_IN_CONTROL>)
    (PATIENT <CHANGED>))))
```

First, as the basic structure on which to found our description, I propose a frame called ACTOR_IN_ACTION, which simply entifies the relation between an *actor* and the *action* that actor performs. The basic structure of this scene is thus of the right sort for a subject-equi verb, a relation between an individual and a scene. Other Equi verbs that would be natural further specifications of this scene: *bother*, *hasten*, *hesitate*, *offer*, *threaten*, and *venture*. SERVING itself is a specification of the ACTOR_IN_ACTION scene which makes two further requirements on the embedded ACTION; first, it involves a change in the *patient*; second, the *actor* must be "not in control," a role which I have simply called *actor-not-in-control*. *Actor-not-in-control* will always be a subject, since it is an elaboration of the *actor* slot.

The requirement that the embedded action involves change rules out cases like the following:

(52) *The stick served to hit the fence.

Recall that we have hypothesized that *hit* does not involve the role *changed*, in order to allow the *instrument* to become direct object. In Chapter 4, we will discuss a number of interesting predictions that follow if the role *changed* constrains a participant to be realized as a nuclear argument rather than obliquely. In the case where some other element was ranked above *changed*, this would constrain the clause to be transitive. The crucial data here involves some somewhat marginal examples, which may challenge Kajita's claim that the downstairs clause must be transitive:

(53) ? The needle served to pierce through the cushion

Under the proposed analysis of *serve*, such an example would also be a challenge to the general claim that a *changed* participant must be realized non-obliquely. The main point here is that complicating the syntactic theory of subcategorization is unnecessary in either case. If the above example is accepted, then Kajita's claim that *serve* takes only transitive clauses is wrong, and a semantic account of its complementation is more desirable. If the above example is not acceptable, then we may still have recourse to a general semantically stated constraint on role realizations: *changed* participants may not be realized obliquely. Nothing special has to be said about the subcategorization of *serve*.

Calling the slot occupied by the controller *actor-not-in-control* in both the embedded and the toplevel scene is not crucial to the treatment proposed. Most importantly, there is no intended claim that an equi controller must bear the same role in both the matrix and the embedded clause. The fact that many equi verbs allow both actors and embedded passives rules this course out. Here, however, it seemed the simplest of the alternatives. Note that *serve* does not allow embedded passives:

(54) *The needle served to be pierced through the cushion.

(55) *The beer served to be chilled.

Both these examples are ruled out by the requirement that the controller must bear the downstairs role of *actor-not-in-control*. This suffices to guarantee it must be "deep" subject in the downstairs clause: there are no verbs which, after passivization, have an *actor* in subject position.

In sum, we have proposed a treatment of *serve* which explains the behavior of the verb at the level of the lexical semantics, without any recourse to special syntactic devices. The fact that *serve* requires a two-participant clause as its complement is simply stipulated in its semantic description with devices we have motivated in a number of cases involving preposition descriptions.

3.4.4 A Note on Figure, Ground, and POS_TRANS

What I want to argue for in this section is that, given the *figure/ground* ranking in our current hierarchy, and given some plausible assumptions about the underlying structure of our POS_TRANS scene, the *patient* in a POS_TRANS scene outranks the *donor*.

To motivate this, we will need to return to the components of POS_TRANS proposed in Chapter 2.

```
(POS_TRANS: CAUSER_SEQUENCE
  (ANTECEDENT:COMPONENT
          (TRANSFERENCE
             (SOURCE)
             (FIGURE)))
  (CONSEQUENT:COMPONENT
           (POSSESSION
            (POSSESSOR)
            (PATIENT))))
```

The crucial thing point here is that TRANSFERENCE is a component of POS_TRANS and TRANSFERENCE has a slot called *figure* in it. What I had in mind in using that slot name in TRANSFERENCE was that TRANSFERENCE be an extension of ORIENTATION_IN_SPACE. I am thus proposing the following unpacked figure scene for TRANSFERENCE:

```
(TRANSFERENCE: ORIENTATION_IN_SPACE
  (FIGURE)
  (SOURCE <GROUND>))
```

As before this frame will also be the figure scene for the preposition *from*. Now I have claimed that TRANSFERENCE is a meaning of *from* appropriate even for non-spatial verbs like *buy*. Therefore, we will need some very general interpretation of ORIENTATION_IN_SPACE that does not limit it to conventional space. That is, there must be other kinds of spaces one can be oriented in besides conventional three-D Euclidean Space.

Let us concentrate here on the meaning of *from* relevant for verbs like *buy*. For *from* to make sense with *buy*, there must be such a thing as a POSSESSION space, a space in which there is no very useful notion of distance, but where there are distinct points corresponding to distinct possessors. A preposition like *over* is limited to other kinds of spaces, so that the sentence "The book is over John," has no "possessive" interpretation. In contrast we have, "The book is from John."

Suppose we interpret that as meaning "The book was once in John's possession." Then a reasonable interpretation of *from* is that *figure* is oriented with respect to a ground such that at some previous time, *figure* occupied the point in space defined by *ground*. In the example, we mean POSSESSION space, and therefore at some previous point in time, John possessed the book. Note that this decription incorporates an asymmetry between possessor and possessed. In this space, *possessors* are locations; possessed things are objects that can occupy them. How can we make this asymmetry part of the representation of TRANSFERENCE_GROUND (the ground scene for TRANSFERENCE)? More important, how can we distinguish this important asymmetry in TRANSFERENCE from the symmetry of VERTICAL_ORIENTATION_IN_SPACE, which was the ground scene for OVER and UNDER?

I propose that TRANSFERENCE_GROUND make explicit reference to the notion of a point-in-a-space, as opposed to the objects occupying it. Suppose that TRANSFERENCE_GROUND had two slots in addition to *figure* and *ground*, namely *figure-point* and *ground-point*, corresponding respectively to the point in space occupied by the *figure* and the point occupied by the *ground*. These notions are implicit in ORIENTATION_IN_SPACE, but there is no reason in that scene to individuate them into their own slots. The crucial difference for TRANSFERENCE is that one of the objects in the orientation scene is fixed in space. That is, if we are to think of possession as a kind of space with points corresponding to possessors, then "John" defines a fixed point in possession-space. Any object at that point belongs to John (including, perhaps, Albert, who defines a different point in possession-space). The difference with locating objects in physical space is that in most contexts we don't think of objects as defining fixed points in physical space. With all this in mind, I propose the following unpacked ground scene:

```
(TRANSFERENCE: ORIENTATION_IN_SPACE
  (SOURCE <FIGURE>)
  (FIGURE-POINT (PAST (= <GROUND-POINT>)))
  (GROUND)
  (GROUND-POINT(FIXED-LOCATION <GROUND>)))
```

Here I have made the *figure-point* equal the *ground-point* at some time in the past. I have also claimed that there is a functional relation FIXED-LOCATION, between *ground* and *ground-point*, FIXED-LOCATION must, of course, be set to the contextually appropriate space.

One of the chief virtues of this definition is that it constructs a role *source* within the TRANSFERENCE frame, without any reference to motion. The basic asymmetry of *from-ness* is attributed to the fact that the *ground* must determine a fixed point in some contextually relevant space. But the TRANSFERENCE_GROUND scene does not select any corresponding fixed-point for the *figure*. This does not rule out the possibility that the *figure* may possibly have such a fixed point in another context; possessors can possess other possessors. It is simply that in a sentence like "This slave is from Mary," we are interested in Mary as a possessor, not the slave. Similarly, in a sentence like, "This table is from Rome," we are interested in Rome as a fixed location, even though, in another context, the table can be viewed as a location.

With all this given, our description of TRANSFERENCE predicts that *figure* outranks *source*, because *source* is an elaboration of *ground*. The POS_TRANS scene, using TRANSFERENCE as a component, will inherit this ranking, and thus, unless a higher ranking role intervenes, *patient* will outrank *donor*. In verbs like *buy* and *sell*, a higher ranking role does intervene; the paticipant that is *donor* is also an *actor*, and that participant becomes subject.

One might now wish to extend this concept of possession space to the POSSESSION scene itself, also a component in POS_TRANS, and call the *possessor* a *ground* and the *patient* a *figure*. Such a move has a certain appeal, but it cannot be made in the POS_TRANS scene per se, if we are to use POS_TRANS as a component in figure scenes, and if we are to maintain uniqueness. We would then have a scene with the role *ground* assigned to both the *donor* and the *recipient*. In short, only one thing at a time can be regarded as *ground* in a figure scene or a component of a figure scene.

What, then, is the motivation for having an asymmetric treatment at all, for claiming that there is a ranking chosen in the TRANSFERENCE scene, but not in the POSSESSION scene? The relevant evidence is in verbs involving possession and tranference of possession. We have the following kinds of pairs:

(56a) John has a book
(56b) The book belongs to John

(57a) Alan gave the book to Sue.
(57b) Alan gave Sue the book.

Pairs like *have* and *belong* suggest that neither *possessor* and *patient* are preferred for subjecthood by the Hierarchy; the English Dative Movement alternation suggests the same thing for direct objects. We will take a closer look at Dative-Movement in the next chapter.

3.5 The Semantics of Valence

In this section we do two things. First, we present the procedure that implements the statements of the Saliency Hierarchy, and determines, as far as it is possible to determine them, possible subjects and direct objects for verbs. Next we present the procedure that actually marks verbs for possible prepositional complements, selecting only complements which are semantically compatible with the verb. These things taken together constitute a semantic characterization of a verb's possible valences; henceforth, we will refer to the particular configuration of nuclear terms and subcategorized-for complements that a verb syntactically selects as its valence. As we shall see, nothing in the current framework prevents a single lexical entry from selecting more than one valence.

3.5.1 A Hierarchy for Verbs

In the subsection on *instruments* we whittled the Saliency Hierarchy down by one statement. Before presenting the actual operation of the hierarchy on lexical entries, we will need to set aside two more statements, at least provisionally.

To begin with, I do not propose at this time to try to represent the phenomenon of definiteness. Clearly the appeal in the seventh statement in the Hierarchy is to something that is not a lexical semantic category. That Fillmore allows himself this is due, first of all, to some major differences of emphasis in the model he is building; his "scenes" are textual entities built up quite apart from the lexicon, or indeed, any linguistic structures. Although my scenes have a non-linguistic status as well, my proposal for implementing the Saliency Hierarchy involves reference to logical predicates, and these have little status outside the lexicon.

I thus propose simply to eliminate the claim about definiteness from consideration at present. Independently of lacking the means to handle such phenomena, I have some doubts that they should be handled with same kinds of mechanisms. Some very rough correlations between definiteness and grammatical function have often been noted in the literature (for example, subjects tend to be definite), but there are clearly parameters other than definiteness and subjecthood involved.

David Justice and Carl Pollard have independently supplied me with examples of predicates that simply seem to reject indefinite arguments:

(58) ?A unicorn was upsetting.

(59) ?A man was fat.

There are of course, numerous predicates that take indefinite subjects quite comfortably:

(60) A man is sitting along in his room.

The question here seems not so much one of subjecthood as of particular lexical semantics. The cases that have been dubbed Fillmore's Mystery by Peter Sgall (Sgall, et al, 1973), but which are actually due to Gruber (see Gruber 1976, p. 140), add another layer of difficulty, since what is presumably the same lexical item has different definiteness requirements in different valences.

(61a) Roman made the log into a canoe.
(61b)*Roman made a log into the canoe.
(61c) Roman made a log out of the canoe.
(61d) Roman made the log out of the canoe.

Minimally, there seems to be an interaction here among the lexical semantics, the nuclear term assignments, and what Halliday calls the Informational Level, that level at which notions like given and new come into play. I propose that the Saliency Hierarchy as such simply state constraints on the mapping from participant roles to grammatical roles, much as the original 1968 Subject Hierarchy did, without reference to any facts about the particular realizations of those roles in a sentence, such as definiteness.

Moreover, for simplicity's sake, I propose to also omit statement 5 in the hierarchy, "A complete or individuated element outranks a part of an element." This covers examples like "I picked him up by the ear." The technical problem is simply one of creating slots that represent "parts of" the contents of some of some other slot. This is an exercise that will not be particularly illuminating here, nor is the semantics of the scenes that should be involved particularly clear to me.

Below I list the statements left, along with frames that provide the necessary slots:

1. An *Actor* element outranks other element.

```
(ACTION
 (ACTOR)
 (PATIENT))
```

2. An *Experiencer* outranks other elements.

```
(INTENTIONAL_ATTITUDE
 (EXPERIENCER))
```

3. A *changed* element outranks other elements.

```
(CHANGE
 (CHANGED))
```

4. A *Figure* outranks a *ground*.

```
(ORIENTATION_IN_SPACE: THING
  (FIGURE)
  (GROUND))
```

5. A *Superior* element outranks an *Inferior*.

```
(RANKING
```

(SUPERIOR)
(INFERIOR))

The only scenes which the above hierachy will have anything to say about will be those which are extensions of one of the above five frames.

The implementation is rather simple, although the reader interested in a close examination of the technical details might wish to review 1.9, where the definitions for predicate denotations are given. Recall that the kind of lexicon assumed there had lexical entries that associated three things, a phonological representation, a morphosyntactic representation, and an interpretation for the lexical item, part of which is always the lexical semantic representation proper, a figure frame.

What the hierarchy does is place some constraints on the interpretation of the predicate. The predicate denotation of a lexical head that takes arguments is a sequence of a frame and slots. The slots in the denotation of the predicate correspond directly to particular predicate positions, and those positions, because of the phrase structure rules that build up the semantics of sentences, correspond in turn to particular grammatical functions.[2] Thus there is a mapping

---

2. Currently, the possible grammatical functions that can be signalled by the position of a slot in a denotation include only subject and object. In Chapter 5, I propose a new addition to the list, XCOMP.

from certain slots to grammatical function. The hierarchy defines which slots get top priority.

This can be modeled with the following sort of procedure. We will discuss only verbs here, though the general procedure carries over quite straightforwardly to other categories, given a Saliency Hierarchy for those categories. Recall that transitive verbs will be three-place predicates, and intransitive verbs will be two-place predicates. We are now engaged in stating what is predictable about their denotations. First we recognize a certain stipulation. Each lexical item begins by being associated with a particular frame in the frame representation for our English-speaking culture, that frame being its figure frame. Furthermore, the denotation of each lexical predicate is constructed from its figure frame. The figure scene, then, is always given. Let us think of predicate denotations as sequences, with one-place predicate denotations being one-place sequences (such denotations will be necessary for non-argument-taking lexical heads, say, *lamp*). Then, for all open-class lexical items, the first member of the sequence will always be its figure frame. The task of the Saliency Hierarchy is to constrain the possible choices of other members of the denotation sequence, given that they must be chosen from slots within the figure frame.

Imagine that the "choice" between a two- and three- place predicate (i.e., intransitive and transitive) is made in advance, that is, either by stipulation, or by factors independent of the operation of the hierarchy.

It will be helpful to consider the operation of the Hierarchy as a kind of redundancy rule, which fills in the missing parts of predicate denotations wherever possible — in much the same way as phonological redundancy rules fill in predictable features.

Consider a typical intransitive verb, say, *run*. Its denotation will be a pair consisting of the RUNNING frame and a slot, unspecified until our redundancy rule applies. Call that slot the subject slot, since it must correspond to subject position. We must now find the subject slot among the actor slots in the figure scene. By active slots I mean slots that haven't been used up yet in building the predicate denotation. We shall also refer to active participants, meaning those participants still associated with active slots. Since we're just getting started in this example, all the slots and participants in RUNNING are active. The implementation of statement one in the hierarchy, then, is to examine the RUNNING scene, and if it is an extension of ACTION, make the *actor* the subject slot (note: *actor* will always be a toplevel slot in a scene that is an extension of ACTION). If there is an *actor* it becomes the second member of the denotation sequence, and we simultaneously render all the slots associated with the same participant in RUNNING inactive (so as not to use them again later, if we happen to be looking for more denotation slots). Let us refer to the slots that mark the same participant as some slot S mentioned in the Hierarchy as the S slots. Thus, if RUNNING is an extension of *actor*, we put *actor* into the predicate denotation and render all the *actor* slots inactive. If RUNNING is not an extension of ACTION, then we move on to the second statement in the hierarchy. We ask if RUNNING is an extension of INTENTIONAL_ATTITUDE. If so, we make *experiencer* the subject slot, if it is still active, and render all the *experiencer* slots inactive. And so on. Until all available positions in the predicate denotation are filled or until all the statements in the hierarchy are exhausted. In the case of RUNNING there is only one available denotation position, presumably an ACTOR.

For a transitive verb like *take* there will be two available denotation positions, the second being the direct object slot.

Consider a simplified version of the entry for *take*

```
</tek/: [+ V, -N]:
<(TAKING
  (AKO (ACTOR_RECIPIENT))
  (REFERENT (TAKING-G))
  (ACTOR_RECIPIENT)
  (ACTOR <ACTOR_RECIPIENT>)
  (DONOR)
  (PATIENT)), UNSPECIFIED, UNSPECIFIED>>
```

The colons here separate the three parts of the lexical entry, the last part being of principle interest; it is a triple consisting first of a simplified figure scene for *take*, and then of two other unspecified elements; these will become the subject and object slots when our hierarchy redundancy rules fill them in.

Statement 1 in the hierarchy will be applicable to the above entry. It licenses the *actor* slot to become the subject slot. So we have:

```
</tek/: [+ V, -N]:
<(TAKING
  (AKO (ACTOR_RECIPIENT))
  (REFERENT (TAKING-G))
  (ACTOR_RECIPIENT)
  (ACTOR <ACTOR_RECIPIENT>)
  (DONOR)
  (PATIENT)), ACTOR, UNSPECIFIED>>
```

At this point all the *actor* slots become inactive; this includes *actor* and actor_recipient. The statement about *Experiencers* will clearly not apply to this entry. More problematic is the statement about the *changed*. We have not until now used the slot *changed* in constructing any lexical entries; the only substantive claim we have made about it is that movement is a kind of *change*; but in chapter 2 we argued that the POS_TRANS scene ought to be distinguished from scenes involvin physical movement. Thus, there is no particular reason to believe *changed* is a slot in the TAKING scene. This will continue to be the case even after we discuss the *changed* slot in the next chapter, a large part of which will be devoted to motivating and exploiting it.

The next statement, the one about *figure* and *ground*, will apply; in the last section, we unveiled a proposal whereby *donor* is an elaboration of *ground* and *patient* is an elaboration of *figure*.

Following through on that proposal means that TAKING will have *figure* as a top level slot. The fourth statement of the verbal hierarchy says "A figure outranks a ground." This only determines a choice if the active slots include both *figure* and *ground*. In fact, with TAKING, only two active participants are left, one with the role *figure*, one with the role *ground*. Given that a three-place denotation has been chosen for *take*, *figure* must occupy the last denotation position Therefore that must be the direct object slot. A more complete TAKING entry would be:

```
</tek/: [+ V, -N]:
<(TAKING
  (AKO (ACTOR_RECIPIENT))
  (REFERENT (TAKING-G))
  (ACTOR_RECIPIENT)
  (ACTOR <ACTOR_RECIPIENT>)
  (DONOR)
  (PATIENT)), ACTOR, FIGURE>>
```

We have now defined a complete interpretation for the predicate TAKING in any frame model. It must be the triple consisting of the TAKING frame and the slots *actor* and *figure*, which correspond in the fully unpacked frame to the *actor_recipient* and the *patient* respectively. Note that the choices dictated by the hierarchy depended only on structures that were common to all ACTOR_RECIPIENT verbs; we would thus expect that any transitive ACTOR_RECIPIENT verb would chose exactly the same participants as subject and object.[3]

This seems to be right; verbs like *buy and acquire* all fit the frame *NP V NP from NP*, with *actor* and *figure* in subject and object position, respectively.

Note the difference between the statement involving *figure* and *ground* and the ones before it. The statement that an *actor* outranks other elements entails that *actors* outrank all other participants. But *figures* outrank only *grounds*. *This means that some unranked role, not mentioned at all in the hierarchy, could win out over a figure*. The obvious candidate is *possessor*, with verbs like *give* and *sell*. For both these verbs the *ground* is also an *actor* and will already be safely in the subject slot by the time the *figure* clause in the Hierarchy is consulted. There will be no active *ground* for the *figure* to outrank and its fate will be indeterminate. In such cases, the Hierarchy offers an option; in chapter 4, I will sketch an analysis that claims that one consequence of that option is the valence alternation called Dative Movement.

---

3. Within the bounds of the Hierarchy, this is a reasonable expectation, but not a certainty. It is possible to have a verb that is AKO ACTOR_RECIPIENT but also has some other salient role not present in *take*. Suppose, for example, the *donor* was also *changed*; then the *donor* would become direct object in preference to *patient*. Nothing in the current set-up forbids such a verb.

3.5.2 Subcategorization

A last remaining concern of lexical entries is the question of subcategorization. Let us adopt the following rather humdrum principle: a verb with n core participants subcategorizes for n-1 things. Subjects will not be subcategorized-for, but will always be supplied by the phrase structure rules. One way to subcategorize for a core participant is to realize it as a direct object. Whether a particular head realizes a given core participant as a direct object is, as far as we are concerned here, a matter of stipulation. That stipulation is encoded into the denotation assigned the lexical head of a predicate. If a head has a triple as its denotation, it will be transitive, and will automatically select for a phrase structure rule of the form:

<V1 -> V N2 ....>

The exact means of implementing this selection is not particularly important here; but let us suppose for specificity that every verb with a 3-place denotation is redundantly marked +TRAN, which is a feature compatible only with rules of the above form. Whether anything follows the N2 above will depend on whether there are any other subcategorization features on the head.

To make this completely precise, we recall some terminology introduced in 2.4.2. There we defined a participant as a maximal elaboration set, where an elaboration set was a set of participant slots in some frame such that for any pair in the set, one slot was an elaboration of the other. That definition in turn rested on the notion of a participant slot. Neither *reference* nor *ako* count as participant slots. In addition, neither component slots nor subscenes count as participants. When we do want embedded scenes to count as participants, as we did with SERVING, and will in general with heads that have "propositional" participants, those scenes will be neither components nor subscenes.

The question before us now is the one we started with, preposition selection. We have already defined the interpretations of lexical heads so that they yield well-defined sentences only when combined with semantically compatible preposition meanings. But the notion of semantic compatibility applies only to core participants, and thus, to subcategorized-for complements. What we need to do, then, is make a connection between the syntactic marking on a head that selects its preposition complements, and its semantic compatibility possibilities.

This can be done with one basic principle:

(1) Compatibility: every lexical entry occurs in an interpretrable sentence.

We also need to impose the conditions of completeness and uniqueness to which we have been appealing all along. Completeness is not a condition on subcategorization as such, but on the relationship between an entire verb valence and all core participants. It is closely related to a principle I will call Availability, which we implicitly appealed to in the procedure that selected nuclear terms. This is the principle that guarantees that no participant occurs twice in the same valence. Thus:

(2) Completeness: all core participants must either be subjects or subcategorized-for, or optional. Optional participants must be subcategorized for or subjects in some valence.

(3) Availability: only active participants can be subcategorized-for or made subjects.

Uniqueness is simply a condition on lexical frames:

(4) Uniqueness: the intersection of the participants in a lexical frame must be null (Recall that participants are maximal elaboration sets).

With these principles given, syntactic complement marking can proceed freely. Exposition will be simpler if we think of complement marking as occuring "after" the hierarchy has operated. Consider the verb *take*, then, with the entry given for it above. *Take* has three core participants; it must thus subcategorize for two things. After the Saliency Hierarchy operates the only active participant is the one assigned the role *donor*. Let us consider three possible syntactic markings:

(1) We mark *take* WITH-3. Suppose marking a head WITH-3 means it subcategorizes for PP complements marked with instrumental *with*. But *instrumental with* is not in the compatibililty set of TAKING (MANIPULATION is not a component of TAKING and TAKING is not AKO MANIPULATION), and therefore every sentence built up with this subcategorization would have an undefined denotation. Thus, by Compatibility, this is not a possible subcategorization. (but note that *instrumental with* may still appear as an adjunct).

(2) We mark *take* TO-3, where T0-3 means a head subcategorizes for complements marked by *to* in the the *possessor* meaning. POSSESSION *is* in the compatibility set of TAKING, but the participant marked by *to* is the *possessor*, and *possessor* is not among the active slots in TAKING; it has already been realized as subject. By availability, this is not a possible subcategorization.

(3) We mark *take* FROM-2, where FROM-2 means a head subcategorizes for complements marked with *from* in its *source* meaning. *Source* is an element of the only active participant, and thus among the active slots. Therefore, this subcategorization is fine.

A few words now about syntactic indeterminacy. The procedure sketched out is not generative, in the sense that it does not produce all and only the subcategorizations of English. What it is intended to be is a characterization of possible subcategorizations, leaving options in just those places where the grammar leaves options, where language learners both big and small must resort to memorizing.

Two principal areas of flexibility should be noted. First, where prepositions compete for the same semantic territory, the theory has nothing to say:

(62) They thirsted for enlightenment.

(63) They thirsted after enlightenment.

In my private lexicon, both the prepositions *for* and *after* are compatible with *thirst*; but only *for* is compatible with *long*. The syntactic marking convention that would be needed here is one feature that allows either preposition for *thirst*, say, AFTER-FOR, and another that allows only *for* for *long*, say FOR. Both are possibilities given the above characterization of subcategorization.[4]

Next, there are numerous cases where the use of a particular preposition with a particular verb is hard to motivate. One of my favorite examples:

(64) He doted on her.

While the use of *on* here may not be a stunning surprise, it is hard to imagine predicting it. At the very limit, given a lexicon and a syntactic theory where verbs and prepositions need to be separate

---

4. Meg Withgott (personal communication) has suggested that these facts be handled with some mechanism either analogous to or identical with the mechanism that handles morphological pre-emption or "blocking." This is the principle appealed to explain, for example, the absence of *mans* as a plural of *man* in the presence of the irregular *men*. Following a parallel account here would offer some means of characterizing certain subcategorizations as "productive." Suppose *for* was the productive means of marking *karman*; then only exceptional heads like *hanker* would mark *karman* with *against*, and only those heads would need to be specially marked. Still more exceptional would be those heads like *thirst* that took both *for* and *against*; such heads would have to be doubly marked.

entries, we may need to have preposition meanings which are only compatible with one head. On the face of it, this may seem like a mere terminological variant of syntactic selection. But it is not a terminological variant at all if we conclude that because there are some cases of idiosyncratic preposition selection, then all prepositon selection is pidiosyncratic. This line leads us to throw preposition meanings away altogether, and that in turn leads to an intolerable loss of generalization.

It seems far preferable to say that semantic selection is itself a pervasive phenomenon, operating at various degrees of productivity, which, at the lower limit, turns into the phenomenon of idiomaticity.

4. Valence Alternations

The title of this chapter is a bit misleading since my concern will not be all types of valence alternation, but only that type that exhibits some regularity across heads, in other words, alternations that might be reasonable candidates for lexical rules:

(1a) John and Mary met.
(1b) John met with Mary.

(2a) Bill cleared the room of junk.
(2b) Bill cleared the junk out of the room.

(3a) Anne loaded the truck with hay.
(3b) Anne loaded hay onto the truck

(4a) An oak tree developed out of the acorn.
(4b) The acorn developed into an oak tree.

(5a) Harry beat the stick against the fence.
(5b) Harry beat the fence with the stick

(6a) Rita sent Alice a robin.
(6b) Rita sent a robin to Alice.

I will limit my discussion to those rules which are exemplified above, the unifying theme being that these alternations seem to have fairly clear semantic domains. This eliminates from consideration old favorites like passive.

The principal problem of this chapter is that of drawing some distinctions among these various cases of semantically governed valence

alternation. Given that we have the means of associating more than one valence with a particular lexical entry (for example, because of optional constituents in frames), and given that we need morphological rules, how do we tell which way to handle the above alternations? It would be theoretically desirable to have some way of distinguishing true morphological alternations from simple cases of valence options. In this chapter, we will show how the framework already given allows us to represent all of the above valence alternations as valence options in single lexical entries. We will also discuss the possibility that the mechanisms for representing valence options are too powerful. It is particularly significant that some of the alternations above are the sort handled in other languages with affixation.

In pursuing accounts of these phenomena, the methodological imperative is that our results be consistent with satisfactory accounts of the lexical semantics of heads and prepositions — where the notion "satisfactory" includes an account of basic compatibility facts.

In 4.1 we will deal with a pair of relatively simple examples of independent interest, first Dative Movement, then what I have called Instrument Promotion, the advancement of Instruments to direct object with the verbs of impingement. In 4.2 we will deal with the other rules en masse, focusing on the alternation exhibited in ().

4.1 Optional Advancement

4.1.1 Instrument Promotion

Let us begin by reviewing what the hierarchy has to say about the MANIPULATION scene introduced in the last chapter for verbs of impingement and the preposition *with*. Recall that in MANIPULATION_T, the template scene for the prepositions, there were no optional elements; let us assume that all the verb templates are built on a nearly identical scene, MANIPULATION_T', which differs only in that the *instrument* is optional.

```
(MANIPULATION_T': CAUSED_EVENT
  [INSTRUMENT]
  (CONSEQUENT (DIRECTED-ACTION
                (ACTOR)
                (PATIENT))))
```

Note that for MANIPULATION_T' to be compatible with MANIPULATION_T, the preposition scene, the notion of constituent defined in 2.4.2 will have to ignore optional structure. That is, MANIPULATION_T and MANIPULATION_T' will have to count as having the same structure in order for them to be semantically compatible.

Let us begin by considering what happens to the verbs of impingement for valences where the optional *instrument* is present. As far as the Hierarchy goes, these verbs are rather trivial: there are three participants to deal with, but only one role, the *actor* role, that is mentioned in the Hierarchy. Thus the *actor* becomes subject.

Assuming that the option *transitive* has been chosen, there will be two different denotations licensed by the hierarchy:

(A) <MANIPULATION, ACTOR, INSTRUMENT>
(B) <MANIPULATION, ACTOR, PATIENT>

(A) and (B) line up alphabetically with the following examples:

(7a) John beat the stick against the fence.
(7b) John beat the fence with the stick.

The theory of possible valences developed so far says that any verb which is an extension of the above scene may exhibit either or both valence possibilities, if its own template scene introduces no new salient roles.

Let us consider choice (B) first. In choice (B), the *patient* will be direct object. Assume for simplicity that the lexical scene for *beat* has MANIPULATION_T' itself as its template, and references some more fully specified version of MANIPULATION. *Instrumental with* has MANIPULATION_T as its template scene, and is thus semantically compatible with *beat*. By Compatibility, it can therefore be subcategorized by *beat* to mark the *Instrument* role. Thus all the participants of the figure frame have found a home.

In order to consider choice (A), we will have to say something about *against* and *on*, the two prepositions that mark *patient* for the verbs of impingement. In Chapter 3, we simplified a bit when we took the MANIPULATION scene as a description of the common situational content among the verbs of impingement. In addition to manipulating one object to act on a second, the impingement scene involves the manipulated object coming into contact with that second object. It is chiefly this second component which licenses the appearance of *on* and *against*:

(8) The ball bounced on the table.

(9) The rock banged against the wall.

These are verbs of impingement in their intransitive incarnations. Here there can be no question of manipulation, yet *on* and *against* are still appropriate. The contact need not involve an *actor*, but it does involve a voyage. One object has arrived from elsewhere. As the ground scene that both prepositions will access I propose:

```
(ENCOUNTERED-CONTACT:CAUSAL-SEQUENCE
 (ANTECEDENT: COMPONENT
   (UNDERGOING
    (PATIENT)))
 (CONSEQUENT:COMPONENT
   (CONTACT
    (THEME <^ ANTECEDENT PATIENT>)
    (TARGET))))
```

What we have thus far is this: one object is undergoing something (perhaps hurtling through the air); as a result it comes into contact with another. Note that this representation makes no reference to movement. Perhaps the ground scenes should stipulate movement, but that will not affect the present discussion, because none of the figure scenes for verbs of impingement will reference any roles related to movement. This is crucial because we are treating movement as a kind of change. If we were to view the *theme* in the above representation as moved in a figure scene, then it would be ranked by the Saliency Hierarchy; since *instrument* must be aligned with *theme* for the verbs of impingement, this would incorrectly predict that those verbs can choose only the valence in (A) above.

The exact status of the role *moved* will be discussed in 4.3.1.2 For the time being, we will simply assume by hypothesis that the *instrument* with verbs like *hit* is not "viewed " as moving in the figure scene.

Since ENCOUNTERED-CONTACT and MANIPULATION are both AKO CAUSAL-SEQUENCE, we can create a new frame, AKO both, which simply merges the requirements each makes on its slots. This frame, call it IMPINGEMENT, will be a constituent in the ground scenes for all our verbs of impingement.

```
(IMPINGEMENT: MANIPULATION; ENCOUNTERED-CONTACT
  (ANTECEDENT
    (DIRECTED-ACTION: UNDERGOING; ACTION
      (ACTOR)
      (PATIENT)))
   (CONSEQUENT:COMPONENT
     (DIRECTED-ACTION-CONTACT: DIRECTED-ACTION; CONTACT
       (ACTOR)
       (THEME <↑ ANTECEDENT PATIENT>)
       (TARGET <PATIENT>))))
```

The simplest assumption to make about a template scene for the prepositions *on* and *against* is that it is the ENCOUNTERED-CONTACT scene;[1] for the verbs, we will want something compatible with both ENCOUNTERED-CONTACT and MANIPULATION_T' (the figure scene for *instrumental with*). This will serve:

```
(IMPINGEMENT-T: MANIPULATION_T'; ENCOUNTERED-CONTACT
  [-1 ANTECEDENT:COMPONENT
       (UNDERGOING
         PATIENT <^ INSTRUMENT>) ]-1
  (CONSEQUENT:COMPONENT
    (DIRECTED-ACTION-CONTACT
      (ACTOR)
      [-1 THEME <^ ANTECEDENT PATIENT>  ]-1
      (TARGET <PATIENT>) )))
```

This frame contains a new notational convention, indexed square brackets. This is to record that the various optional structures in the frame are related, that, in fact, there is only one option; either leave in all mention of the *instrument*, or take it out. There is no option, say, just to leave out the *theme* role in the *consequent* scene, but leave in the entire *antecedent* subscene. When there are independent optional constituents in the same frame, their square brackets will have different indices.

This new convention deserves some comment; first of all, the aim of the brackets is to say that all roles that are elaborations of roles inside the optional *antecedent* slot must be omitted when the *antecedent*

---

1. This is the first time we have made a template scene equal a ground scene; formally, this is done simply by having the value of the AKO slot equal the value of the reference slot. This makes the Rule of Referenced Structure apply vacuously.

slot is omitted. That cannot just be a convention because presently we will want to have roles that are optional independently of their elaborations. On the other hand, we shall never need to have arbitrary chunks of frame structure be optional; for example, we shall never want to omit two participants simultaneously. The bracket convention in principle would allow this, which suggests it is too powerful. We shall return to this point in Chapter 5.

I will assume that the template scene for *hit* is IMPINGEMENT-T. I also assume that *hit* references some further specification of IMPINGEMENT, that the template scene for *on* and *against* is ENCOUNTERED-CONTACT, and that the template scene for *instrumental with* is MANIPULATION_T.

Since *hit* has two denotation possibilities, it will have two possible valences, because choices A and B will leave different participants active. We must thus assume that a single lexical entry may have different syntactic feature matrices, corresponding to its different subcategorizations. Moreover, each of those feature matrices must be linked to a particular predicate denotation. Thus, instead of having a lexical entry be a simple triple, we shall have it be a triple consisting of a phonological representation, a figure scene, and an n-tuple; the n-tuple consists of pairs of predicate denotations and syntactic representations, with the convention that the syntactic representations differ only in their subcategorizations, and the predicate denotations differ only in options allowed by the Saliency Hierarchy and the figure frame. An oversimplified version of *hit*:

```
<hit,
(HITTING:IMPINGEMENT-T
  (HITTER)
  (HITTEE)
  [INSTRUMENT]),
<<<HITTING, HITTER, INSTRUMENT>, [+V, -N, TRAN, ON-
  AGAINST]>,
 <<HITTING, HITTER, HITTEE>, [+V,-N, TRAN, (WITH)]>>
```

Here, the syntax associated with the first denotation requires an NP complement followed by a single prepositional phrase headed by either *on* or *against*, while the second denotation requires an NP, and allows an optional *with* PP, or perhaps better, either a *with* PP or a nothing.

A word is in order here about the interpretation of optionality in a generic frame. To put an optional slot in a generic frame means that an individual instance of that frame may or may not have a value for the given slot. How, then, do we prevent the wrong kind of individual frames from showing up to instantiate *hit* when it has its instrument complement? That is, suppose we have the sentence, "John hit Bob with a stick." How do we keep from getting an instantiating frame that has no value for its *instrument* slot.

We keep from getting such a frame because our interpretation of the sentence disallows it. Consider the logical representation:

(EXISTS* SIGMA (EXISTS X (AND (HITTING SIGMA JOHN BOB)

```
(STICK X)
(WITH SIGMA X))))
```

The denotation of this sentence is a non-empty property set just in case there is a hitting situation whose *actor* is John and whose *patient* is Bob, and whose *instrument* is some entity that is a stick. Let us call such situations satisfying situations. We shall say a situation S satisfies a property set just in case it is one of the "generators" of that property set. A property set P has a set of generators G if all and only the sets containing members of G are in P. The property set corresponding to *a walking man* is a set of sets containing walking men. The set of walking men is the generator set G. The property set corresponding to the above logical representation is the set of sets containing a situation in which John hits Bob with a stick. Situations in which John hits Bob with a stick are thus satisfying situations.

Any hitting situation which satisfies the above sentence of logic must have its instrument slot filled. If there are no such hitting situations available, then no hitting situations in the frame model matches the one described, and the property set is empty.

The syntactic requirements on a head thus specify which kind of instantiating situations will satisfy it. A predicate whose interpretation is <HITTING, ACTOR, INSTRUMENT> can only be satisfied by HITTING situations with fully specified *instruments*. Similarly, if a head optionally takes instrument complements (like the second of our above denotations for *hitting*), only situations with with their instrument slots filled can satisfy the logical representation of a sentence in which the optional instrument complement has been included.

We have thus sketched an account of a small group of "instrument promotion" verbs that does not posit a lexical rule of instrument promotion, but simply leaves the different valences as options of grammatical realization. Such an account does not constitute a claim that the alternative realizations have no linguistic significance. Fillmore 1977a points out that the sentences:

(10a) I hit the stick against Harry
(10b) I hit the stick against the fence

differ in naturalness. (a) is more marked because in some way Harry seems to be viewed less as an animate being than as a physical object on which the stick happens to be impinging. There is a general tendency for animates to rank higher wherever possible, and given that, taking the option of giving an animate low rank inevitably communicates something. The feature animate thus has a status something like the feature definite; it participates in certain conventions about how the information in a clause is organized (within the options offered by the grammar), and violations of those conventions can themselves be informative.

Nothing in the account we have given compels any impingement verb to take both options. Thus, we would expect to find exceptions to the pattern. A likely candidate:

(11a) He covered the bed with the bedspread.
(11b) *He covered the bedspread on the bed.

Interestingly, I find no exceptions that go the other way, that is, impingement verbs in which the *instrument* may be direct object, but not the *patient*.[2] This may well be a reflection of the fact the valence in which *instrument* is direct object is in some sense more marked. If this is so, the treatment given here suggests that the account of why such constructions are more marked belongs in the theory of the information structure of the clause, and not in theory of how lexical semantics affects nuclear realizations.

I mentioned in the last chapter that one of the strongest arguments for a non-syntactic account of such a valence alternation is the lack of any morphological reflex. Indeed, this is the crucial property that Marantz 1981 notes in proposing a non-lexical rule account of Dative Movement (the actual mechanism he appeals to is analogy). Note that like Dative Movement, Instrument Promotion applies to only a very small semantically defined set of verbs, and the possibility of the valence option is dependent on there being

---

2. *Put* might seem like just what we want, but unlike other impingement verbs, *put* requires no contact between the VP participants:

(i) John put the bedspread under the bed.

prepositions to mark either of the possible oblique roles. Of course, the inventory of prepositions (or case markings) will differ from language to language. So, too, will the inventory of valence options.

I thus want to claim that the existence of regularities like "instrument promotion" and "dative movement" (as we shall see in the next section) is due to two factors:

(1) options left open by the hierarchy.

(2) the available complement marking apparatus of the language.

Suppose, as may be the case, that Dative Movement is a much more widespread phenomenon cross-linguistically than Instrument Promotion with verbs of impingement. The reason for this might well be that the complement-marking apparatus for Dative Movement is much more widespread than the complment marking apparartus for instrument promotion. In other words, markings semantically equivalent to *possessive-to* and the double object construction may be much more common than markings semantically equivalent to *instrumental with* and *contact on* and *against*. Surely there are cross linguistic tendencies in lexical semantics just as there are in syntax; and one of the basic assumptions of the framework adopted here is that the semantics of complement markers is a fundamental part of lexical semantics.

4.1.2 Dative Movement

Much of the literature on Dative Movement has proceeded under the assumption that it is meaning-preserving. There are a number of important examples that challenge this assumption, discussed in Green 1974 and Oehrle 1976. A small sampling from Oehrle 1976

(12a) Max is teaching the class trigonometry
(12b) Max is teaching trigonometry to the class

(13a) The doctor gave Mary an attractive skin
(13b) The doctor gave an attractive skin to Mary

(14a) Nixon gave Mailer a book
(14b) Nixon gave a book to Mailer.

Let me begin with the verb *teach*. The sentences in () alternate between what Oehrle calls an activity and a causal reading. The causal sense is paraphrasable roughly as "cause to know or learn." The activity sense, as Oerhle puts it, "corresponds to an activity associated with this goal."[3] The bottom line, truth conditionally speaking, is noted by Green. (a) entails that the class leasns some trigonometry, (b) is neutral on this point.

One line to take is that there are two verbs *teach*, differing in semantics and valence. Call the version of *teach* in (a) *activity teach* and the version in (b) *causal teach*. A striking piece of evidence for

---

3. p. 72

an analysis with two separate verbs was noted by Oerhle. There are differences in selectional restrictions on the subject position, depending on whether the prepositional costruction or the double object construction is chosen:

(15) Visiting Tijuana taught the children the value of the dollar.

(16) *Visiting Tijuana taught the value of the dollar to the children.

There are selectional differences with respect to what is taught as well. Oehrle notes that in general the prepositional construction is suitable only with academic subjects, where the double object has a broader application.

If we continue to speak of two verbs *teach*, then there is some evidence that *activity teach* shows both valences.

(17a) He taught French.
(17b) He taught the children.
(17d)*Visiting Tijuana taught the children.
(17e)*Visiting Tijuana taught the value of a dollar.

The natural source for (a) is activity *teach*, the natural source for (b) causal *teach*, on an account where each takes the oblique constituent optionally. But (d) and (e) suggest that *activity teach* has no optional arguments, so where does (b) come from? Calling both complements of *activity teach* optional, and allowing it to take both valence options solves this problem.

A similar line will serve for (). (a) is ambiguous between a reading on which Mary has had an operation, and a reading on which she is the recipient of bizarre gift. (b) has only the bizarre reading. Again, let us suppose there are two verbs *give*, one the garden variety transference of possession verb, the other with a meaning paraphrasable as "endow with". Once again, different selectional restrictions help support this view:

(18a) The accident gave John an unattractive face.
(18b)*The accident gave an unattractive face to John.

The final example involves a special reading for (a): Nixon, either voluntarily or involuntarily, is a necessary cause in Mailer's writing a book. This reading is much clearer with an event as subject.

(19) Nixon's resignation gave Mailer a book

Again, the prepositional construction is not grammatical when the subject is an event. The same account as before will suffice; there are two verbs *give*, one meaning very roughly "necessary cause" which allows event subjects, the other meaning "possession transference" and requiring animate subjects.

A pattern is beginning to emerge:

(20a) Her veiled look sent the barkeep a warning.
(20b)? Her veiled look sent a warning to the barkeep.

(21a) A careful reading showed the scholar the awful truth.
(21b)? A careful reading showed the awful truth to the scholar.

(22a) The eerie light lent the officer a vulpine air.

(22b)? The eerie light lent a vulpine air to the officer.

(22a) Her weary eyes told the prelate the whole story.
(22b)? Her weary eyes told the whole story to the prelate.

The judgements are not all equally secure here, but they give unmistakable evidence of a trend; the prepositional valence has extra restrictions on it that disfavor inanimate subjects.

In each case an analysis that claims there are two verbs instead of one is observationally adequate. The problem with such an analysis as it stands is that it misses a common semantic thread uniting all the verbs:

> (1) In each case the selectional restrictions of the double object construction were broader; events were allowed in subject position; and the meaning of the verb in that valence was something like CAUSE to X, where X was a semantic component shared by the verb in both valences. Double object *give* means "cause to have"; double object *teach* means "cause to know".
>
> (2) Oehrle points out that the prepositional valence meanings have in common what he calls the "transference" property. In our terms, they posit a specific relationship between the *donor* and the *patient*, which holds prior to the POS_TRANS situation. For ordinary *giving* this is possession; for *teaching* this is knowledge. This "presupposition" is suspended in the double object valence. "Visiting Tijuana" doesn't know "the value of the dollar."

However, there is a feature of the example with *teach* which does not seem to have a systematic status. This is the "completion" aspect of the double object reading. In "He taught the class trigonometry," the class learns some trigonometry. The only other verb which seems to have related sense shift is *throw*. Another example of Oehrle's:

(23a) He threw the ball to the catcher, but it went wide.
(23b)*He threw the catcher the ball, but it went wide.

I am not going to try to treat this aspect of the semantics of the dative alternation, since convincing cases seem to be hard to come by. What is striking about the "completion" reading of the double object construction with these two verbs is its likeness to what Steven Anderson 1971 calls the "holistic" reading with verbs like *load*, referring to some examples first discussed in Partee 1964:

(24a) He loaded hay onto the truck.
(24b) He loaded the truck with hay.

In (b), but not (a), the truck must be completely filled by the load. In 4.3.1.2 I will propose a treatment of these cases in which the role *totally-affected* is crucial. The *goal* ("the truck") becomes direct object when it (optionally) occupies the *totally-affect* slot. One might suggest a similar line with a verb like *teach*. In the case where the constituent realizing the *pupil* role is direct object, that participant is "changed;" in particular their state of knowledge is changed. While I have no objection to this treatment for *teach*, it is does not seem to go through with other Dative Movement verbs, and here we are concerned with the semantic properties of the class as a whole.

I propose to capture the relevant semantic facts by tinkering with the ground POS_TRANS scene. Once again, we will add an optional constituent:

```
(POS_TRANS: CAUSAL-SEQUENCE; CONDITIONED-SCENE
  [PRECONDITION: SUBSCENE
    (POSSESSION
     (POSSESSOR <DONOR>)
     (PATIENT))]
  (ANTECEDENT: COMPONENT
    (TRANSFERENCE
     (SOURCE <DONOR>)
     (FIGURE <PATIENT>)))
  (CONSEQUENT: COMPONENT
    <SCENE>
    (POSSESSION
     (POSSESSOR <RECIPIENT>)
     (PATIENT))))
```

Here we have complicated POS_TRANS by making it both a CAUSAL-SEQUENCE and a CONDITIONED-SCENE (the scene CONDITIONED-SCENE was introduced in 2.5.1), a scene with two slots, *precondition* and *scene*. The *precondition* essentially stipulates that the *source* possess the *patient*; that requirement, however, is optional.

In essence, my proposal is this: with the prepositional valence, POS_TRANS will be required to meet the precondition; some lexically specific form of POSSESSION will have to hold between *source* and *patient*; that form of POSSESSION may well selectionally restrict the *source*. To guarantee that the *precondition* is met in the prepositional valence, we shall modify our treatment of *to*. In Chapter 2 we provisionally accorded *to* the meaning POSSESSION on the basis of verbs like *belong*, despite the fact that most of the verbs compatible with *possessor to* involved not just possession, but acquisition. The following ACQUISITION frame constitutes an about-face:

```
(ACQUISITION: CONDITIONED_SCENE
 (PRECONDITION: SUBSCENE
   (POSSESSION:UNDERGOING
    (POSSESSOR <^ DONOR>)
    (PATIENT <^ PATIENT>)))
 (SCENE: COMPONENT
   (POSSESSION:UNDERGOING
    (POSSESSOR <RECIPIENT>)
    (PATIENT))))
```

This is simply a relation between two possessions, where one is a precondition for the other; but nothing about the manner of ACQUISITION has been specified. Let this be the template scene for TO. Now suppose the above POS_TRANS scene is the template for all POS_TRANS verbs. Then sentences using *acquisition to* will only have satisfying POS_TRANS scenes in which the *precondition* slot is filled. I assume all the various POS_TRANS verbs will have ground scenes that may differ considerably, as long as they are all extensions of the POS_TRANS scene above. Among those differences will be various specifications of just exactly what kind of POSSESSION is at issue. Consider *tell*; *tell* is a POS_TRANS verb involving transference of information; so that the particular kind of POSSESSION involved will be knowledge. The idea is that whenever *tell* appears in its *to* valence, the precondition will be in force, and the *teller* will be required to know the *told*. But one of the selectional restrictions on knowing is that the knower be a possible cognizer. Hence the contrast:

(25a) John's face told the sergeant the grim truth.
(25b) *John's face told the grim truth to the sergeant.

Faces don't know things, so in (b) the precondition is implausible.

We turn now to the question of the double object construction itself. In GPSG, there is a fairly straightforward, although unconventional, way of a adding a particular kind of interpretation to a particular syntactic structure. Make it part of the semantics of the phrase structure rule.

```
<V1 ->  V[D-OBJ] N2 N2[D-OBJ]: (lambda sigma
                               (lambda x
                                 (and  (N2 (lambda z (V  sigma z
                                 x)))
                                       (N2[D-OBJ] (lambda y
                                                   (D-OBJ sigma
                                 y)))))))>
```

I have here treated the construction as parallel with the prepositions as possible. There is a syntactic feature D-OBJ that selects for this construction, just as there is a syntactic feature TO that selects for T0-phrases. There is a predicate D-OBJ, just as there is a predicate TO. The only thing missing is a phonological realization; one might in fact claim that this treatment amounts to hypothesizing a null preposition. Since I have no further syntactic business to transact, I will remain neutral on this point.

A point I can not remain neutral on, however, is associating the predicate D-OBJ with a particular interpretation in the frame model. The simplest way to do this seems to posit a lexical entry missing its syntactic and semantic component, essentially, an entry relating a predicate to a frame slot pair. There are other alternatives here which might be more compatible with a view on which logical predicates are dispensable; one might, for example choose to make D-OBJ a logical constant (since, like all lexical items, it has the same interpretation in every frame model), or assign it as the interpretation of a feature piggybacked onto the second noun phrase in the double-object rule. For simplicity, I have chosen the alternative that tangles us up in the least amount of extra apparatus. Assume then, that in the lexicon the predicate D-OBJ is paired with the following frame-slot pair:

```
<(POSSESSION
  (PATIENT)
  (POSSESSOR)), PATIENT>
```

The frame here is simply the POSSESSION frame which was previously our interpretation for *to*. If we did think of D-OBJ as a null-preposition, then the slot would correspond to its object. Thus, D-OBJ is the inverse of our old interpretation of TO. It is the possessed thing rather than the possessor that is "object" of the preposition. Note that TO, even its new version, is an extension of POSSESSION. If D-OBJ were thought of as a preposition, these representations would amount to a claim that the Saliency Hierarchy for prepositions shares at least one property with the Saliency Hierarchy for verbs: it does not enforce a preference between *possessors* and *patients*; for one predicate, *patient* wins out over *possessor*; in the other *possessor* wins out.

Note that POSSESSION cannot be the only interpretation of the double object construction in English. Verbs like *cost* and *envy* seem to partake of some different semantics entirely. The construction is polysemous, just as prepositions are. Thus, given the above treatment, there will have to be other D-OBJ predicates, and other phrase structure rules introducing the double object construction.

We will conclude our treatment of datives with a sample lexical entry. *sell* is an obvious candidate. The frame given below is a simpified version of figure frame finally adopted in Chapter 2:

```
<sell:
 (SELLING: DONOR_ACTION
   [PRECONDITION
    (POSSESSION
     (POSSESSOR <DONOR> <ACTOR> <SELLER>)
     (PATIENT <GOODS>))]
  (ANTECEDENT: COMPONENT
    (TRANSFERENCE
     (SOURCE <DONOR>)
     (FIGURE <PATIENT>)))
  (CONSEQUENT: COMPONENT
    <SCENE>
    (POSSESSION
     (POSSESSOR <RECIPIENT> <BUYER>)
     (PATIENT)))),
<<SELLING, ACTOR, PATIENT> [+V,-N, TO]>
 <SELLING, ACTOR, POSSESSOR> [+V,-N, D-OBJ]>>>
```

The critical portions of this entry are the pairs of predicate denotations and feature matrices at the end. Two possibilities are listed. The first makes *patient* the direct object and subcategorizes for TO. But the new TO frame places requirements on the *precondition* that are only satisfied by an instance of SELLING that has the optional *precondition* slot filled in:

(EXISTS* SIGMA (EXISTS X (AND (SELLING SIGMA JOHN X)

```
                                    (BOOK X)
                                    (TO SIGMA MARY))))
```

The fact that TO is predicated of sigma guarantees that whatever situation satisfies this sentence must have its *precondition* filled. On the other hand a double object paraphrase gives:

```
(EXISTS* SIGMA (EXISTS X (AND (SELLING-2 SIGMA JOHN MARY)
                              (D-OBJ SIGMA X)
                              (BOOK X))))
```

D-OBJ requires only that *possessor* and *patient* slots be filled. Thus there is no requirement that the optional material be present.

This seems to be consistent with greater semantic flexibility of the double object construction. It is also consistent with the cases where the two valences seem to be perfect paraphrases:

(26a) John gave Mary a book.
(26b) John gave a book to Mary,

On the absolute paraphrase reading of both sentences, the interpretation will involve POS_TRANS scenes which include the optional POSSESSION scene.

Crucial to the treatment being proposed here is the assumption that the POSSESSION scene in the precondition slot was the source for extra selectional restrictions in the prepositional valence. But the POS_TRANS frame has another subscene, the TRANSFERENCE scene, which has the same participants, and which offers another domain where the relationship between them may be restricted. Thus, some

POS_TRANS verbs seem to require animate participants in both valences:

(27) Mary read me Tolstoy

(28) Mary read Tolstoy to me.

(29) * Mary's look read me the handwriting on the wall.

(30) * Mary's look read the handwriting on the wall to me.

The restrictions maintained by *read* may be thought of as being introduced in the TRANSFERENCE subscenes of the READING frame, a non-optional portion of the frame, and thus applicable in either valence.

The treatment of Dative Movement proposed here involves the interaction of a number of different aspects of lexical description:

> (1) The Saliency Hierarchy has nothing to say about *patient* or *possessor* or their elaborations among the POS_TRANS verbs.
>
> (2) There are complement markers in English for both *patient* and *possessor*.
>
> (3) *to* brings along with it a certain presupposition of a relation between the *donor* and *patient*. This feature is really independent of points (1) and (2). The treatment of Dative Movement would have been similar, but essentially the same, without it.

The sort of view taken here of valence alternations suggests that there ought to be a number of loopholes left open by the Saliency Hierarchy, particularly in the assignment of direct objecthood, which allow verbs to select more than one valence option. This suggests that there will be idiosyncratic cases of valence alternation, limited to even smaller domains than Instrument Promotion and Dative Movement:

(31a) John credited Andrea with the victory.
(31b) John credited the victory to Andrea.

(32a) Rupert blamed Anya for the disaster
(32b) Rupert blamed the disaster on Anya.

(33a) Kropotkin played Kuryakin at tennis.
(33b) Kropotkin played tennis with Kuryakin.
(33c) Kropotkin played Kuryakin two games of tennis.

(34a) Rhonda supplied vodka to the Finns,
(34b) Rhonda supplied the Finns with Vodka.

(35a) Bogdan presented a plaque to Jasia.
(35b) Bogdan presented Jasia with a plaque.

(36a) John replaced his adventurousness with wisdom in middle age.
(36b) John substituted wisdom for his adventurousness in middle age,

Ultimately viewing processes like Instrument Promotion and Dative Movement as simple valence options comes down to this: it is hard to imagine a theory of the semantics of nuclear terms flexible enough to allow options like those above, which could draw a principled line between those alternations and alternations like Dative Movement. The critical distinction is one which all theories find difficult to draw, the distinction between productive and non-productive operations. The account I have chosen says that these kinds of alternations may arise whenever the issue of direct objecthood is unsettled; the productivity of a valence alternation involving different direct object realizations is then hung on the productivity of ways of marking the oblique arguments. Both *possessive to* and the double object construction are productive ways of marking oblique arguments that fall in a certain semantic domain. In the relevant meanings, the prepositions marking oblique arguments in () - () offer less productive ways.

Before closing the discussion of Dative Movement, two relatively strong arguments for its status as a lexical rule need to be mentioned. First, there is the fact, noted by Oehrle, that Dative Movement seems to have a morphologically characterizable class of exceptions in the right semantic domain, namely, verbs that are +Latin. Oerhle's list:

(37) return, transfer, convey, deliver, reveal, explain, report, submit, restore, exhibit (Oehrle omits "donate")

This is a striking fact. If Dative Movement is a morphological redundancy rule, this condition on its application is rather natural, since the feature +Latin constrains the environment of a number of affixation processes. The only way to state this in the current framework would be with what in what in GPSG is known as a feature co-occurrence restriction (see Gazdar, Pullum, Sag 1981):

+LATIN -> -D-OBJ

Such statement are never very theoretically appealing, and this one makes use of a feature +LATIN which has no other motivation that I know of as a syntactic feature. However, I am less worried than I might be by these verbs. First, there seem to be counterexamples, *offer* and *assign*. Second, the "constraint" whatever its source, does not seem to play a role in productive applications of Dative Movement.

Wasow 1977 cites an example of Dative Movement with a coined verb, which happens to be +LATIN: "He satellited me a letter."

The second point is more troubling; there seem to be no instances of verbs in the right semantic domain which take the double object construction but not the prepositional construction. We noted a parallel fact for Instrument Promotion; there are no verbs of impingement that allow the *instrument* as direct object, but not the *patient*. This evidence that one of the valences in each alternation appears to be marked would be very naturally explained with a directional morphological redundancy rule. I confess that the only ways I can think of to represent the markedness here all involve adding some mechanism to the valence selection process that looks very much like a derivational rule. I will return to this point in the conclusion of this chapter.

We have now seen two "rules" where systematic valence alternations could be explained in terms of options allowed by the Saliency Hierarchy and available complementation possibiltiies. In 4.2, we will investigate Goal Promotion, a different kind of valence alternation which involves changing a role to which the Hierarchy must be sensitive.

4.2 Advancement involving Change

4.2.1 Goal Promotion

I want to begin with a celebrated valence alternation first noted in Partee 1964:

(39a) John loaded hay onto the truck.
(39b) John loaded the truck with hay.

Call this alternation Goal Promotion. The crucial feature for our discussion here is what Anderson 1971 calls the holistic reading of (b). In contrast with (a), the truck described in (b) must be completely filled.

The key property distinguishing this alternation from those described in 4.1 is that describing the semantic change involves crucial reference to elements ranked on the Saliency Hierarchy. Evidence that what is at issue is intimately connected with the semantics of nuclear termhood has been collected in Anderson 1971:

(40a) John climbed up the moutain
(40b) John climbed the mountain

(41a) A yellow roadster traveled on this road last night.
(41b) A yellow roadster traveled this road last night.

(42a) John chewed his steaked.
(42b) John chewed on his steak.

(43a) The student committee voted for a strike.
(43b) The student committee voted a strike.

(44a) The press secretary read from his prepared speech.

(44b) The press secretary read his prepared speech.

(45a) John punched at Bill
(45b) John punched Bill.

Other pairs that present similar options: *shoot/shoot at*, *push/push against*, *pull/pull on*, and *scratch/scratch at*. All of these examples loosely be described as cases of promotion to nuclear termhood. In each instance, there is a contrast in the interpretation of the role of one participant when that participant is realized obliquely and when that participant is promoted. Advanced to nuclear termhood, a participant comes to be completely affected. This is what Anderson calls the holistic reading.

At present there is way to capture Anderson's generalization in the current framework. We have thus far let the choice between transitive and intransitive be a stipulation from valence to valence for any verb. If we required any participant marked *changed* to be realized as a nuclear term, then the above array of facts might begin to make sense. Suppose each of the above verbs was given an optional *changed* role, but that the participant associated with *changed* was also associated with some obligatory role. Then, by completeness, each verb would have to have some valence in which *changed* was realized, and *changed* would have to be a nuclear term. Given the presence of an *actor* in each of the above examples, *changed* would have to be direct object. Such a stipulation for *changed* would be more plausible if we could extend it to all the roles in the Saliency Hierarchy. In the case of *actor*, there is of course no problem, at least with verbs; I know of no troublesome examples involving *figure*, but *experiencer* remains problematic; we discussed a number of cases of "inversion" in Chapter 3 in which *experiencer* was realized obliquely. I leave this point open, since it does not affect what follows.

Anderson also notes that the holistic reading does not in general extend to Dative Movement (although we have noted one verb, *teach*, where it may be relevant). He cites this as evidence that the rule of Dative Movement applies after the level of Deep Structure (or after whatever level determines the holistic interpretation). The concept of ordered levels crucial to Anderson's EST framework is not so important here, but a sensible question in any framework is whether there is or should be a formal distinction in kind between Goal Promotion and Dative Movement. We shall see that it is possible to give Goal Promotion an analysis that does not make a formal distinction. In chapter 5, however, I will sketch an anlysis where slightly different assumptions about the grammar rules involved entail what amounts to a formal distinction. It is not entirely clear to me which course is preferable; the most obvious way to draw a distinction is to call Goal Promotion a morphological redundancy rule, and Dative Movement a simple valence option. We will discuss that alternative in the conclusion of this chapter.

4.2.1.1 The Patient Valence

Following are some examples of Goal Promotion:

(46a) Bees swarmed in the garden
(46b) The garden swarmed with bees.

(47a) He jammed pencils into the jar
(47b) He jammed the jar with pencils.

(48a) She hung drapes on the wall.
(48b) She hung the wall with drapes.

(49a) Tourists flooded into the city
(49b) The city flooded with tourists

(50a) He spread butter on the bread.
(50b) He spread the bread with butter

(51a) We sprinkled flowers over the floor.
(51b) We sprinkled the floor with flowers.

(52a) They showered gifts onto the queen
(52b) They showered the queen with gifts

(53a) They sprayed gas into the room
(53b) They sprayed the room with gas.

(54a) He packed sulfa powder into the wound.
(54b) He packed the wound with sulfa powder.

A fact that has often been remarked about these pairs is that in one valence there is a large degree of freedom in the choice of prepositions from head to head; in the other valence, the only choice is *with*. Let us call the valence with a free choice of prepositions the *patient* valence, and the valence with *with* the *goal* valence. Sometimes the *patient* valence gives us a large number of preposition choices, even with one verb:

(55) He sprinkled flowers under the door.
over her head.
around the room.
behind the bed.

(56) He spread lime behind the bushes.
under the oak.
around the yard.

Note that some of these examples are not even approximate paraphrases of the *goal* valence:

(57) He sprinkled the bed with flowers

(58) He sprinkled flowers under the bed.

For *sprinkle,* in fact, the only *goal* prepositions that do seem to have paraphrases in the *goal* valence are *over* and *around,* depending on the exact topology of the *goal*:

(59) He sprinkled flowers around the room.

(60) He sprinkled the room with flowers.

(61) He sprinkled flowers over the child.

(62) He sprinkled the child with flowers.

But the fact that the *patient* valence selects for multiple prepositions in one syntactic slot raises a problem we have not yet discussed. The problem is that our current definition of semantic compatibility does not allow us to select for a family of meanings in one slot. If A is an extension of B, in general extensions of A are not. So if we have some frame PUTTING with a component labeled only LOCATIVE, that does not give us compatibility with all locative prepositions; in fact it gains us compatibility with none. Presumably all LOCATIVE prepositions are further specifications of the LOCATIVE scene. They are thus not in the compatibility set of PUTTING.

This leaves us two alternatives. First, we could revise the definition of semantic compatibility as follows: if A is compatiole with B, A is compatible with anything that is AKO B. This would ailow further specifications of LOCATIVE into the compatibility set of PUTTING. It would also predict that if a head was compatible with a preposition P, it would be compatible with P', where P' had a more specific meaning than P. A possible case of this is the pair, *over* and *about* in the meanings illustrated in the following pair of sentences:

(63) They had a fight about who would go.

(64) They had a fight over who would go.

over in this sense means *bone-of-contention*, *about* means *topic*; the former can be viewed as a special case of the latter, and, indeed, there are a number of heads involving conflict which are compatible with both.

Another pair of sentences with the same flavor is a pair we looked at in Chapter 1:

(63) He decided on the boat.

(64) He decided against the boat.

These prepositional phrases seem to take up the same syntactic slot, since they cannot be syntactic sisters, but they can be coordinated. The very fact that they are antonyms shows that the relevant preposition meanings must have a lot in common; an easy way to capture that fact would be to have some more general scene, ON_AGAINST, which had as further specifications both ON and AGAINST, where ON and AGAINST, differed in just the features that made them antonyms. If we revised compatibility in the proposed way, then DECISION could be an extension of ON_AGAINST and compatible with both prepositions.

A different solution to the problem of valences that allow families of prepositions is to treat the prepositions as predicative, that is, not as arguments of the head, but predicates in their own right which take another participant as their argument.

In terms of PUTTING, the difference between these two answers to the problem can be thought of in terms of as a single annotation to the LOCATION slot. On the first account, LOCATION is a component, and the embedded scene yields participants of the top level scene no different from any other participants. Only the definition of semantic compatibility has been generalized. On the second account, LOCATION will be treated as a participant. Its treatment in the logic will differ, because it will be subsumed to the treatment of control. Other than that the semantics on the frame level will remain the same.

The treatment for predicatives will be outlined in chapter 5. Under a predicative analysis of the *patient* valence, either Goal Promotion entails a formal augmentation of the frame-notation, or it is a morphological redundancy rule involving zero-derivation. For the present we will assume an extended definition of semantic compatibility which allows us to treat the prepositional complements of the *patient* valence as we have treated prepositional phrase arguments all along.

Before we can state a rule relating the valences in Goal-promotion, it is crucial that we can handle both valences individually — that they be coherent subcategorization frames in the system we have developed thus far. The reason is that both valences occur quite independently of Goal promotions:

(65a) John filled the glass with water
(65b)*John filled water into the glass.

(66a) John poured water into the glass.
(66b)*John poured the glass with water.

In this subsection, we will focus on the *patient* valence.

First, what is the semantic class we are dealing with? All of the verbs at hand involve the introduction of a substance or a collection into a confined space or onto a surface. Borrowing a term used in Davison 1980 in discussing a similar rule in Hungarian, let us call the relevant scene the APPLICATION scene. Roughly we have:

```
(APPLICATION: RESULTATIVE; UNDERGOING
 (MATERIAL <UNDERGOER>)
 (RESULT: COMPONENT
  (ORIENTATION_IN_SPACE
   (FIGURE <^ MATERIAL>)
   (GROUND))))
```

The idea is this: something happens to some material; as a result it becomes oriented in some way with respect to some point in a space.[1] A little more specifically, we might hazard: the something that happens involves collecting the material. This is about as specific as we can hope to be for a scene whose ultimate descendants will be lexical scenes for both *load* and *swarm*. The *ground* in the *result* scene will of course be what we have informally called the *goal*, corresponding to the truck in (), and the garden in (). Note that for both *load* and *swarm* this participant is optional. For *jam* it is not:

(67) *He jammed the pencils.

(68) He jammed the pencils into the jar.

I thus assume that the optionality is something introduced in further specifications of the APPLICATION scene. Note that the roles *figure* and *ground* determine the grammatical realizations of the two participants in the APPLICATION scene. As the scene stands *material* outranks *ground*, because *material* is an extension of *figure*.

Now, many of the verbs we are concerned with introduce a

---

1. The observation that the semantics of these verbs involved the notion result was made by Fillmore in 1981, in a seminar lecture.

further component of motion. It will thus be useful to examine a particular instantiation of APPLICATION, as an example of how movement is introduced.

```
(LOADING:APPLICATION; ACTION
 (LOADER <ACTOR>)
 (LOAD <MATERIAL>)
 (RESULT:COMPONENT
   (MOVEMENT: ORIENTATION_IN_SPACE
       (FIGURE <CHANGED><↑ MATERIAL>)
       (GROUND))))
```

What happens here is that a new participant is introduced, an *actor*, and the ORIENTATION_IN_SPACE is further specified to be a MOVEMENT. We might want to choose a scene a bit more specific than MOVEMENT, given that not all "movement" prepositions are suitable with *load*:

(69) We moved around the track

(70) ?He loaded the hay around the tire.

But the exact specifications of this scene are not critical.

While we are dealing with the semantic unit result, we might as well pick up a loose end from 4.1. One valence of the verb *hit* that we have not dealt with is very much like the *patient* valence of the Goal-Promotion verbs:

(71) He hit the ball across the park.

Suppose to represent this possibility, we simply add an optional *result* to the IMPINGEMENT scene. Then we would have:

```
(IMPINGEMENT-T: MANIPULATION-T;
                ENCOUNTERED-CONTACT;
                RESULTATIVE
  [-1 ANTECEDENT:COMPONENT
       (UNDERGOING
         PATIENT <↑ INSTRUMENT>) ]-1
  (CONSEQUENT:COMPONENT
    (DIRECTED-ACTION-CONTACT
       (ACTOR)
       [-1 THEME <↑ ANTECEDENT PATIENT>  ]-1
       (TARGET <PATIENT>) ))
  [-2 RESULT: COMPONENT
   (MOVEMENT
    (FIGURE <CHANGED> <THEME>)
    (GROUND))]-2 )
```

Note that this has an interesting effect. When the optional *result* component is included, then *theme* is *changed*. This means that in that valence it will outrank *instrument* and *ground* both, so that both will have to be oblique. Instrument promotion will no longer be possible when the *result* is included. This correctly predicts the unacceptability of (71+1) on the reading where hitting the ball causes it to go across the park:

(72) *He hit the bat against the ball across the park.

4.2.1.2 Goal-valence

The first problem to tackle is the particular meaning of *with* involved in the Goal Promotion rule. Consider the following examples:

(73) The room teemed with people.

(74) The room throbbed with excitement.

(75) The room was crawling with roaches.

(76) John's plan was fraught with risk.

(77) The garden was alive with bees

(78) John was dripping with sweat.

(79) The room filled with people.

A substance or collection fills a space or covers a surface. None of these examples are obvious participants in the Goal Promotion rule, but the examples we have seen that are fit the pattern. The participant marked with *with* fills a two- or three- D space; the fact that the verb *fill* takes this preposition in this meaning suggests something like this as the preposition scene:

```
(FILLING:THING
 (MATERIAL)
 (GOAL))
```

As yet we have proposed no grounds for relating the role *material* in this FILLING scene with the role *material* in the APPLICATION scene of last section. This will be done below. The above examples in isolation suggest that *goal* always outranks *material*, but the following examples argue otherwise:

(80) Water filled the glass.

(81) The sheet covered the bed.

One might try to analyze the subjects in these examples as *actors*, parallel to "the hammer" in:

(82) The hammer broke the vase.

However, the "stative" senses in both () and () argue strongly against that analysis. "Water filled the glass," can be a paraphrase of "The glass was full of water." It seems to me that the intuition that ACTIONS are disjoint from STATES is important enough to rule out this approach. I will thus take the position that Saliency Hierarchy says nothing directly ranking the roles *goal* and *material*.

Let us turn now to the problem of relating the FILLING scene with the APPLICATION scene of last section. There, we took the position that in the Patient valence, *material* outranked *ground* because it was an elaboration of *figure*. However we decide to relate the two valences, something must overrule that ranking in the Goal valence. What I propose is that this something be the role *changed*.

The term *changed*, however, is not the happiest one when applied to the case of a truck loaded with hay; it is even less happy when applied to sentences which have a clearly stative sense ("The garden swarmed with bees). If the term *actor* is inappropriate for states, then surely so is the term *changed*. Perhaps a better name for the feature we want here is *totally-affected*, or *exhibiting total affectedness*. And perhaps what we are calling *changed* in the Hierarchy might better be decomposed into two features, one involving movement, the other totality of affect. Suppose we made the simplest possible revision here, inserting both features into the place in the Hierarchy previously occupied by *changed*. Let us temporarily defer the question of which of the two new roles ranks higher: *moved* or *totally-affected*.

It is not hard to guess what scene will underlie all *goal* valences: it is the FILLING scene augmented with the role *totally-affected*. Call the new scene FILLING_WITH:

```
(FILLING_WITH: FILLING
 (MATERIAL)
 [TOTALLY-AFFECTED<GOAL>])
```

One may or may not wish to account for the subjecthood of the *goal* in examples (82-9) - (82-3) by associating their governing heads with the FILLING_WITH scene; I leave that question open.

To represent the Goal Promotion verbs, we must create one frame that combines the information of the APPLICATION scene with the FILLING_WITH scene:

```
(APPLICATION: RESULTATIVE; UNDERGOING; FILLING_WITH
  (MATERIAL)
  (RESULT:COMPONENT
   (ORIENTATION_IN_SPACE
    (FIGURE <↑ MATERIAL>)
```

```
    (GROUND <↑ GOAL>)))
  [TOTALLY-AFFECTED <GOAL>])
```

The idea behind this composite scene is fairly simple. Suppose we imagine that this is the template scene LOADING; When the optional *totally-affected* slot is realized, *Goal* will outrank *material*. Since the scene is compatible with FILLING (the scene for *material with*), we will have the makings of the *goal* valence. When the optional slot is not realized, *material* will outrank *goal* (since it is *figure*, and *goal* is *ground*), and we will have the makings of the *patient* valence.

Note that this set-up forces a decision on us about the relative ranking of *moved* and *totally-affected*. In the actual LOADING scene, the *result* will not be an ORIENTATION_IN_SPACE scene, but a MOVING scene; and in that case *material* will be *moved*. This means that in order to get the *goal* valence for *load*, we must assume that *totally-affected* outranks *moved*.

This is one of the ways in which the choice between a predicative PP analysis and a generalization of the notion compatibility makes a difference in our analysis of Goal Promotion. If we took the predicative analysis, *result* would not be a component slot, but a participant slot. In that case, *moved* would not be a slot in the top-level frame, and no choice between the relative rankings of *totally affected* and *moved* would be necessary (we might even continue to assume they were different elaborations of the same underlying slot).

This treatment of Goal Promotion does not seem to differ much from the treatment of dative movement. The similarity can be illustrated by looking at the lexical entry for *load:*

```
<lod:
(LOADING: APPLICATION;ACTION
  (LOADER <ACTOR>)
  (LOAD <MATERIAL>)
  (RESULT:COMPONENT
   (MOVEMENT: ORIENTATION_IN_SPACE
    (MOVED <FIGURE> <↑ MATERIAL>)
    (GROUND <↑ GOAL>)))
  [TOTALLY-AFFECTED <GOAL>]):
<<LOADING, ACTOR, TOTALLY-AFFECTED>, [+V,-N, TRAN , WITH]>
 <LOADING, ACTOR, MOVED>, [+V, -N, TRAN, LOC]>>>
```

There is a gross oversimplification in this entry. As written, all participants must be realized (even if they are sometimes realized with differing sets of roles). But we also have:

(83) John loaded the truck.

(84) John loaded the hay.

This is clearly not a case of what we called syntactic omissibility in chapter 3. Thus, in order to permit these possibilities, we shall have to complicate the LOADING scene by adding two separate optionality components, one for the *patient*, one for the *goal* (just in case it is not also *totally-affected*). This can be done using the indexed square brackets we introduced in the treatment of optional *instruments:*

```
(LOADING: APPLICATION;ACTION
  (LOADER [actor])
  [-2 LOAD [material]]-2
  (RESULT:COMPONENT
```

(MOVEMENT: ORIENTATION_IN_SPACE
[-2 MOVED [figure] <↑ MATERIAL>]-2
[-3 GROUND <↑ GOAL>]-3))
[-1 TOTALLY-AFFECTED <GOAL>]-1)

Now the convention is that optional material may be discontinuous, and that all the instances of material between square brackets of the same index constitute single optional constituents. But different optional constituents are presumably independent of each other. The above representation thus gives us eight possibilities. We need to make sure that this frame, taken together with the above lexical entry, gets the right results, in particular, that it does not allow incoherent results. In the following list, "+" before a number n indicates a frame realization where the optional constituent indexed n has been included; "-" indicates a realization where the optional constituent has been left out:

(1) [+1, +2, +3]. This is as before. It gives us sentences like "He loaded the truck with hay."

(2) [+1, -2, +3]. Not possible because the *totally-affected* slot contains a procedure that requires position 2 to be filled. *goal = totally-affected*.

(3) [+1, -2, -3]. Not possible for the same reason.

(4) [+1, +2, -3]. This give us sentences like "He loaded the truck."

(5) [-1, +2, +3]. Sentences like "He loaded hay onto the truck."

(6) [-1, -2, +3]. Sentences like "He loaded hay."

(7) [-1, +2, -3]. Not possible with either predicate. <LOADING, ACTOR, TOTALLY-AFFECTED> automatically fills *totally-affected*. <LOADING, ACTOR, MOVED> automatically fills *moved*.

(8) [-1, -2, -3]. Not possible for the same reason.

Thus, the above frame, taken together with the syntactic options allowed in the lexical entry, predicts the right configuration of valences.

One possible objection to this lexical entry is also an objection to the kind of entry we had for datives and impingement verbs in the last section. It is associated with two different logical predicates and therefore with two different meanings. Therefore, what we have is merely an abbreviation for two lexical entries, no matter how you look at it. This point of view, however, depends on the traditional model theoretic view of what a meaning is. In the framework being developed here, logical predicates are a way of encoding certain facts about the grammatical function of a lexical item. These predicates are not semantic objects; rather they are closer in spirit to the F-structures of LFG. Of course they do not encode as much information as a lexical F-structure; many of the properties of a lexical item stated in that theory as grammatical function are captured here with syntactic features. But logical predicates do critically encode information about nuclear terms; in this more modest grammatical domain they function just as F-structures do; they are pointers from the syntactic realization of a lexical item to the right place in the semantics. The real semantics is the lexical scene.

It is nevertheless true that we could have written the above

APPLICATION frame without the optional slot, and written a lexical redundancy rule that said, when A is a lexical item with the following semantics, then A plus a zero affix is a lexical item with with same semantics plus the slot *totally-affected*. We would in that case want to add *totally-affected* to the figure scene of A (and perhaps to its ground scene).

Two questions arise here. One: what makes a lexical entry a lexical entry, and when do we have two? Two: what does it really means to have optional constituents, and why do we bother to have them?

I want to address only the second question in this section, because it is a little simpler. One answer can be stated in terms of our representational ontology. Sometimes we wish to say that there is a single scene which may or may not have an individuated part of a certain type. But with or without that part an instantiating situation is still the same type of scene.

Another answer is more practical, from the point of view of the working grammarian. Optional constituents in abstract scenes let us make important generalizations about lexical items. To have a generic scene with an optional part shared by a number of lexical items means that for all those lexical items, that part is optional. Suppose we tried to argue that a scene with an optional constituent is really an abbreviation for two scenes, and that we could always say the same thing with two scenes. Scenes are semantic objects. Once semantic objects are distinct there are no guarantees about their realizations. Each of those new pairs of objects might very well get pronounced in different ways; if such pairs of scenes are realized by the same phonological bundle, then that is an accident. Under a single scene representation we have made the claim that semantically defined cases of optionality are not accidents.

Looked at the second way, frames with optional constituents really make a kind of morphological claim; semantic objects with and without a certain piece of structure get pronounced the same. Looked at the other way, they constitute an ontological claim; objects with and without this piece of structure are still the same kinds of objects. One of the underlying assumptions of this dissertation is that these two different ways of looking at things are really reflections of each other. Particular cultures recognize specific regularities among situations. Those regularities define scenes. Scenes in turn may define words. Thus the fact that two distinguishable pieces of semantic structure are pronounced the same is evidence (although not conclusive evidence) that they participate in a single scene.

What I have argued, then, is that treating *load* as a single lexical entry is completely consistent with the direction we have been pursuing all along. This is nothing more than a plausibility consideration.

What it means is that if we want evidence that *load* should really be viewed as two separate entries, we will need purely grammatical evidence. The nature of the lexical representations themselves does not decide the issue.

Some evidence of that form will be considered in the conclusion of this chapter, and in Chapter 5.

4.2.2 Other rules

4.2.2.1 Container promotion

There is a rule completely parallel to Goal Promotion which has, as it were, just the opposite semantics. Some examples:

(85a) He emptied the glass of milk.
(85b) He emptied milk out of the glass.

(86a) He drained the corpse of blood.
(86b) He drained blood out of the corpse.

(87a) He cleared the room of the junk.
(87b) He cleared the junk out of the room.

Where Goal Promotion involved movement of material to a two- or three-D Goal, this rule involves movement of the material out of three-D spaces. Let us call the space the *container* and the rule *Container-promotion*. Again, there are holistic and non-holistic readings. In (), the glass must be completely empty, while () may describe an ongoing or incomplete process. It is apparent, just as it was with *with* in Goal Promotion, that a productive meaning of the preposition is involved:

(88) This book is devoid of interest.

(89) Tom robbed Lefty of his dignity.

(90) The man is bereft of any human feeling.

(91) She relieved the adjutant of all his duties.

Let us represent this meaning of *of* with the following simple scene:

```
(EMPTYING: THING
  (MATERIAL)
  (CONTAINER))
```

And let us choose something quite parallel to the APPLICATION scene to represent the common source for the Container-promotion verbs.

```
(REMOVAL:RESULT; EMPTYING;UNDERGOING
 (MATERIAL)
 (RESULT:COMPONENT
  (ORIENTATION_IN_SPACE
    (FIGURE <↑ MATERIAL>)
    (GROUND <↑ CONTAINER>)))
 [TOTALLY-AFFECTED <CONTAINER>])
```

Lexical entries will parallel those of the Goal Promotion verbs.

Note that REMOVAL is so parallel to APPLICATION that it is easy to construct a scene that abstracts over both. First we need a source for both FILLING and EMPTYING. Call it MATERIAL-TRANSFERENCE:

```
(MATERIAL-TRANSFERENCE: THING
  (SPACE)
  (MATERIAL))

(EMPTYING: MATERIAL-TRANSFERENCE
   (CONTAINER <SPACE>)
   (MATERIAL))

(FILLING: MATERIAL-TRANSFERENCE
```

```
(GOAL <SPACE>)
(MATERIAL))
```

Taking this route, both preposition meanings are further specifications of a single abstract scene involving the relationship of material to space. This is a very simple example of the general pattern known as antonymy. Antonymic words have identical semantics except for one crucial feature; and in differing in this feature they set up a simple paradigm of two members.

Having supplied a common source for both EMPTYING and FILLING, we can now also supply a common source for APPLICATION and REMOVAL. Call this scene MATERIAL-MANIPULATION, suggesting a certain conceptual connection with the MANIPULATION scene for *instruments*:

```
(MATERIAL-MANIPULATION; MATERIAL-TRANSFERENCE;
 UNDERGOING; RESULT
  (RESULT: COMPONENT
    (ORIENTATION_IN_SPACE
      (FIGURE <↑ MATERIAL>)
      (GROUND <↑ SPACE>)))
  [TOTALLY-AFFECTED <SPACE>])
```

Suppose now that APPLICATION is AKO this scene and simply specifies *space* to be *goal*, and that REMOVAL is AKO this scene and simply specifies *space* to be *container*. Then we have, in effect, collapsed the two "rules" of Goal Promotion and Container-Promotion.

4.2.2.2 Symmetric predicates

There are numerous difficult problems connected with the handling of symmetric predicates. The only thing that will concern us here is the alternation exhibited in the following examples:

(92a) Fred and Bertha agreed
(92b) Fred agreed with Bertha

(93a) Fred and Bertha argued
(93b) Fred argued with Bertha

(94a) Fred and Bertha collided
(94b) Fred collided with Bertha

In each of these pairs the sentence with conjoined subjects is truly symmetric, but the sentence with *with* is not. Dowty 1972 shows this for the verb *collide*:

(95a) The truck collided with the lamppost
(95b)?The truck and the lamppost collided.

Examples for the other verbs are easy to find:

(96) Fred always agreed with Bertha; Bertha never agreed with Fred

(97) Fred always argued with Bertha; Bertha never argued with Fred.

Let us propose a scene for these verbs, leaving aside the question just how it fits in with the general scheme of scenes we have bee developing:

```
(COLLECTIVE-ACT: ?
  (COLLECTION)
```

```
(INITIATOR ( => <COLLECTION>))
[COMITATOR ( => <COLLECTION>)])
```

A new procedure has been added to our list of procedural attachments. It is called "=>" and is interpreted to mean "is included among." This is simply a generalization of the procedure "=" to which we have appealed all along. Rather than requiring that a value of one slot A equal a value of another B we may now require that the value of A be "included in" the value of B. This will only be appropriate when the value of B is a collection, that is, an object which consists of other objects in the ontology. This assumes an ontology where there is an entity corresponding to "John and Mary", to which the individual "John" and "Mary" bear some specially defined relationship we will call "included-in". I am not prepared to offer the details of any such treatment, but something like the ontology of Link 1983 seems approriate; all we need here is to assume that a satisfactory semantics of plurals will have recourse to some kind of plural entity. Following Link, I have called such an entity a collection.

The *collection* slot is thus a slot which adds a role but not a participant. The COLLECTIVE-ACT scene counts as having only two participants, one optional, and the two slots associated with those participants may jointly fill another non-particpant slot.

We may also assume that the slot *collection* requires that it be filled by a collection. Thus, if the optional *comitator* slot is unrealized, the *instigator* slot alone will have to supply a collection. This will admit the first two of the following examples, and rule out the third:

(98a) Fred and Bertha agreed.
(98b) The committee agreed.
(98c) *Fred agreed.

Note that a number of similar verbs do appear to be fully symmetric in both valences:

(99a) Fred and Bertha played tennis.
(99b) Fred played tennis with Bertha

(100a) Fred and Bertha talked
(100b) Fred talked with Bertha.

(101a) Fred and Bertha fought
(101b) Fred fought with Bertha

Although *talk* sometimes seems to exhibit slight asymmetries:

(102a) ?Bertha talks with the walls.
(102b) *Bertha and the walls talk.

It appears that for *fight* and *play*, at least, we shall want to allow for complete symmetry. Note that this can be done in a ground scene with slots that take multiple values. A possible ground scene for *play*:

```
(PLAYING-G: COLLECTIVE-ACT
  (COLLECTION)
  (INSTIGATOR1 (=> <COLLECTION>)
               (<COMITATOR2>))
  (COMITATOR1  (=> <COLLECTION>)
               (<INSTIGATOR2>)))
```

The figure scene for *playing* will reference this ground along PATH1 <> (see 2.5.1).

4.2.2.3 Origin Promotion

At issue here is the valence alternation in the following pairs:

(103a) Fred made the log into a canoe
(103b) Fred made a canoe out of the log.

(104a) Fred molded the clay into a statue.
(104b) Fred molded a statue out of the clay.

(105a) A lowly fisherman developed into a champion
(105b) A champion developed out of a lowly fisherman.

Suppose the relevant meanings for *into* and *out of* are:

```
(STATE-ASSUMPTION:THING
  (NEW-STATE)
  (ORIGIN))

(STATE-DEPARTURE:THING
  (OLD-STATE)
  (FATE))
```

The simplest template scene for the relevant verbs is something like:

```
(STATE-CHANGE:STATE-ASSUMPTION;STATE-DEPARTURE
  (OLD-STATE <ORIGIN>)
  (NEW-STATE <FATE>))
```

Now, if the Saliency Hierarchy says nothing about the roles *old-state* and *new-state*, then either role is an allowable direct object. Thus *make* might have as a lexical entry:

```
</mek/:
(MAKING:STATE-CHANGE;ACTION
 (ACTOR)
 (NEW-STATE)
 [OLD-STATE]):
<<<ACTOR, OLD-STATE>, [+V, -N, TRAN, INTO]>,
 <<ACTOR, NEW-STATE>, [+V, -N, TRAN, (OUT-OF)]>>
```

This accounts for the following valence judgements:

(106) John made the log into a canoe.

(107) John made a canoe out of the log.

(108) John made a canoe.

(109) *John made the log (where "log" is *old-state*)

(110) *John made

(111) *John made into a canoe.

(112) *John made out of the log.

Note that there are a number of verbs that might be thought of as "exceptions" to this rule. *Shape, turn, transform,* and *metamorphose* all take only the *into* valence. *fashion, whittle, sculpt, knit,* and *cast* all take only the *out of* valence. Moreover, there seems to be a semantic split. The first group are all verbs focused on the fact of state-transformation; the particular means are not specified. The second group contains verbs which specify a manner of effecting the transformation, and constrain the medium; some select the type or material of their *old-state*; whittling is ordinarily done on wood, knitting with yarn, casting with metal. *Fashion* is a bit less specific, but its most literal use still suggests work done by hand; the manner in which the transformation is affected is constrained.

One way to capture this semantic split is to make it part of what distinguishes STATE-ASSUMPTION from STATE-DEPARTURE. That is, STATE-ASSUMPTION may be a scene which highlights the fact or result of transformation; STATE-DEPARTURE a scene which focuses on the manner. I do not propose any details here, because they do not really affect questions of valence alternation. But the natural account that would follow on such a distinction in scenes is to make the first group of verbs AKO STATE-DEPARTURE, the second AKO STATE-ASSUMPTION. Only verbs that exhibited both valences need be AKO both scenes.

Note that on this account the fact that the *old_state* becomes direct object with a verb like *fashion* could be due to two different things:

(1) Chance.

(2) the fact that there is no available means of marking *old_state* if it is oblique.

4.5 Conclusion: semantic options versus lexical rule

The chief point of this chapter has been to present a plausibility argument that a number of regular, semantically governed valence alternations could be captured in frame representations that gave rise to various kinds of realization options: options left open by the Saliency Hierarchy, optional participants, and optional roles. This possibility in turn raises a theoretical problem.

The theory seems to have two mechanisms for describing the same phenomena, single frames with realizational options, and morphological redundancy rules. Where such free choices are quite congenial to, say, a computational linguist working on a practical implementation, they are anathema to the theorist, because they indicate an overabundance of theoretical apparatus.

We can make the dilemma clearer by outlining three possible positions differing in how much of the burden of accounting for valence alternations is laid on the morphology. All three positions will assume that the theory needs morphological redundancy rules, both for rules that change grammatical function, like passive, and for cases of classical derivation, like *un-* prefixation. They will also assume that the theory needs some account of optional participants. Here, then are three possible theoretical courses sketched within those assumptions, with the version that lays the most burden on the morphology coming first:

(1) All possible semantically systematic valence alternations must be treated by morphological redundancy rule. (Only participants can be optional).

(2) Only constituents that do not contain material mentioned in the Saliency Hierarchy can be optional. The intuitive thrust of this claim is that material mentioned in the Hierarchy is somehow essential to the ontology of scenes; and that any situations that differ in some salient role must be different types of scenes. Enforcing this constraint means that rules like Goal Promotion and Container-Promotion must be morphological redundancy rules involving zero-derivation.

(3) (3) There are no category-preserving morphological redundancy rules involving zero-derivation.

Position (3) resolves the dilemma because then any systematic valence alternation must be treated as realizational options allowed by the lexical semantics. Position (1) resolves the dilemma by stipulation; do it by rule. It has the advantage of being a strong position, and, in at least one version, an easily falsified one. Position (2) as it stands does not appear to resolve the dilemma. It constrains some of the analyses in this chapter to be morphological redundancy rules, but others are unaffected. In particular, the analyses of Instrument Promotion, Dative Movement, and Origin-promotion, and Symmetric Predicates can all stand as proposed. The reason is that in each of these cases, either a nonsalient participant was optional or there was no optionality at all; the valence alternation was explained solely in terms of a realization option allowed by the Saliency Hierarchy.

Position (1) says that all possible semantically systematic valence alternations would have to be treated by morphological redundancy rule. One way to acheive this result is simply to forbid single lexical entries to have more than one denotation. The problem that immediately arises is what to do in the cases where the Hierarchy has nothing to say, with, say, verbs like *blame*. One can, of course, maintain that such verbs yield lexical entries, but then one will be charged with redundantly storing the same lexical-semantics and phonological representation in two different places. If, in answering this charge one resorts to some kind of shared structure among different the lexical entries for *blame,* then it is hard to see how this really differs from a single lexical entry. What a proponent of (1) really needs, in order to have an interesting position, is some criterion for individuating lexical entries, and some reason for claiming that "semantically systematic" alternations need to be governed by morphological rule.

The interesting version of (1), it seems to me, is the one that claims that Saliency Hierarchy is a complete algorithm which imposes a strict ordering of roles on every head, and that the nuclear terms must be chosen according to this ordering. Then *all* valence alternations involving nuclear terms would have to be done by lexical rules, whether semantically governed or not. That is, in any case where a single head form had two valences, either it would have two different meanings in those valences, or one of the valences would violate the hierarchy and would have to be derived by relation-changing rule. This version of

(1) explains why *every* systematic alternation must be a morphological rule; the first version only stipulated it.

In this guise, (1) is a stronger hypothesis than (2), but I think it is arguably wrong.

Consider one case where (1) differs from (2). Under position (1) Instrument Promotion would have to be a lexical rule; under (2) it may have the treatment we gave. Assume that Instrument Promotion does not change meaning; in effect this means that the rule is merely a relation-changing rule (like Passive). (1) predicts that none of the semantically relevant verbs will exhibit only the "derived" valence. This is because (1) stipulates that there is a unique basic valence licensed by the Hierarchy for each verb's semantics. In the case of the verbs of impingement and Instrument Promotion this seems to be right; there is no impingement verb which takes the *instrument* as direct object which does not also take the *patient* as direct-object. But the (1) position holds that there will always be such a "winning" valence, and this does not seem to be the case.

We noted, for example, that in the case of Origin-Promotion, both valences exist independently of the alternation:

(113a) K. metamorphosed into some strange sort of vermin.
(113b)*A strange vermin metamorphosed out of K.

(114a) John whittled a statuette out of wood
(114b)*John whittled wood into a statuette.

Of course Origin-promotion is not a problem for (1) if it is taken to be an alternation that involves a change in semantics, because then both valences could be licensed by the hierarchy. But among the verbs that *do* take both valences, there seems to be no independent reason to posit a systematic semantic change.

More generally, the problem with (1) is that there just seem to be too many cases like *blame* (a number of example were given in () - ()), where very local valence alternations are possible. (1) might be tuned to allow for scattered, idiosyncratic exceptions to the complete ordering of the Saliency Hierarchy, but each such exception that cannot be linked to a morphological rule challenges the assumption that the Hierarchy completely decides the semantics of nuclear terms.

In sum, (2), although weaker, seems a much more plausible position. Within the scope of (2), it is always possible to capture any particular prediction made in (1) by strengthening the hierarchy and calling a particular alternation a lexical rule. For example, to capture the fact that verbs of impingement will never take only the valence on which *instrument* is direct object, we need only change the hierarchy so that instruments can not ordinarily become direct objects (let *patient* be ranked, for example), and then license Instrument Promotion as a relation-changing rule. A parallel account will capture the fact that within the semantic domain of the Dative Movement verbs, there are none that take only the double object construction.[1]

Let us now consider (3). (3) rules out all cases of category-preserving zero-derivation. It thus amounts to the claim that all cases of so-called zero-derivation within categories can be handled with semantic representations that countenance different realization options.

It will be worthwhile examining a a celebrated case of this sort that presents certain problems for (3). This is the productive alternation between transitive and intransitive valences that has sometimes been called the English Causative rule. This involves verbs like *open, turn, break, fill, crack, melt, cool, stop, start,* and *move.* One very simple proposal for handling this is really an echo of Fillmore 1968:

```
(DIRECTED-ACTION-CHANGE:DIRECTED-ACTION; CHANGE
  [ACTOR]
  (PATIENT<CHANGED>))
```

If all of the above verbs incorporated the above DIRECTED-ACTION-CHANGE scene into their lexical structure, we could have single lexical entries yielding both valences (note that this

---

1. The idea of semantically constrained relation-changing rules is certainly not new. This is how Jackendoff 1972 proposes to treat Passive. And Wasow 1980 proposes a whole class of such rules (including one of his two passive rules), which he calls minor rules (borrowing a term from G. Lakoff).

treatment violates position (2)}.

But there are two classes of verbs for which this treatment is not really satisfactory. Halliday 1967 distinguishes among the cases of transitive/intransitive alternation three distinct types:

Nuclear:
(115a) John opened the door.
(115b) The door opened.

Descriptive:
(116a) He marched the prisoners across the yard.
(116b) The prisoners marched across the yard

Effective:
(117a) The clothes washed
(117b) He washed the clothes

The idea of Halliday's division is that some verbs are basically transitive (effective), some basically intransitive (descriptive), and some are truly neutral (nuclear). The above DIRECTED-ACTION-CHANGE frame is intuitively a satisfying representation only for the last class, and, indeed, all our paradigm examples of the Causative rule seem to be nuclear.

It is always difficult to argue what the "basic" nature of a verb is, but the following fact suggests that the transitive valence of *march* has a special status:

(118) ?The prisoners were marched.

Some sort of complement makes the passive much more acceptable:

(119) The prisoners were marched across the compound.

The necessity of a complement with the passive of the Descriptive cases parallels a fact about the Effective cases, a number of which sound much more acceptable with a following adverb.

(120) Cockroaches don't kill easily.

The markedness of the Effective cases is much clearer. It seems uncontroversial that we want our basic entry for a verb like *kill* to be transitive.

A nice argument that orthogonal processes govern the Nuclear and Effective cases is Halliday's observation that some verbs seem to swing both ways.

(121a) This silver shines.
(121b) This silver shines easily.

(b) has a reading paraphrasable as "It is easy to polish this silver." One way to account for such data would be to handle *shine* with something like the above DIRECTED-ACTION-CHANGE frame and then, contrary to (3), derive an intransitive version from the transitive version by lexical rule.[2]

Supposing for the sake of argument that a distinction did have to be made. How would we make it under proposal (3)? Consider the descriptive class. Short of generating a new frame, there is no way in the current frame notation to represent valence addition. Note that even a rule relating frames is unsatisfactory, since no relation stated on a purely semantic level guarantees that the related objects will be pronounced the same. To capture the notion of valence addition, we need to have our hands on some morphology.

The Effective class poses much the same problem; detransitivization can not be represented in a single frame.

If we rule out the possibility of a zero-derivation rule, then the only recourse left open is a syntactic rule, and this is in fact the treatment counseled in Keyser and Roeper 1982 for the Effective cases. In their framework it would be difficult to conceive of a parallel treatment for the descriptive cases, but there is no principled obstacle to a valence increasing syntactic rule (in GPSG, such a rule could be

---

2. For those who control a distinction between intransitive *lie* and transitive *lay* in their dialect, the contrast between descriptive and effective readings will have morphological reflexes:

(i) This rug lies well.
(ii) This rug lays well/easily.

I am indebted to Charles Fillmore for pointing out this example.

easily formulated using metarules, if one could find a plausible semantics). The disadvantage of such a recourse in GPSG is that it is difficult to determine what principles in that framework distinguish processes treated by lexical rules from processes treated by metarule. We have only shifted the domain of the problem; we have not solved it.

I have no general treatment to propcse for these three alternations, if indeed they represent three separate processes. My purpose here is to sketch some of the problems which would arise in a fully developed version of (3), problems which could be avoided under (2).

Hypothesis (3) takes on a very different complexion when we consider it in the light of some cross linguistic facts. Consider again the Causative rule. It is well-known that a number of languages handle the same semantic alternation with a morphological affix. Turkish and Japanese, for example, both have causative suffixes which attach to a verb stem meaning "open" to yield a new verb with a new participant that mean roughly "cause to open." Other languages may relate the same semantic material, but with the morphological markedness going in the other direction. Thus, Polish has a basic transitive verb meaning "open", and creates an intransitive version by attaching a reflexive clitic; this verb form, called the middle, may also be viewed as the output of a morphological process.

A consequence of position (3), then, is that it keeps us from treating causativization in English with the same grammatical device as either causativization in Turkish and Japanese or middle-formation in Polish. Clearly, where there is an affix there must be a morphological rule; position (3) entails that English, with no affix, has no such rule. What are the benefits of such a position? What are the compensating benefits of some version of position (2)?

Essentially, there are two interesting questions here: first, what can the semantics of morphological rule involve? Second, what can the semantics of a single lexical entry contain?

Position (3) makes some interesting predictions about what can fit into the semantics of a single head — given some fixed formalism for lexical representations. For example, the notational devices we have introduced thus far do not allow there to be dependencies among separate optional constituents. Imagine a lexical representation in which two participants were in complementary distribution; when one was present, the other had to be absent, and vice versa (we shall encounter an occasion for using such complementary constituents when we deal with predicative PP's in chapter 5). Given the current formalism, position (3) entails that definable classes of heads with such complementary valences do not exist. Note that even with the same formalism, such heads might exist under position (2). Position (2) would allow two such complementary valences to be related by a rule of zero-derivation. Position (3) states that there will be no non-category-changing zero-derivation processes at all; this includes processes that would introduce one participant and remove another.

It is thus possible to conceive of predictions that would follow from position (3), although they appear to be of a negative character. The drawback of position (3) is that it can only say something about zero-derivation processes; it can say nothing about morphological processes in general.

I want to argue that position (2) can make make semantic claims about what sorts of valence alternations are mediated by morphological processes; moreover in doing so it also defines a class of valence alternations that do not need to be mediated by morphological processes.

To give a simple example to begin with, (2) rules out the DIRECTED-ACTION-CHANGE scene we suggested above as an analysis of the English Causative alternation. This is because the optional constituent in that scene is *actor*, a role mentioned in the hierarchy. (2) says that DIRECTED-ACTION-CHANGE must really be two scenes. This means that if a language is going to express a systematic relationship between those two scenes, it must do so by a morphological rule. Thus, under (2), the fact that that rule in English involves zero-derivation is just an accident. It is thus encouraging to a proponent of (2) to find that numerous languages use an affix to express the causative relation.

Of the analyses presented in this chapter, (2) rules out only Goal Promotion and Container Promotion; both of these valence alternations were captured with a single frame that involved an optional slot *totally-affected*, a role mentioned in the Hierarchy. The gist of (2) is that situations that differ in a salient slot must be instances of different scenes. In a way, (2) constitutes a claim about the individuation of scenes; as a consequence, it is also a claim about the individuation of lexical items. The two different valences of *load* must, under (2) belong to different verbs.

To relate such valences systematically, we are then compelled to resort to a morphological redundancy rule; I will propose such a rule in Chapter 5.

The payoff of such a treatment is largely in its cross-linguistic prespective. English is not a morphology-rich language; therefore the existence of zero-derivation processes in English is not surprising. In languages with more morphological apparatus, we would expect to find the similar relations between lexical items mediated by some kind of affix. In the case of Goal Promotion, a modest cross-linguistic survey involving Polish, Russian, and Hungarian, is promising. The following Hungarian examples are from Davison 1980:

(122a) Ra-takartam a takaro-t az agy-ra
onto-spread1sPa
the blanket-acc
the bed-onto
I spread the blanket on the bed.

(122b) Be-takartam a takaro-val az agy-at
-instr.
-acc.
I covered the bed with the blanket.

(123a) Be-toltom a viz-et a pohar-ba/medence-be.
into-pour-1sPa
the water-acc
the glass-into/pool-into.
I poured water in the glass/the pool.

(123b) Fel-toltom a medence-t/a pohar-at viz-zel.
upto
-acc.
-acc.
instr.
I filled up the pool/the glass with water

In both these Hungarian pairs, the same stem with different prefixes takes valences that parallel the English Goal Promotion alternation. The semantic shift also parallels the English semantic shift; that is, in the *goal* valence, with an instrumental, the Goal is totally affected.

A parallel example in Polish:

(124a) W-pychałem pierz-ę do poduszk-i.
into--push-impf1sgPa.
feathers-acc
to pillow-gen.
I stuffed the feathers into the pillow.

(125) Wy-pchałem poduszkę pierzem.
compl-pushpf1sg.Pa.
pillow-acc
feathers-instr.
I stuffed the pillow with feathers.

Here not only is there a prefix change, but we also have a change in the stem corresponding to a change from imperfective to perfective aspect. In Polish, and apparently in Russian and Hungarian as well, there is a considerable interaction between the holistic semantics and the grammatical institution of aspect, where aspectual contrasts are often marked with a prefix (almost all prefixed verbs without an imperfectivizing suffix are perfective). Thus, in Polish we find cases of a single perfective form that exhibits both valences, with a paired imperfective that allows only one of the valences:

(126) Ładowałem siano na ciężarówk-ę
Load-impf1sg.Pa hay-acc on truck-acc
I loaded hay on the truck

(127) *Ładowałem ciezarówk-e sian-em
f1sg.Pa truck-acc hay-inst
I loaded the truck with hay.

(128) Naładowałem siano na ciężarówk-ę
Load-pf1sg.Pa hay-acc on truck-acc
I loaded hay on the truck

(129) Naładowałem ciężarówk-ę sian-em
Load-pf1sg.Pa truck-acc hay-inst
I loaded the truck with hay.

Clearly, Goal Promotion is not a unified morphological operation in Polish, but nothing about (2) leads us to expect it will be. All we expect is that the semantic alternations involving the role *totally-affected* will involve different lexical items. If the morphological means are available, the relationship between scenes differing in that role will be expressed morphologically. Just as clearly, to capture the relationship between the appearances of instrumental in these examples we will need one of the semantic representation of Instrumental case to be something very like our FILLING scene.

An example parallel to the last one from Russian:

(130) zatykala probkoj butelku.
*butelku probkoj.
She plugged the cork in the bottle
(131) zatknula probku v butelku.
butelku probkoj

That this semantic domain gives parallel valence possibilities for four languages is clear, just as it is clear that there are significant differences among the languages in expressing the relevant semantics. Perhaps the most striking parallel is one we have not captured in our lexical representations: all four languages have a way of marking the *material* in the FILLING scene which is morphologically identical to their way of marking the *instrument* in the MANIPULATION scene.[3] Our current representations of these scenes show no abstract connection, and this is surely a shortcoming.

As far as (2) is concerned, though, matters are just as expected. Scenes differing in the role *totally-affected* have mapped to different lexical items.

There are two sides to (2), however. The semantic domain directly affected is quite small, and thus there is quite a bit of leeway as to what *can* be packaged into a single entry. Most of the rules we have considered in this chapter involve fairly idiosyncratic features of English, but there is at least one rule, which is fairly well-represented cross-linguistically, whose treatment in this chapter is countenanced by (2). This is Dative Movement. As stated, (2) does not lead us to expect that the semantics of Dative Movement will involve separate lexical entries. That is, we need not expect Dative Movement, if it appears, to involve an affixation process.

---

3. I am speaking a little loosely here. It should be clear from the approach we have taken that there is no guarantee that a lexical scene in one language will be a lexical scene in another. The exceptions must of course be the scenes alluded to in the Saliency Hierarchy, which are proposed as universal. Beyond that, one does expect some semantic trends in lexicalization across language, concepts that are frequently, if not always, marked, and there is always the chance that there is some particular inventory of scenes, outside the Hierarchy, which is universal.

To sum up, in this chapter I have shown how the theoretical apparatus we have developed for lexical semantic description is powerful enough to represent a number of semantically governed valence-alternations as simple realizational options taken by a single lexical entry. Even given this power, however, cross-linguistic considerations might lead us treat some of these alternations as morphological processes involving zero-derivation. As we shall see in Chapter 5, abandoning a realizational options analysis of Goal Promotion allows us to strengthen our definition of semantic compatibility back to its force in Chapter 2, and adopt what is perhaps a more persuasive predicative PP analysis of the *patient* valence.

5. Predication, Control, and Lexical Rules Revisited

In this chapter I investigate the interaction of a general account of predication or control with the phenomena discussed in chapter 4, and with our general framework of lexical representation. The material here is not intended as a complete theory of control; it merely sketches some of the lines such a theory might follow if it were to be consistent with the view of lexical representations adopted here. First a simple account of infinitives is sketched, compatible with the semantics presented in chapter 1. Then this account is extended to predicative prepositional phrases, and the question of the lexical representation of heads with predicative complements is addressed. Finally Goal-promotion is reconsidered in light of a predicative analysis; there are problems which again point in the direction of a lexical rule account.

I use the term predicative here to refer to any complement which is controlled by another one of the head's complements. The classic examples are thus equi and raising VP complements, both infinitival and participial. But there are numerous other examples recognized in the literature involving all the other major categories, and adjuncts as well (see Bresnan 1982). In GPSG (Gazdar, Pullum, and Sag 1980), the term "predicative" is used to denote a syntactic class, basically those complements that occur after the copula *be*. In standard American English this does not include infinitives (and there is some question whether one can give a compositional treatment of the British modal future construction with "is to"). I do not intend the term to be taken as this syntactic class, whatever it may be precisely, but merely as the semantic class of controlled complements. GPSG has no convenient term to refer to the class of subcategorized-for controlled complements; LFG, however, does. In Bresnan 1980, the only syntactic subcategorization information that a governing head involving control needs to specify is the grammatical function XCOMP. I will adopt this term.[1]

---

1. The idea that XCOMPs are what control verbs subcategorize for is implicit in Bresnan 1982 and has a great deal of appeal. Taken together with LFG's principle of functional uniqueness, it correctly predicts that no verb will have more than one controlled complement, even controlled complements of different categories (this prediction was not made in an older version of LFG which allowed functions like NCOMP, PCOMP, and so on). It also countenances verbs that allow controlled complements of more than one category:

(i) I saw John in trouble
(ii) I saw John leave
(iii) I saw John angry.

The catch is that this seems to leave the finer points of selection up to the semantics. This is of course a view I am sympathetic to, but some room for extra syntactic stipulation seems to be necessary in the face of:

(iv) I made John leave.
(v) I forced John to leave.

The existence of minimal pairs like (iv) and (v) suggests that semantics cannot always be relied on to determine the precise syntactic features of a controlled complement, and that subcategorization for XCOMP alone does not give a fine enough set of distinctions.

5.1 Infinitival Complements

I propose we treat the relation between matrix and controlled complement situations as unmediated by a complement marker, that is, as a primitive grammatical relation on a par with subject and direct object. We will use the LFG term and call this relation XCOMP. Under this assumption the infinitive rule and the object control rule become:

```
<V1 -> V[TO] V1: V1>
```

```
<V1 -> V N2 V1:
(lambda sigma
  (lambda x
   (exists tau
    (N2 (lambda y
         [(and (V sigma x y tau)
               (V1 tau y))])]))))>
```

This object control rule will be adopted for the remainder of this chapter. A simple generalization will be proposed in 5.3 to cover all predicatives under the assumption they all have the same types as VP's. A few remarks are in order to explain how some standard phenomena are treated.

First, subject control is minimal variation:

```
<V1 -> V V1:
(lambda sigma
  (lambda x
   (exists tau
         [(and (V sigma x tau)
               (V1 tau x))]))))>
```

Second, the distinction between Equi and Raising should, in our current framework, be a distinction in whether or not the controller has a role with respect to the matrix. To make the principle clear, let us propose provisional figure frames for *believe* and *persuade*:

```
(BELIEVING
  (BELIEVER)
  (PROPOSITION))

(PERSUADING
 (PERSUADER)
 (PERSUADEE)
 (PROPOSITION))
```

Let us assume the above control rule works for both equi and raising verbs. Then the predicates BELIEVING and PERSUADING must have the same -arity. PERSUADING will have the denotation <PERSUADING, PERSUADER, PERSUADEE, PROPOSITION>. Each of its three entity-type arguments will have a slot to fit into. What do we do with BELIEVE? Let us allow predicate denotations to have dummy fillers that do not pick out any slot, and do not affect the truth conditions for the predicate. So the denotation of BELIEVE is <BELIEVING, BELIEVER, DUMMY, PROPOSITION>; using italics to mean interpretation, An atomic formula (BELIEVING T1 T2 T3 T4) will be true just in case *T1* is *AKO BELIEVING*, *T2* is the value of the *believer* slot, and *T4* is the value of the *proposition* slot in *T1*. *T3* goes unmentioned. In contrast, (PERSUADING T1 T2 T3 T4) is true just in case *T1* is *AKO PERSUADING*, T2 is the value of the *persuader* slot, *T3* is the value of the *persuadee* slot, and *T4* is the value of the *proposition* slot.

5.2 Predicative PP's

In this section we will tackle the general problem of how to describe verbs that allow a wide variety of preposition complements in a single syntactic slot.

Let us begin, then, with the paradigm case of a verb with a variety of prepositional complements.

```
(1) John put the book in the box
                      under the box
                      over the box
                      through the window
                      away.
```

Suppose that we analyze the prepositional-phrases here as predicative, that is as syntactic XCOMPs. Then *put* would have the same grammatical properties as an Equi predicate. Schematically the argument structure for *put* is:

```
PUTTING (SITUATION) (NP1) (NP2)  (PP      NP2)
                    SUBJ  OBJ     XCOMP   OBJ
```

In "John put the book on the table," "on the table" will be predicated of "the book". We can interpret that semantic constituent alone to mean that the book is on the table.

That interpretation of ((ON (THE TABLE)) (THE BOOK)) suggests we extend the grammatical function XCOMP to the verb *be*. The simplest semantic representation of a copular prepositional phrase would be just to predicate it of the subject. To get this semantics, or indeed, any semantic representation that has that predication as a constituent, we need to be able to interpret the PP as a predicate in its own right.

The semantic coherence of such an analysis is thus not hard to argue, but XCOMP is a syntactic function. What does such a proposal buy us syntactically? To put it another way, the semantic observations we have made amount to little more than a plausibility argument. But we have seen how powerful our frame representations are. Why can't we encode any relationships between prepositional complements and particular participants in our lexical representations, and dispense entirely with a syntactic notion of XCOMP?

The grammar without XCOMP's goes something like this. *Put* has very lax semantic restrictions on one argument position, and a number of preposition phrases meet it. We adopted this kind of treatment throughout chapter 4, and we noted there that an extension of the definition of semantic compatibility was necessary to make it work. The relationship between the direct object and the preposition is not encoded at all in the argument structure, and we treat prepositional complements of *put* just like all other complements. As for the claim that "The book is in the box" is a semantic constituent of "John put the book in the box:" whatever validity that obervation has can be captured in a frame that looks this:

```
(PUTTING
  (PUTTER)
  (PUT-THING)
  (LOCATION)
  (RESULT: COMPONENT
    (LOCATION_IN_SPACE
     (FIGURE <↑ PUT-THING>)
     (GROUND <↑ LOCATION>))))
```

In other words we can handle the locative complements of *put* just as we handled the *to* complement of *give*. There we recognized a POSSESSION relation that held between *recipient* and *patient*, but we did not encode it into our predicational structure; we kept it covertly as part of the lexical representation.

Inded, the field of the argument can be expanded. With frame representations this powerful, who needs the notion of syntactic control at all? Why can't all XCOMP's be treated the way we treat prepositional phrases, without first being predicated of other constituents in the clause? If there is a relationship between "John" and "to run" in "John tried to run" why can't it be captured in the frame model, in some way parallel to the way we capture the POSSESSION relationship with *give*?

The answer lies in classical arguments for syntactic accounts of control. Consider the following examples (where italicized constituents are intended to be coreferent):

(2a) John persuaded Mary to shoot herself
(2b)*John persuaded Mary to shoot himself
(2c) *John* persuaded Mary to shoot *him*.
(2d)*John persuaded *Mary* to shoot *her*.

(3a)*John promised Mary to shoot herself.
(3b) John promised Mary to shoot himself
(3c)**John* promised Mary to shoot *him*.
(3d) John promised *Mary* to shoot *her*.

It is not important here which particular account of disjoint reference and the distribution of reflexives is embraced. The important thing is the crucial information of which syntactic form has been used has been lost by time a frame model interpretation is built. Any account of these facts needs access to the morphological forms used and the control facts. Whatever level of linguistic description that may be, it must be distinguished from the frame model as we now understand it.

This brief excursus into elementary syntax has helped recall the motivation for a syntactic theory of control for VP's. The same kinds of considerations should help motivate a theory of control for PP's.

(4) *John* put the book behind *him*.
?behind himself.

(5) *John* gave the book to himself.
**him*.

Although the judgement of the unacceptability of the reflexive in () does not seem completely secure to me, the contrast between () and () in the case of the non-reflexive pronouns seems unmistakable. The only possibility with *give* is disjoint reference, while *put* clearly allows coreference. On an account where the PP is predicated of the direct object, and where disjoint reference only applies within a single clause nucleus, this fact would be explained.

Thus far, I have tried to put the case entirely in syntactic terms. Given that there are controlled VPs and APs, (and the arguments for both are essentially identical), there are some compelling arguments for extending the notion to PPs on the basis of logical interpretation. For certain verbs, prepositional complements alternate with either VP complements or AP complements, or both:

(6) I want him in London
to leave
thirty pounds lighter.

(7) Imagine John in London
happy

(8) The snowstorm turned the city white
into a crystal palace.

(9) I saw John drunk
leave
in a bar.

For all these verbs, either we posit separate lexical entries especially for the prepositional phrases, or we accept the notion that a PP can be controlled, and give all the complements a uniform treatment.

The price for such generalizations of specific forms of analysis is a greater number of alternatives everywhere in the grammar. Old analyses may have to be rethought; new analyses will always present an extra decision for the working grammarian. Where do we draw the line? AP and VP complements will always be predicative; since they denote properties in everyone's theory, they must eventually be brought home to some participant, whether in the clause or supplied by the grace of anaphora. But PP's present a special problem. Sometimes they will mark core participants; sometimes they will be predicatives. Which is which? We have suggested three properties that distinguish predicative PP's:

(1) Alternation with a number of other PP's, such as the family of Locative PP's appropriate with *put*.

(2) Alternation with complements of other, clearly predicative categories, such as VP and AP.

(3) Apparent violations of disjoint reference.

Unfortunately, (1) and (2) are really just heuristics; they were useful in helping us decide there were such things as predicative PP's, but there is no principled reason to conclude that a PP is *not* predicative, even if it fails both these tests. While (3) seems more promising, in practice constructing plausible examples is often just a case of semantic potluck.

(10) She kept her hands over her

(11) He held the wrench under him

(12) She sprinkled beer nuts over herself/?her

(13) The giant robot loaded us into ?it/?itself

(14) He pulled her to him/*himself.

(15) She hit the ball against ?her/?herself

Even though there seem to be serious problems in exactly circumscribing the domain of predicative PP's, I am going to assume that they are a necessary part of our description of complements. In the next section, I will explore some possible consequences of admitting them into our lexical semantics.

5.3 Frame representations of Predicative PP's

Suppose we make a trivial revision of our object control rule, to make it apply cross categorially to all predicatives:

```
<V1 -> V[α] N2 XP[α]:
(lambda sigma
  (lambda x
   (exists tau
    (N2 (lambda y
          [(and (V sigma x y tau)
                (XP tau y))])]))))>
```

This rule generalizes the old V1 complement rule to all predicatives. The syntax has been adjusted accordingly, with α ranging over some appropriate subcategorization features. Alternatively, the syntax might be:

```
<V1 -> V[(SUBCAT  α)] N2 [α]>
```

Here SUBCAT is a feature on heads introduced in Pollard 1983, which takes as values syntactic categories that are subcategorized for. Either of these syntactic treatments will suffice for our purposes here. The idea is simply to schematize over all cases of object control, whatever particular syntactic mechanism is used. The following examples all count as object control:

(16) Alan saw Marsha running.

(17) Marsha saw Alan drunk.

(18) Marsha made Alan giddy.

(19) Tom persuaded Marsha to leave.

(20) Anne knocked Alan off his feet.

The last example involves what will be our principle topic this section, a predicative PP.

The first problem with the above semantics is that it assumes that all object-controlled complements have the same type as VP's. As yet, there are no PP meanings that have this type. The simplest way to arrange this is simply to let the creation of predicative PP denotations be another option in the mapping from frames to predicates. This gives us a total of three denotational options for an arbitrary preposition frame:

(1) subcategorized-for. Predicate denotes a frame/slot pair.

(2) adjunct. Predicate

(3) predicative. Predicate denotes a frame/slot/slot triple.

Given the denotation of a predicative preposition, a predicative PP will have exactly the type of a intransitive verb, that is, of a VP. We have assumed that for a uniform treatment of control, predicative PP's are of the same same type as VP's. But note that denotations of predicative prepositions are of the same type as as adjuncts.

Here, we give an alternative version of our semantics for adjunct PP's, that allows adjuncts and predicatives to have the same denotations and be treated uniformly.

Suppose that, in accordance with their three-place denotations, adjunct prepositions were three place predicates (in chapter 1, we made them 1-place predicates). This gives us an extra variable, corresponding to the adjunct situation, to bind off in the adjunct rule.

```
<V1 ->  V1 P2: (lambda sigma
                 (lambda x
                   (exists tau
                          (and (V1 sigma x)
                               (P2 tau sigma)))))>
```

As an example, I offer the translation for "Beatrice longed for a Buick in Rome:"

```
(EXISTS* SIGMA
        (EXISTS TAU
                (EXISTS X (AND (LONGING SIGMA BEATRICE X)
                               (BUICK X)
                               (LOCATION T SIGMA ROME)))))
```

Here *tau* is a LOCATION_IN_SPACE situation.

We turn now to the question of the frame semantics for the heads. Let us consider a very schematic version of the frame for KNOCKING:

```
(KNOCKING:IMPINGEMENT-T
 (ACTOR)
 (TARGET <PATIENT>)
 (RESULT (MOVEMENT
```

```
(FIGURE <CHANGED>)
(GROUND))))
```

Let us now consider the problem of mapping this into a predicate with the proper denotation. What we want is a denotation completely parallel to that of *persuade,* which was, <PERSUASION, PERSUADER, PERSUADEE, PROPOSITION>. For KNOCKING, the analogous denotation would be <KNOCKING, ACTOR, TARGET, RESULT>. The key point is that in the predicate and in the frame, *result* must be treated as a participant. It is thus an ordinary, unannotated slot, neither a *component*, nor a *subscene*.

Now consider our scene for Goal-Promotion, the APPLICATION scene:

```
(APPLICATION: RESULTATIVE; UNDERGOING; FILLING-WITH
  (MATERIAL)
  (RESULT:COMPONENT
   (ORIENTATION_IN_SPACE
    (FIGURE <↑ MATERIAL>)
    (GROUND <↑ GOAL>)))
  [TOTALLY-EFFECTED <GOAL>])
```

Note that here, *result* is a component. Under the treatment for Goal-promotion proposed in chapter 4, the *result* slot does not define a participant in either of the valences.

Suppose now that we wished to claim that the Patient valence involved predicative PP's, on the basis of data like the following:

(21a) He sprinkled the glitter onto the tree.
(21b) He sprinkled the glitter into the tree.

(21c) He sprinkled the glitter under the tree.
(21d) He sprinkled the glitter over the tree.

As noted in the last section, such data are far from decisive, even when their grammaticality is not an issue. But, given that predicative PP's do have some role in the grammar, it is not clear whether a predicative or non-predicative analysis is favored. What I want to do here, without pretending to decide the issue, is to explore some of the consequences of a predicative analysis of Goal-Promotion.

Let us assume, then, that the Patient valence involves predicative PP's. (There is also the possibility that the Goal valence is predicative, but the line of argument pursued here is unaffected by that possibility).

Here is a version of APPLICATION compatible with a predicative analysis, with none of the optional constituents yet marked:

```
(APPLICATION: RESULTATIVE;FILLING_WITH
  (MATERIAL)
  (TOTALLY-AFFECTED <GOAL>)
  (RESULT
   (ORIENTATION_IN_SPACE
    (FIGURE <↑ MATERIAL>)
    (GROUND <↑ GOAL>))))
```

The only difference between this and the scene we settled on in Chapter 4 is that the annotation *component* has been removed from the *result* slot. *result* is now a participant.

The problem arises when we try to write optionality back into this frame. It has three participants, *material*, *goal*, and *result*. This means for a verb like *load*, which adds an *actor*, there are four participants. Consider the Goal-valence. We will have no trouble filling the *actor*, *material* and *goal* slots. But what do we do about the *result* slot? By completeness, either that slot can be filled, or it must be absent in the Goal-valence.

Consider the first possibility. It will not do to say that in the Goal-valence the *figure* slot and the *ground* slots are automatically filled, and that in turn fills the *result* slot. The fact is that to fill a slot means to give it a determinate value, and specifying a set of participants does not define a particular scene. We might alternatively write the semantics of *load* so that it was really a four participant verb in the Goal-valence (that is, the denotation of the predicate would be a quintuple). For a sentence like "John loaded the truck with hay," the four participants would be an *actor* John, a *goal* truck, some *material* hay, and a *result* ORIENTATION_IN_SPACE scene (specifically an INTO scene). The problem is, of course, where would the semantics that specified the INTO scene come from? There is no extra preposition from which to extract another situation variable. The only possibility would be to have a feature or the syntactic rule itself supply the semantics, semantics that would in any case be redundant. Moreover, the kind of semantics involved would be the semantics of control. That is, *hay* would be the controller of an added INTO scene. Thus, whatever syntactic predictions our ultimate theory of control made ought to extend to *hay* and whatever other constituents of the INTO scene are realized; the only candidate is the direct object. The following examples are both bizarre, but the second seems to enjoy a clear edge in hopelessness:

(22) We loaded it into itself.

(23) *We loaded itself into it.

The fact is that obliques in English never control direct object reflexives; if our account of control is to follow from our account of grammatical relations, and our account of grammatical relations depends on the way predicates are semantically combined, then making the RESULT scene a participant in the Goal valence has insuperable drawbacks.

The other possibility is to arrange to have the *result* participant absent whenever the *totally-affected* participant is present. The problem with this solution is that it entails an augmentation of our frame formalism. We need a way of saying that two frame constituents are in complementary distribution. There are various ways one might go about doing this. The more important question is whether one should. In the conclusion of Chapter 4, we discussed one way in which the individuation of scenes could be constrained, by imposing the requirement that scenes not have optional constituents that included salient roles. We refrain from adopting such constraints only at the risk of complicating the theoretical task of differentiating scenes. Any augmentation of the formalism we already have for constructing scenes further complicates that task. Allowing complementary constituents into frames is one such augmentation. Unless such a device were very carefully constrained, any two scenes A and B could be collapsed into a single scene which allowed A and B to be realized in turn.

There is a "cute" variant here that would accomplish the necessary work. This is to have *totally-affected* be a constituent that appears along with the annotation "component" on the *result* slot. The frame:

```
(APPLICATION: RESULTATIVE; UNDERGOING; FILLING-WITH
  (MATERIAL)
  (RESULT: [-1COMPONENT]-1
   (ORIENTATION_IN_SPACE
    (FIGURE <↑ MATERIAL>)
    (GROUND <GOAL>)))
  [-1TOTALLY-AFFECTED <RESULT GOAL>)]-1)
```

Thus, when *totally-affected* is present, *result* is a component, which makes it a non-participant, and not grammatically realized; instead, the slots inside of *result* must be grammatically realized.

The rules of the game technically allow this move, because we have not yet formalized the notion "constituent" crucially appealed to in the phrase "optional constituent." Yet it seems clear that this move involves a considerable extension of the intuitive idea. We first introduced the convention of indexed brackets for cases like the following:

```
(IMPINGEMENT-T: MANIPULATION-T; ENCOUNTERED-CONTACT
  [-1 ANTECEDENT:COMPONENT
       (UNDERGOING
         PATIENT <↑ INSTRUMENT>) ]-1
  (CONSEQUENT:COMPONENT
    (DIRECTED-ACTION-CONTACT
       (ACTOR)
       [-1 THEME <↑ ANTECEDENT PATIENT>  ]-1
       (TARGET <PATIENT>) )))
```

Here we are interested in making the whole component *antecedent* scene optional. The second pair of indexed brackets represents the fact that when the component *antecedent* scene is absent, one of the roles associated with one of its participants is also absent. Some such marking of this option is necessary, since we have in general allowed roles to be optional independent of their participants (this is how *totally-affected* works). What we have not allowed (until now) is an optional constituent that does not consist of one of the two following things:

(1) Optionality constraint

(2) One or more roles involving the same participant.

(3) A scene and one or more roles involving participants in that scene.

The proposed "cute" treatment of Goal-Promotion thus depends on a new kind of optional constituent consisting of two rather arbitrarily linked pieces of frame structure, a role and the specification of a slot type on a slot that involves a different participant. This bears a certain suspicious likeness to the device of complementary constituents; the main feature both ideas share is that they involve defining a kind of control structure for the frame, dictating which pieces will be realized when. They really encode the same information that a lexical rule would: a frame with structure A implies a frame with structure B.

Of course we could interpret optional constituents in the same way, but we are working under the assumption that some kind of optionality is a necessary part of lexical descriptions. Sometimes a role defined in a frame will not have an individuated value. The appealing thing about the Optionality Constraint defined above is that it limits the definition of an optional constituent to something like our intuitive understanding of optionality. But adopting that constraint means one of two things: either we abandon the predicative analysis for Goal-promotion verbs, or we make Goal-Promotion a lexical rule.

There is an independent consideration arguing for the second of these alternatives. This is the fact, noted in Chapter 4, that not all instances of the Patient valence are paraphrases of the Goal-valence:

(24a) He sprinkled the bowl with dust.
(24b) He sprinkled dust onto the bowl.
(24c) He sprinkled dust around the bowl

(a) and (b) are paraphrases (modulo the difference attributable to the presence in (a) of the role *totally-affected*). (c) is not a paraphrase of either. One way to represent this is to say that the presence of the role *totally-affected* constrains the type of the ORIENTATION_IN_SPACE scene that fills the *result* slot. In particular it must be a scene involving covering the surface of, or filling the interior of, the *goal*. This is very similar to what we called a FILLING-WITH scene before (except that FILLING-WITH was not AKO ORIENTATION_IN_SPACE).

The treatment for Goal-promotion proposed in Chapter 4 did nothing to make this semantic constraint on the Goal valence explicit:

```
(APPLICATION: RESULTATIVE; UNDERGOING; FILLING-WITH
  (MATERIAL)
  (RESULT:COMPONENT
   (ORIENTATION_IN_SPACE
    (FIGURE <↑ MATERIAL>)
    (GROUND <↑ GOAL>)))
  [TOTALLY-AFFECTED <GOAL>])
```

In fact, as a semantic characterization of both valences of the Goal-promotion verbs, this frame is highly suspect, because it is already AKO FILLING-WITH. As we have just seen, there are instances of the Patient-valence where the notion of filling is irrelevant. Again, we always have the option of making the APPLICATION frame not be AKO FILLING-WITH and making the optional constituent into something more complicated, but this inevitably seems to involve us in some optionality mechanism which violates the Optionality Constraint.

It may simply be more natural to have a lexical rule something like the following:

```
<(APPLICATION: RESULTATIVE; UNDERGOING
```

```
  (RESULT:COMPONENT
   (ORIENTATION_IN_SPACE
    (FIGURE)
    (GROUND))))>

zero-derivation
=============>

<(APPLICATION: RESULTATIVE; UNDERGOING
  (RESULT:COMPONENT
   (FILLING-WITH: ORIENTATION_IN_SPACE
    (MATERIAL)
    (GOAL)
    (TOTALLY-AFFECTED <GOAL>))))>
```

Note that there is a morphological operation (though a vacuous one) relating not frames but frames surrounded by angle brackets. This is to capture the fact that these are lexical statements, not merely implicational statements about frames. If this was only a statement about frames, nothing would guarantee that the pairs of related frames realized lexical items pronounced the same way. Presumably the same format could be extended in cases where the morphological operation was more substantive, although matters would be complicated somewhat if the same kind of rule is to be extended to derivational morphology in general, since we would then wish to say something about the frame representation of the affix.

Note that the above lexical frame has no syntactic component, no new specification of syntactic features for the lexical item. This is because the syntactic features of both valences of the Goal-promotion lexical rule are predictable from the lexical semantics. A possible strong constraint on semantically-governed lexical rules is that they never include syntactic statements.

We can sum things up by comparing the conclusions in the last section of chapter 4 with the conclusions of this section. In the conclusion of chapter 4 we suggested that requiring optional constituents not to include salient roles might have interesting cross-linguistic results. In particular it characterized a set of valence alternations that, if regular, had to be treated as morphological redundancy rules, which in turned characterized a kind of semantic relatedness that might be mediated by affixation. Dative Movement and Instrument Promotion were unaffected by those considerations, as were our treatments of most of the other valence alternations discussed in Chapter 4 (I will turn to some exceptions in a moment). The considerations brought to bear in this chapter, chiefly a predicative analysis of the Goal-promotion verbs, point to the same conclusion. Goal-promotion should be a lexical rule. Again, most of the other alternations treated in Chapter 4 are unaffected by this consideration, since they did not involve valences with a large choice of prepositions.

The obvious exception is Container-Promotion, which also involves the role *totally-affected* and which we subsumed to Goal-Promotion at one point. Nothing said here excludes a uniform analysis of Goal-Promotion and Container-promotion in English; a predicative analysis would, however, have to treat the Source valence as predicative, even though only two prepositions are possible.

There is another exception and this is the treatment of verbs of impingement briefly sketched in 4.3.1.1. There we posited an optional *result* component linked to the role *totally-affected,* which correctly predicted which participant must be direct object in "John hit the ball over the fence," and correctly blocked instrument promotion. A predicative analysis of this valence is attractive because it allows a number of prepositions; on that analysis *result* would be not a component, but a participant and the same sorts of problems that we noted for a predicative analysis of Goal-Promotion would arise; again, these problems could be solved by resorting to a zero-derivation rule that created the resultative valence for verbs of impingement. Again, the requirement that optional constituents not include salient roles also points in that direction.

To sum up, a number of independent considerations point to a treatment of Goal Promotion as a genuine lexical rule. This does not mean, however, that all of the valence alternations discussed in Chapter 4 need to be lexical rules. As we noted at the end of Chapter 4, English allows a number of idiosyncratic valence alternations that have no status as rules, and can be quite easily described as options available within a single lexical entry.

In the final analysis, some valence alternations seem to best be described as different syntactic options for realizing the same core participant. Perhaps the simplest case for such options is a kind of valence alternation we have not yet discussed, but which is quite common among English verbs: the possibility of realizing a propositional argument as an ordinary NP, as a controlled complement, or as an embedded finite clause:

(25) John expected an earthquake.

(26) John expected there to be an earthquake.

(27) John expected that there would be an earthquake.

Each of these examples exhibits what is arguably a different subcategorization, yet all arguably involve the same main verb. I leave as a question for future research an account of these three valences which could relate them to a single lexical entry with one semantic representation. The relationship of alternative valences for propositional complements is, it seems to me, an important problem for any general semantic theory of valence.

REFERENCES

Alexander, D. and W.J. Kunz. 1964. **Some Classes of Verbs in English.**. Linguistics Research Project, Indiana University, Principal Investigator, F.W. Householder. Indian University Linguistics Club, Bloomington.

Alexander, D. and W.J. Kunz. 1965. **More Classes of Verbs in English.**. Linguistics Research Project, Indiana University, Principal Investigator, F.W. Householder. Indian University Linguistics Club, Bloomington.

Amritavalli, R. 1979. *The Representation of Transitivity in the Lexicon.* Linguistic Analysis 5, 71-92.

Amritavalli, R. 1980. *Expressing Cross-Categorial Selectional Correspondences, An Alternative to the X-bar Syntax Approach.* Linguistic Analaysis 6.3: 305-343.

Anderson, John M. 1977. **On Case Grammar: Prolegomena to a Theory of Grammatical Relations.** Croom Helm, London.

Anderson, Steven R. 1971. *On the Role of Deep Structure in Semantic Interpretation.*, Foundations of Language 7: 387-96.

Aronoff, Mark. 1976. **Word Formation and Generative Grammar.**. Linguistic Inquiry Monographs, No. 1. MIT Press, Cambrigde.

Barwise, Jon and John Perry. 1981. *Situations and Attitudes.* The Journal of Philosophy. LXXVIII(11): 668-691.

Barwise, Jon and John Perry. 1982. **Situations and Attitudes.** manuscript, Stanford University.

Bennett, Michael. 1974. *Some Extensions of a Montague Fragment of English.*. Doctoral Dissertation. UCLA.

Bresnan, J. W. 1976. *Towards a Realistic Model of Transformational Grammar.* paper presented at at the MIT-AT&T Convocation of Communications. March, 1976, MIT.

Bresnan, J. W. *Polyadicity: Part I of a Theory of Lexical Rules and Representations*. In T. Hoekstra, H. van der Hulst, and M. Moortgat (Eds.), Lexical Grammar. Foris Publications, Dordrecht, Holland.

Bresnan, Joan. 1982. *Control and Complementation*. Linguistic Inquiry 13: 3.

Chafe, Wallace L. 1970. Meaning and the Structure of Language. University of Chicago, Chicago.

Chierchia, Gennaro. 1983. *Outline of a Semantic Theory of Obligatory Control*. Proceedings of the Second West Coast Conference on Formal Linguistics. Stanford Linguistics Association, Stanford.

Chomsky, Noam. 1970. *Remarks on Nominalization*. In Readings in English Transformational Grammar., Jacobs, R. and Rosenbaum, P. (eds.) Ginn, Waltham, Mass.

Clark, Eve, and H.H. Clark. 1979. *When Nouns Surface as Verbs*. Language 55: 767-811.

Davidson, Donald. 1967. *The Logical Form of Action Sentences*. In N. Rescher (ed.). The Logic of Action and Decision. 81-95. Pittsburgh.

Davison, Debora. 1980. *Verbal Prefixing in Hungarian*. University of California at Berkeley M.A. Thesis.

Dowty, David. 1972 Studies in the Logic of Verb Aspect and Time Reference in English. University of Texas Dissertation.

Dowty, David. 1978. *Montague Grammar and Lexical Rules*. In Papers from the Parassession on the Lexicon, Chicago Linguistics Society.

Dowty, David. 1982. *Grammatical Relations and Montague Grammar*. In Jacobson, P. and Geoffrey K. Pullum. The Nature of Syntactic Representation. Reidel, Dordrecht, Holland.

Fillmore, Charles. 1968. *The Case for Case*. In Bach, E. and R. Harms (eds). Universals of Linguistic Theory. Holt, Rinehart and Winston, New York.

Fillmore, Charles. 1971. *Some Problems for Case Grammar*. In Richard O'Brien, S.J. (ed) Monograph Series on Languages and Linguistics. 22nd Annual Roundtable. Georgetown University.

Fillmore, Charles. 1977a. *The Case for Case Reopened*. In Cole, Peter, ed. Syntax and Semantics 8. Academic Press, New York.

Fillmore, Charles. 1977b. *Topics in Lexical Semantics*. In Roger Cole, ed. Current Issues in Linguistic Theory. Indiana University Press, Bloomington.

Friedin, R. 1974. *Transformations and Interpretive Semantics*. In R. Shuy and N. Baily (eds.). Towards Tomorrow's Linguistics., Georgetown University Press, Washington, D.C.

Gawron, Jean Mark, Jonathan J. King, John Lamping, Egon E. Loebner, E. Anne Paulson, Geoffrey K. Pullum, Ivan A. Sag, and Thomas A. Wasow. 1982. *Processing English with a Generalized Phrase Structure Grammar*. Proceedings of the 20th Annual Meeting of the Association for Computational Linguistics, Toronto.

Gazdar, Gerald. 1981a. *Unbounded dependencies and coordinate structure*. Linguistic Inquiry 12: 155-184.

Gazdar, Gerald. 1981b *On syntactic categories*. Philosophical Transactions of the Royal Society of London B 295: 267-276.

Gazdar, Gerald. 1982. *Phrase structure grammar*. In Jacobson, Pauline and Geoffrey K. Pullum (eds.). The Nature of Syntactic Representation. D. Reidel, Dordrecht.

Gazdar, Gerald, and Geoffrey K.Pullum. 1982. *Generalized phrase structure grammar: a theoretical synopsis*. Indiana University Linguistics Club, Bloomington.

Gazdar, Gerald, Geoffrey K. Pullum, and Ivan A. Sag. 1982. *Auxiliaries and related phenomena in a restrictive theory of grammar*. Language 58: 591-638.

Grimshaw, Jane. 1982. *Subcategorization and Grammatical Relations*.. Paper delivered at the First Annual West Coast Conference of Formal Linguistics, Stanford University.

Goldstein, Ira and R. B. Roberts. 1977. *The FRL Primer*. AI Memo 408, MIT, July, 1977.

Goldstein, Ira and R.B. Roberts. 1979. *Nudge, a Knowledge-based Scheduling Program*. In Metzing, Dieter (ed.). Frame Conceptions and Text Understanding. Walter de Gruyter, New York.

Grimshaw, Jane. 1979. *Complement Selection and the Lexicon*.. Linguistic Inquiry: 10 pp. 279-326.

Grimshaw, Jane. 1982. *Subcategorization and Grammatical Relations*. Paper delivered at the First Annual West Coast Conference on Formal Linguistics.

Green, Georgia, 1971. Semantics and Syntactic Irregularity. Indiana University Press, Bloomington.

Gruber, Jeffrey S. 1976. Lexical Structures in Syntax and Semantics. Noth Holland, New York.

Halliday, Michael A.K. 1967. *Notes on Transitivity and Theme in English 1*. Journal of Linguistics 3.37-81.

Hankamer, Jorge and Ivan A. Sag. 1979. *Deep and Surface Anaphora*. Linguistic Inquiry 7: 391-426.

Hirst, Graeme. 1983. *A Foundation for Semantic Interpretation*. Procceedings of the 21st Annuial Meeting of the Association for Computational Linguistics, Cambridge, Mass.

Hirst, Graeme. In preparation. A Foundation for Semantic Interpretation, with Word and Case Disambiguation. Doctoral Dissertation, Department of Computer Science, Brown University.

Hjelmslev, Louis. 1961. **Prolegomena to a Theory of Language.** Translated by Francis J. Whitfield. University of Wisconsin Press, Madison.

Hofstadter, Douglas R., Gray A. Closman, and Marsha J. Meredith. 1981. *"Shakespeare's Play Weren't Written by Him, But by Someone Else of the Same Name:" An Essay on Intensionality and Frame-Based Knowledge Representation Systems.* Indiana University Linguistic Club, Bloomington.

Jackendoff, Ray. 1972. *Semantic Interpretation In Generative Grammar.* Camridge, MIT Press.

Jackendoff, Ray. 1974 *A Deep Structure Projection Rule.* Linguistic Inquiry 5: 481-506.

Jackendoff, Ray. 1975. *Morphological and Semantic Regularities in the Lexicon.* Language 51:639-671.

Jackendoff, Ray. 1976. *Toward an Explanatory Semantic Representation.* Linguistic Inquiry 8.1: 89-150.

Jackendoff, Ray. 1977. X-bar Syntax: A Study of Phrase-Structure. (Linguistic Inquiry Monograph No.2). MIT Press, Cambridge, Mass.

Kajita. 1967. A Generative-Transformational Study of Semi-Auxiliaries in Present-Day American English. Sanseido, Tokyo.

Kaplan, R. M. and J. Bresnan. 1982. *Lexical Functional Grammar: A formal System of Grammatical Representation.* In Bresnan, J. (ed.). The Mental Representation of Grammatical Relations. MIT press, Cambridge, Mass.

Kamp, Hans. 1980. *ATheory of Truth and Semantic Representation.* In Groenendijk, J.A.G., T.M.V. Janssen, and M.B.J. Stokhof (eds). Formal Methods in the Study of Language: Part 1.. Mathematisch Centrum, Amsterdam.

Kay,Martin. 1979. *Functional Grammar.* In Chiarello et al eds. Proceedings of the Fifth Annual Meeting of the Berkeley Linguistics Society.

Katz, J.J and J. A. Fodor. 1963. *The Structure of a Semantic Theory*. Language 39: 170-210.

Katz, J.J., and Paul Postal. 1964. An Integrated Theory of Linguistic Descriptions. MIT Press Cambridge.

Keyser, Samuel Jay and Thomas Roeper. 1982. *On Middle Verbs in English*. MIT manuscript.

Kiparsky, Paul and J.F. Staal. 1969. *Syntactic and Semantic Relations in Panini*. Foundations of Language 5: 83- 117.

Kiparsky, Paul. 1982. *Lexical Morphology and Phonology*. In Yang, I.S. (ed). Linguistics in the Morning Sun. Seoul, Hanshin.

Kiparsky, Paul. 1983. *Word Formation and the Lexicon*. In Ingemann, F. (ed). Proceedings of the 1982 Mid-America Linguistics Coneference.. University of Kansas, Lawrence, Kansas.

Klein, Ewan, and Ivan A. Sag. 1982. *Semantic Type and Control*. In Barlow, M., D. P. Flickinger, and I. A. Sag (eds). Developments in Generalized Phrase-Structure Grammar. Indiana University Linguistics Club, Bloomington.

Kuno, Sesume. 1973. *Constraints on Internal Clauses and Sentential Subjects*. Linguistic Inquiry 4: 363-386.

Lakoff, G. 1970 *Irregularity in Syntax*. Holt, Rhinehart, and Winston, New York.

Langacker, Ronald. 1983. Foundations of Cognitive Grammar: Chapters I and II. Indiana University Linguistics Club, Bloomington.

Lindner, Susan Jean. 1981. A Lexico-Semantic Analysis of English Verb Particle Constructions with OUT and UP. University of California at at San Diego Dissertation.

Link, G. 1981. *The Logical Analysis of Plurals and Mass Terms*. Paper presented at the Konstanz conference on Formal Semantics.

Marantz, Alec. 1981. On the Nature of Grammatical Relations. Doctoral Dissertation. MIT.

McCarthy, J. and P. Hayes. 1969. *Some Philosophical Problems from the Standpoint of AI*. Machine Intelligence 4.

Minsky, Marvin. 1975. A Framework for Representing Knowledge. In P.H. Winston, ed. The Psychology of Computer Vision. New York, McGraw-Hill.

Montague, Richard. 1970. *The Proper Treatment of Quantification in English*. In Montague 1974.

Montague, Richard. 1974. Formal Philosophy. Thomason, R., ed. New Haven, Yale University Press.

Nichols, Johanna. 1975. *Oblique Case*. In Proceedings of the First Annual Berkeley Linguistics Society.

Nichols, Johanna. 1983. *On Direct and Oblique Cases*. In Proceedings of the Ninth Annual Berkeley Linguistics Society.

Oehrle, Richard. 1975. The Grammatical Status of the Dative Alternation. Doctoral Dissertation. MIT.

Ostler, Nicholas. 1980 A theory of Case Linking and Agreement. Indiana University Linguistics Club.

Panevova, Jarmila. 1974. *On Verbal Frames in Functional Generative Grammar: Part I*. Prague Bulletin of Mathematical Linguistics 22: 3-40; Part II, PBML 17-52 (1975).

Partee, Barbara. 1964. Subjects and Objects. MIT Dissertation.

Pollard, Carl. 1983. *Generalized PHrase Structure Grammars, Head Grammars, and Natural Language*. Manuscript, Stanford University.

Pollard, Carl. In preparation. Doctoral Dissertation. Stanford University.

Perlmutter, David. 1975. *Working 1's and Inversion in Italian, Japanese, and Quechua*. In Chiarello, Christine, et al. (eds) Proceedings of the Fifth Annual Meeting of the Berkeley Linguistics Society. University of California at

Berkeley.

Rooth, Mats and Barbara Partee. 1982. *Conjunction and Type Ambiguity*. In Flickinger, Daniel, Macken, Marlys, and Wiegand, Nancy(eds). Proceedings of The First West Coast Conference on Formal Linguistics.

Selkirk, Elisabeth O. 1982. The Syntax of Words. Mit Press, Cambridge.

Sgall, Petr, Eva Hajicova, and Eva Benesova. 1973. Topic, Focus, and Generative Semantics. Taunus, Kronenburg.

Sgall, Peter. 1980. *Case and Meaning*. Journal of Pragmatics 4: 525-536.

Siegel, D. Topics in English Morphology. Doctoral Dissertation. MIT.

Talmy, Leonard. 1975. *The Syntax and Semantics of Motion*. In Syntax and Semantics, Vol. 4. New York, Academic Press.

Wasow, Thomas. 1977. *Transformations and the Lexicon*.. In Culiconver,P., Wasow, Thomas, and Akmajian, Adrian. Formal Syntax. Academic Press, New York.

Wasow, Thomas. 1980. *Major and Minor Rules*. In Teun Hoekstra, Harry Van der Lust, and Michel Moortgat, eds. Lexical Grammar. Foris Publications, Dordrecht.

Williams, Edwin.1975. *Small Clauses In English*.. In John P. Kimball, ed. Syntax and Semantics 4, pp. 249-73. New York, Academic Press.

Zimmer, Karl. 1964. *Affixal Negation*. Doctoral Dissertation. Columbia University.